Princes, Pastors and People:

The church and religion in England 1529–1689

Susan Doran and Christopher Durston

ROUTLEDGE

London and New York

First published 1991
by Routledge
11 New Fetter Lane, London EC4P 4EE

Simultaneously published in the USA and Canada
by Routledge
a division of Routledge, Chapman and Hall, Inc.
29 West 35th Street, New York, NY 10001

Typeset in 10/12pt Times by
Falcon Typographic Art Ltd,
Edinburgh & London
Printed and bound in Great Britain by
Clays Ltd, St Ives

British Library Cataloguing in Publication Data
Doran, Susan
Princes, pastors and people: the church and religion in
England 1529–1689
1. England. Christian church. Reformation
I. Title II. Durston, Christopher
274.2

Library of Congress Cataloging in Publication Data
Doran, Susan
Princes, pastors and people: the church and religion
in England, 1529–1689 / Susan Doran and Christopher
Durston
p. cm.
Includes bibliographical references and index.
1. Church of England – History – 16th century.
2. Anglican Communion – England – History – 16th
century.   3. Church of England – 17th century.
4. Anglican Communion – England – History – 17th
century.
5.   England – Church history – 16th century.
6. England – Church history – 17th century. I. Durston,
Christopher, 1951–.   II. Title.
BR756.D67 1991
274.2'06–dc20 90–24215

ISBN 0–415–05963–1. — ISBN 0–415–05964–X

For Bathsheba, Jacob, Joel and Luke

Contents

Preface

This book is primarily intended for use by undergraduate students, sixth formers and sixth-form teachers. Unlike most textbooks, it is structured thematically rather than chronologically. The authors hope that this will allow it to be read both as a single whole and also as a series of free-standing, self-contained essays. For this reason, we have listed books providing further detailed reading material at the end of each chapter (except the Introduction and Conclusion) rather than in a long bibliography at the end of the text. While this thematic approach has necessarily involved a certain amount of overlap between chapters, this has been kept to a minimum and has been used to reinforce some of the most important points. We feel that a major advantage of this structure is that it will make it easier for those preparing for seminars or researching specific essay topics to direct and focus their reading.

Inevitably, a certain amount of technical ecclesiastical language is incorporated in the text, but in all cases a definition is provided, either in the body of the text itself or in the Glossary. Quotations and references to specific historians are given a conventional note number in the text and explained in the Note section at the end of chapters before the Suggestions for Further Reading section.

Acknowledgements

All writers of historical textbooks rely very heavily on the specialist studies of their fellow historians. We would like, therefore, to acknowledge our debt and express our thanks to the many Tudor and Stuart historians whose researches and publications are mentioned in the text or in the Suggestions for Further Reading. We would also like to thank our colleague at Strawberry Hill, Christopher Harper-Bill, with whom we have had numerous lively discussions on the religious history of late medieval and early modern England during the period of the book's creation. We are particularly grateful to Michael Beech, Charles Carlton, Barry Coward, Michael Foley, Nicholas Tyacke, and Rosemary O'Day, all of whom read drafts of part or all of the text. They have saved us from many errors and indiscretions. For those that remain we are, of course, entirely responsible. At Routledge, Claire L'Enfant was always helpful and supportive.

Our spouses, Alan and Ros, deserve special thanks. For a long period they were subjected to an increased burden of familial duties, inflated telephone bills, and the almost constant preoccupation of their partners. Despite this, they offered a great deal of advice on the contents and style of the book, and as always provided invaluable encouragement and support. Finally, the authors would like to thank each other; not only have they emerged from the hazardous pursuit of co-authorship still on speaking terms, they remain friends.

1 Introduction

This study of the religious history of England during the early modern period commences in 1529, a year which proved a fundamental turning-point in the fortunes of the church and religion in England. The autumn of 1529 not only saw the fall from power of Cardinal Thomas Wolsey, who had dominated religious and political life in England for the previous fifteen years, but also the beginning of the first session of the Reformation Parliament. The members of this parliament immediately set about introducing legislation to reform abuses within the English Catholic church, and during the course of the next seven years they passed a series of statutes which would lead that church into schism and formalize its break with the Roman papacy, which has lasted down to the present day.

The immediate spur to both these events was the marital dilemma faced by the English king, Henry VIII. As is well known, Henry wanted to be rid of his wife, Catherine of Aragon, in order to marry a lady of the court, Anne Boleyn, with whom he had fallen in love in 1526. An annulment of his marriage was deemed essential not only because Anne had steadfastly refused to become the royal mistress, but more importantly because Henry was deeply anxious about the succession. The only surviving child of his marriage to Catherine was a daughter, Mary, and unless Henry was able to produce a legitimate son, the realm was likely to suffer a disputed succession on his death and, if Mary were to marry a foreigner, might even lose its independent status. As early as 1524, Henry had given up all hope of Catherine bearing another child, and by the time he became infatuated with Anne Boleyn two years later, he had already begun to convince himself that his wife's failure to give birth to a son who survived infancy was a sign that his marriage to his brother's widow was sinful, in that it had broken the laws concerning affinity laid down in the Old Testament Book of Leviticus (chapter 20: verse 21).

The following year, Henry and Wolsey began negotiations with Rome, aimed at securing an official papal annulment of the king's marriage; by 1529, however, it was clear to all involved that the pope had no intention of allowing Henry to put Catherine aside (see Chapter 4).

The principal victim of Henry and Anne's anger and disappointment at the failure of the negotiations was Thomas Wolsey. In October 1529, the cardinal was charged with the offence of praemunire, of introducing an illegal foreign authority into England through his acceptance of the office of papal legate *a latere*. A few days later, parliament met and some MPs took advantage of Wolsey's disgrace to air their grievances against the church. Instead of siding with the bishops who protested at this action, Henry put his weight behind the anti-clerical agitation and agreed to pass legislation reforming the church in a number of relatively minor ways. Yet neither at this stage nor for the next eighteen months did he have any clear plans to launch a full-scale attack on the church or to break with Rome. In the immediate aftermath of Wolsey's fall from power, his advisers offered him a range of options on how to obtain the annulment and Henry responded by trying a number of different schemes. Only in 1532 did he alight on the policy of the royal supremacy: the idea that the English monarchy had enjoyed an unlimited authority over the church within its realm for centuries and only now needed to start exercising this on a more regular basis.

Geoffrey Elton has consistently argued that this revolutionary new strategy was the brainchild of the recently appointed secretary to the privy council, Thomas Cromwell, who should thus be seen as the sole architect of the Henrician Reformation. More recent research, however, has revealed that the radical theories justifying the supremacy were being promoted at court by members of the Boleyn faction as early as the summer of 1531, well before Cromwell became the king's chief minister (see Chapter 4). But if Cromwell was not the architect of the Reformation in England, he was its main builder, for without question the implementation of the policy was his achievement; he masterminded the legislation which severed the ties with Rome, manoeuvred the statutes through parliament, sponsored a propaganda campaign to encourage obedience to the changes, and launched a programme of coercion against those refusing to comply.

Although Henry's desire to have a new wife and greater control over the English church was the primary incentive for the schism, Cromwell and the members of Anne Boleyn's faction were also keen to bring about reform of the church (see Chapters 4 and 6). Sharing the humanist outlook of the continental reformer, Desiderius

Erasmus, they were in favour of allowing the laity easy access to English translations of the Bible, placing a greater emphasis on preaching, and instituting simplified forms of worship, stripped of superstitious practices such as the worship of relics and images. Through the influence of Cromwell and the new Archbishop of Canterbury, Thomas Cranmer, the 1530s witnessed a number of reform initiatives of this nature. However, when Cromwell fell from power in 1540, a conservative backlash ensued; several purges of heretics followed and little further progress towards religious reform was made until after Henry's death.

The accession to the throne of the minor, Edward VI, in 1547 brought to power at court a reform group led by the new king's uncle, Edward Seymour, Duke of Somerset. During the course of the next two years, Somerset's government brought about a number of Protestant reforms, including the dissolution of the chantries and the introduction of an English Prayer Book and a new liturgy for the mass. In 1549, Somerset was replaced as effective head of the government by John Dudley, Duke of Northumberland, and from then on the Reformation took an even more radical direction. The authorizing of a new ordination service for the clergy in 1550 was followed two years later by the appearance of a second Edwardian Prayer Book, and by the last months of Edward's reign the country was officially Protestant. This new Protestant church was, however, extremely precarious, for its survival was threatened by Edward's ill-health and the fact that the heir to the throne, Catherine of Aragon's daughter Mary, was a staunch Catholic. Consequently, during the last months of his life Edward conspired with Northumberland to exclude his half-sister from the throne and to elevate instead the duke's Protestant daughter-in-law, Lady Jane Grey. Although Jane's hereditary claim was weak, she was initially recognized as queen in many parts of the realm, and it took Mary several weeks to organize an effective *coup d'état* and take control of the throne. Once in power, she immediately set about turning the clock back to 1529 by returning England to papal jurisdiction, restoring Catholic forms of worship, and reintroducing the old heresy laws. Despite her subsequent burning of nearly 300 committed Protestants, her efforts to reimpose Roman Catholicism were ultimately doomed by the brevity of her reign and her failure to produce a Catholic heir. In November 1558, she was succeeded by her half-sister Elizabeth, who within a few months of coming to the throne had authorized a new religious settlement which once again left the country officially Protestant.

At one level, therefore, the English Reformation was undoubtedly 'an act of state', or perhaps more accurately acts of state – a series of changes initiated by monarchs and imposed by them upon their subjects. It also, however, involved conversions at grass-roots level, for in the course of the sixteenth century the people of England ceased to be overwhelmingly Catholic and became predominantly Protestant. The question of how quickly and how voluntarily this process of 'Protestantization' was accomplished has seriously divided Reformation historians over the last thirty years; it will be discussed in detail in Chapter 6. One view put forward by A. G. Dickens in the mid-1960s held that because Protestantism greatly appealed to the many lay people who had been alienated by the formalistic, clerically dominated Catholicism of the later middle ages, the Protestantization of the country was achieved very quickly. Dickens declared that: 'Long before Henry VIII broke with Rome numerous developments were preparing Englishmen for some sort of religious and ecclesiastical change or crisis.' Among these long-term influences he included the deplorable state of the late medieval Catholic church, a widespread and deeply-rooted anti-clericalism, and the indigenous English heresy of Lollardy, which had both fuelled lay anti-clericalism and prepared the ground for later Protestant doctrines. Thus, he argued, when Henry VIII quarrelled with the pope over his marriage, he was able to use a pre-existing anti-clericalism as a stick with which to beat the church, and when he subsequently embarked on the official Reformation, the greater part of the political nation readily gave him their support. According to the Dickens view, opposition to Henry's ecclesiastical policies was negligible, being restricted to the unrepresentative northern backwoodsmen who joined the 1536 Pilgrimage of Grace, and a few saintly martyrs, such as the London Carthusians, Sir Thomas More, and John Fisher, Bishop of Rochester.

Dickens' reading of the English Reformation held sway for nearly two decades, but in the early 1980s Christopher Haigh and Jack Scarisbrick began to challenge and revise his interpretation of events. Both denied that the underlying causes of the Reformation which he had identified had actually existed, claiming that rather than being an institution in terminal decline, the late medieval Catholic church had been 'a lively and relevant social institution', displaying 'growing and vigorous' forms of piety. They also dismissed Dickens' evidence for the existence of widespread anti-clericalism and heresy on the eve of the Reformation, and argued that the vast majority of the laity were both well satisfied with their parish priests and orthodox in their doctrinal beliefs. Furthermore, they doubted whether the new, austere Protestant beliefs had in fact appealed to the laity, suggesting instead that Protestantism proved highly unpopular and was only imposed on the English people through force, by means of a government-sponsored process which met with great difficulties, and was only completed late in Elizabeth I's reign.

Much of the work of these and other 'revisionist' historians has proved invaluable, and many of their findings have been incorporated into subsequent chapters of this book. Most importantly, they have demonstrated that the late medieval church was functioning effectively, and that historians have been misguided in relying too heavily on the testimony of condescending sixteenth-century intellectuals like Erasmus who were so hostile towards superstitious and non-biblical religion, while ignoring the perspective of the contemporary rural parishioners, who participated happily in this type of unsophisticated religious life and seemingly gained great spiritual comfort from the various rituals of the liturgical year. The revisionists have also encouraged historians to focus more attention on the conservatives and the committed Catholics, whose opposition to the policies of Henry VIII and his Protestant successors has too often been overlooked or underestimated.

On the other hand, some of the original assertions of the revisionists are themselves now in need of revision. Haigh's denial of the existence of anti-clericalism on the eve of the Reformation is a case in point. It may well be true that there is little evidence of a widespread parochial anti-clericalism in the early sixteenth century, if by that we mean an endemic lay hostility towards the local priesthood. There is, however, clear evidence of the existence of both literary anti-clericalism and the corporate anti-clericalism of specific interest groups with a power and influence well beyond their numbers (see Chapters 4 and 8). Other areas where the revisionists appear to have overstated their case will be identified and discussed in the following chapters.

Thanks to the work of the revisionists, no future history of the English Reformation will end in 1559. Elizabeth's reign is now seen to be of crucial importance because it saw the completion of the Protestantization of the English people and witnessed the creation of a uniquely English style of Protestant church which was later to be labelled Anglicanism. Elizabeth was determined to preserve within her church a number of liturgical features which were roundly condemned by more radical Protestants as popish, and throughout her reign she consistently thwarted the efforts of those who sought to bring English Protestantism more closely into line with its continental counterpart. Some of her bishops and prominent lay subjects, meanwhile, were engaged in a process of creating a learned Protestant ministry and imposing a godly discipline on the parishes. On Elizabeth's death in 1603, therefore, her successor James I became head of an English church which included a wide spectrum of religious opinion. Despite his mother's Catholicism, James had received an impeccably Protestant upbringing in Calvinist Scotland, and was personally extremely interested in religious issues. Shortly after arriving in England, he responded to a petition from a number of Puritan ministers by calling a theological conference at Hampton Court Palace, at which he took the chair for a series of debates between his bishops and the representatives of those looking for reform. In the event, however, rather than witnessing yet another religious *volte face*, James's reign saw the continuation and consolidation of the ecclesiastical policies set in train by Elizabeth. For this reason, the years 1559 to 1625 need to be viewed as a distinct religious period, during the course of which the Elizabethan church founded in 1559 gradually came to acquire a deep hold on the affections of the English people.

James worked closely with his bishops, and in particular with George Abbot, whom he appointed Archbishop of Canterbury in 1611. By turning a blind eye to the activities of moderate Puritan laymen and clergy while at the same time dealing harshly with Presbyterian extremists, king and archbishop ensured that the first fifteen years of Abbot's primacy were some of the most tranquil in the religious sphere during the entire century following the break with Rome (see Chapter 7). The absence of serious internal religious discontent during these years is illustrated by the lack of parliamentary concern. Even during the later years of the reign, when Europe was embroiled in the early stages of the Thirty Years' War and James's MPs were calling for active English intervention on behalf of Protestants abroad, there were very few complaints in parliament about the state of religion at home.

Although historians have differed somewhat less in their interpretations of the religious history of the Elizabethan and Jacobean periods than in their views on the turbulent years between 1530 and 1560, there have, none the less, been a number of notable areas of dispute. The most important of these controversies has arisen over the theological nature of the established state church, and in particular over the prevalence and popularity of the doctrine of predestination – the belief that humankind is divided into immutable groups of the saved and the damned, and that an individual's salvation depends not on his or her actions while on earth, but rather on a predetermined and arbitrary decision by God (see Chapter 2). Some historians, most notably Nicholas Tyacke, have argued that between 1560 and 1625 this doctrine was accepted unquestioningly by all the leading officials, theologians, and teachers of the Elizabethan church. R. T. Kendall and Peter Lake have refined this position by drawing a distinction between a moderate majority of 'credal' predestinarian Protestants and a smaller group of more intense 'experimental' predestinarians. However, the view that there was a predestinarian orthodoxy in the Elizabethan church has been challenged by another group of historians, which includes Peter White, Kevin Sharpe, and George Bernard. They have argued that Elizabeth's church contained a variety of acceptable doctrinal positions, that predestinarianism never managed to achieve the dominance accorded it by Tyacke, and that at no time during the sixty-five years between 1560 and 1625 was the idea that good works could be an aid to salvation anything other than a perfectly orthodox belief. One of the chief reasons why these issues have been so hotly contested is that they have enormous bearing both on the significance of the religious changes introduced under Charles I and on the possible causes of the English civil war.

Sometime before he became king in 1625, James I's son Charles had adopted as his personal religion a conservative version of Protestantism known as Arminianism; he had done so either because he disagreed with the doctrine of predestination, or more probably because he found the austere liturgy of undiluted Calvinism distasteful. Arminianism had also been adopted by a small group of clerics within the Jacobean church who, as well as questioning the doctrinal basis of Calvinism, had sought to reintroduce into church worship certain decorative features and ceremonies most commonly associated with Catholicism. Aware that Prince Charles was the key to their bid to take control of the church, shortly before James's death the Arminian polemicist Richard Montagu entitled his new theological work *Appello Caesarem* – An Appeal to Caesar. Once he had come to the throne, Charles quickly answered this call for religious change by promoting notable Arminians to positions of prominence in both church and state. Disquiet at the new direction of religious affairs soon surfaced in parliament, and over the next few years a growing number of MPs began to speak out against the Arminian threat. In 1629, the intense anxiety and frustration of the MPs erupted into violence, as the Speaker of the Commons was held down in his chair while the House forced through motions condemning the religious innovations.

This incident finally convinced Charles that he should abandon his efforts to work with parliament, and he embarked on a period of personal rule, which lasted until 1640. Throughout the 1630s he continued to lend his wholehearted support to the Arminian takeover of his church. In 1633, one of the leading Arminians, William Laud, who had been the king's chief religious adviser since the beginning of the reign, was appointed to succeed Abbot as Archbishop of Canterbury, and by the mid-1630s most of the other bishops' thrones were also occupied by Arminians. In alliance with the king, these bishops set out to impose both their theological preferences and their particular brand of ceremonialism on the parish clergy and the laity (see Chapter 7). The large numbers of the English gentry and aristocracy who enjoyed the profits from impropriated tithes were further alarmed when the Laudian ecclesiastical authorities made it clear they would spare no pains in an attempt to recover as much as they could of the church's former wealth and power. Their suspicions and anxieties were further fuelled when both Laud and the Archbishop of York, Richard Neile, were appointed to Charles's privy council, and became intimately involved in the king's plans to achieve a more ordered secular, as well as ecclesiastical commonwealth.

These developments were clearly of some considerable significance; just how considerable, however, depends on the nature of the Elizabethan church that the Arminians set out to change. If one agrees with the view of Sharpe, White, and Bernard that prior to 1625 predestination had merely been one of a number of alternative doctrines vying for supremacy within the church, the rise to power of the Laudians represented little more than another swing of a theological pendulum which had been fluctuating wildly since 1560. As such, it was not something that many people were particularly upset about. If, on the other hand, one accepts Tyacke's argument that predestination was *the* one mainstream belief down to 1625, the Arminians were responsible for an unprecedented attack on a well-established orthodoxy, and their activities accordingly met with great hostility and resistance. Thus, while Sharpe, White, and Bernard do not believe that the Arminians should be blamed for causing the civil war of the 1640s, Tyacke, John Morrill, and other historians have conversely argued that Laud and his fellow prelates should bear a major part of the responsibility for provoking what they regard as 'England's wars of religion'. This controversy will be discussed in more detail in subsequent chapters.

Following the outbreak of civil war in 1642, the revolutionary years of the 1640s and 1650s witnessed the attempts of a succession of governments to impose several quite distinct forms of established church on the English people. During the course of the civil war, the Long Parliament removed from the church all the innovations introduced by Charles and Laud during the 1630s, abolished episcopacy and the Elizabethan Prayer Book, and entrusted the task of devising a new church to the Westminster Assembly of Divines, a committee made up of a small number of MPs and peers, several representatives of parliament's allies the Scots, and over 100 English churchmen. The eventual product of their lengthy discussions was the strongly Presbyterian Directory of Public Worship, which was accepted by parliament in early 1645 as a blueprint for the new ecclesiastical establishment. As well as imposing this Presbyterian liturgy on the country, parliament also attempted to reorganize ecclesiastical government in the localities by bringing parishes together into new administrative groupings presided over by 'classes' (see Chapter 6). Furthermore, in 1648 it passed a restrictive Blasphemy Act, which threatened those convicted of denying the central tenets of Christianity with death, and those dissenting from orthodox Calvinist theology with imprisonment.

The Scots' commissioners in London were far from pleased with this new English church, and one of them referred to it as 'but a lame, Erastian presbytery'. However, if it was too weak and watered down a version of Presbyterianism for the Scots, it none the less proved far too rigid and alien for the majority of the English laity. Although the ceremonies contained in the Directory of Public Worship remained the official liturgy of the English church throughout the period from 1645 to the Restoration, few English parishes appear to have welcomed them with any enthusiasm, and all over the country clergymen continued to conduct services based substantially on the old Book of Common Prayer. The classis system proved equally unpopular; a number of parishes in London, Manchester, Bury, Nottingham, Yorkshire, Essex, and Shropshire were grouped together, and provincial assemblies were established for London and Lancashire. Elsewhere in the country, however, the idea met with at best a lukewarm response, and evidence of the existence of classes exists for only about a quarter of English counties.

Handicapped from the outset by its widespread unpopularity in the country, the new Presbyterian state church soon also lost all official backing from the central government. In the months following the end of the civil war, parliament's New Model Army, which contained large numbers of soldiers who had rejected the Presbyterian establishment in favour of greater religious toleration, grew steadily more and more disenchanted with its masters. Frustrated at the persistent refusal of the MPs to listen to their grievances, at the end of 1648 and beginning of 1649 the army staged a military coup, ejecting the most prominent Presbyterians from parliament, publicly executing the king, and imposing a military regime upon the country. For the next eleven years, the country was under the effective control of the army, and as its commander-in-chief, Oliver Cromwell, and most of his fellow officers were far from convinced of the need for any state church, and firmly opposed to any compulsory religious system, Presbyterianism was consigned to a limited and localized presence.

During the 1650s, England experienced what was probably the freest religious environment of the entire early modern period, within which Protestants who believed in the doctrine of the trinity and refrained from breaking the law were allowed a wide measure of toleration. In 1650, the Rump of the Long Parliament replaced the 1648 Blasphemy Act with their own far less harsh legislation, which although it continued to outlaw the extreme beliefs of disruptive fringe groups such as the Ranters, signalled a far more liberal approach on the part of the civil authorities. In the same year, the Rumpers passed an Act for the Relief of Religious and Peaceable People; this retained the legal requirement on the laity to take part in some form of Sunday worship, but released them from their obligation to attend the local parish church. Throughout the remainder of the 1650s, successive governments presided over a wide diversity of religious practice; large numbers of English men and women continued to frequent only their parish churches, many worshipped solely in gathered congregations of Independents, Baptists, and Quakers, and many more regularly attended both sectarian and parish worship. Official toleration was denied only to Roman Catholics and episcopalian Anglicans, and in practice if they exercised discretion, they too were able to worship without much disturbance.

If the military regimes of the Interregnum were prepared within reason to allow lay men and women to be godly in whichever way seemed most appropriate to them, they did expect them to be godly in some way. Cromwell and his army colleagues considered the improving of the morality of the English people one of the chief priorities of their government, and they made every effort to eradicate a range of popular pursuits which they considered to be sinful, profane, or unseemly. Brothels, gaming-houses, and unlicensed ale-houses were sought out and closed down, a strict Puritan Sunday was enforced, the much-loved festivities associated with Christmas, Whitsuntide, and Mayday were outlawed, and a whole range of rural sports was banned. It can indeed be argued that the strict Calvinists who controlled England during this period were attempting by such means to bring about a cultural revolution (see Chapter 5).

When Charles II returned to England as king in 1660, the old compulsory state church was quickly restored and the freedoms of the 1650s soon vanished. Having gone down with the monarchy in the 1640s and learnt from that experience that its fortunes were closely dependent on those of the crown, the established church was more than ever determined to shore up the monarchy as a means of guaranteeing its own survival. Dr Robert South emphasized this point when he declared shortly after the Restoration that the Anglican church 'glories in nothing more than that she is the truest friend to kings and to kingly government of any Church in the world'. It is also clear that there was a great deal of support for the old church throughout the country, and particularly from the gentry elites of provincial England. Although Charles's own personal inclination was to refound a wide, comprehensive church able to encompass as many of the various denominations of the 1650s as possible, it was soon clear that the king would have to bow to pressure from the bishops, the conservative landowners, and their representatives in the Cavalier Parliament, who wished to see a more narrow restoration. In the event, the restored Anglican church of the 1660s was a conservative, in some respects even Laudian church, which large numbers of Presbyterians, Baptists, and Quakers could not in conscience bring themselves to join. These nonconformists – or dissenters – were no longer, however, simply allowed to opt out and organize their own services, for the legislation of the Clarendon Code passed in the 1660s made any such unauthorized meetings for worship illegal. During the twenty-nine years between 1660 and 1689, many thousands of nonconformists chose to disregard the Code and participate in secret 'conventicles'; many hundreds of them who were caught subsequently languished for years in gaol. Only in 1689, the closing date for this study, were they at last given the legal right to conduct their nonconformist worship in their own meeting-houses (see Chapters 3 and 6).

Over the course of the period between 1529 and 1559, the English church experienced a number of dramatic changes in its nature and status; starting out as a branch of the international Roman Catholic church, it moved to become first an independent, schismatic Catholic church, and later a unique, hybrid Protestant church. After 1560, this new English church was engaged in the task of establishing its traditions and defining its boundaries, a process which lasted well over a century and was only effectively completed by the end of the seventeenth century. It is to the detail of these developments that we shall turn in the following chapters.

2 Theology and liturgy

During the late medieval period, the core doctrinal beliefs of the Roman Catholic church were salvation through faith and works, transubstantiation, and the efficacy of the grace transmitted through the seven sacraments. The church taught that the individual's fate after death was primarily decided by the way he or she acted while on earth. Those who avoided temptation, practised good deeds, and regularly sought forgiveness for their sins through the sacrament of confession would receive the reward of a place in heaven. Before they reached heaven, the great majority of men and women would be required to spend a period in an intermediate location called purgatory, where those destined for eternal bliss would first be subjected to severe punishments for the sins they had committed on earth. It was, however, possible to obtain either partial or total remission of one's time in purgatory through the acquisition of indulgences. These had originally been envisaged as rewards for the undertaking of religious exercises, but during the late medieval period were increasingly also being sold for cash. The individual's attempts to avoid the pitfalls of sin were assisted by the spiritual food of grace, which was transmitted through the seven Catholic sacraments: baptism, confirmation, confession, the eucharist, marriage, ordination, and the last rites. Of particular importance was the eucharist, which involved the miracle of transubstantiation; since the twelfth century, the Catholic church had argued that, although the 'accidents' (or external appearance) of the bread and wine remained unchanged during the mass, the substance of both was turned by the priest at the moment of consecration into the body and blood of Christ. For this reason each Catholic mass was considered a re-enactment of Christ's sacrifice on Calvary. As late medieval Catholics also believed that they could elicit the help of the Virgin Mary and the saints in heaven not only for themselves but also for those in purgatory, intercessory prayers, masses for the dead, and the worship of relics of the saints were all extremely important features of lay piety. Hundreds of chantries and lay fraternities were established with this as their major function.

During the 1520s, this theological orthodoxy came under challenge throughout Europe from the new ideas of the continental reformers, Martin Luther and Ulrich Zwingli, both of whom claimed that the truth of their new theology was evident from scripture and based upon a biblical authority which took precedence over tradition and papal decree. Central to their challenge was the doctrine of justification by faith alone, or solafidianism (from the Latin *sola fide* – 'by faith alone'). They argued that sinners were quite unable to attain salvation through their own merits or through the long process of confession, repentance, and partial purification, and that justification or redemption was obtainable only at a stroke through the gift of faith from God made possible by Christ's sacrifice. As well as eliminating the spiritual importance of good works, this reformed theology of grace and salvation rejected a number of the doctrinal cornerstones of late medieval Catholicism. It discarded purgatory and intercession for the dead, asserting that the damned went straight to hell and the saved directly to heaven. It also rejected worship of the saints and relics, pilgrimages, indulgences, and masses for the dead as futile attempts to purge the sins of the deceased or pile up merit for the living.

Luther and Zwingli also attacked the orthodox theology of the mass. The Catholic miracle of transubstantiation could be performed only by an ordained priest, who then received the body and blood alone at the altar. The laity were merely passive observers and their view of the process was obscured by the rood screen which separated the nave of the church from the chancel. The great majority of them participated in the sacrament only once a year at Easter, when they received the host (or wafer) but not the consecrated wine. While continuing to believe in the real presence of Christ in the bread and wine at communion, Luther rejected transubstantiation for a position which has been labelled consubstantiation. He argued that the bread and wine somehow coexisted with the body and blood, and more importantly that the miracle occurred because of the presence of the faithful and not as a result of the magical powers of the priest. Consequently, he demanded regular communion in both kinds (bread and wine) for the laity, and he denounced private masses celebrated by a priest alone. Zwingli departed still further from the orthodox

Catholic position; although he believed in Christ's spiritual presence among the faithful at communion, he totally rejected the idea of any physical presence of Christ in the bread and wine.

Henry VIII was horrified by what he understood of Luther's theology, and, in an attempt to rebut it during the early 1520s, he wrote with the help of a number of court scholars the theological tract *The Assertion of the Seven Sacraments*, for which he was rewarded by the pope with the title 'Defender of the Faith'. His subsequent break with the Roman church during the 1530s was not the result of any change of heart or conversion to the reformer's views, nor due to any theological differences with the papacy. Henry remained a doctrinal conservative until his death, and as a consequence, although the legislation enacted by the Reformation Parliament brought about a jurisdictional revolution, it created no new theology for the English church. Indeed, the Act of Dispensations of 1534 specifically affirmed Henry's commitment to Catholic doctrine, stating that the king did not intend to 'vary from the congregation of Christ's Church in any things concerning the very articles of the Catholic faith of Christendom'.

None the less, during the period immediately following the schism, both domestic politics and considerations of foreign policy proved an encouragement to religious change and theological experimentation in England. At court, Anne Boleyn and Thomas Cromwell, Henry's vicegerent in spirituals, used their influence to promote reform of the church and to advance those evangelicals who questioned the sacramental power of the priesthood. Furthermore, as Henry VIII had relied on the authority of scripture to justify his annulment, it was difficult for him to resist pressure for the translation of the Bible into English, or demands that doctrine and liturgy should conform to the word of God as revealed in the scriptures. Abroad, the German princes who had reformed their churches along Lutheran lines saw Henry as a potential ally against their common enemy, the Holy Roman Emperor Charles V, but demanded as a preliminary to a political alliance that he accept their Protestant statement of faith, the Augsburg Confession of 1530.

The 1530s, therefore, saw some tentative official moves towards religious reform, although they all reflected the tension between the forces for conservatism and those who looked for change. Typical of the uneasy compromises that resulted was the Ten Articles of Faith laid down by convocation in 1536. On the sacraments, this document accepted the traditional Catholic doctrine that baptism, penance, and the eucharist were 'necessary for man's salvation', but made no mention at all of the other four Catholic sacraments deemed unscriptural by Luther; similarly, its statement on the eucharist was left sufficiently vague to be interpreted as either transubstantiation or consubstantiation. On purgatory and prayers for the dead, the Articles were also ambivalent, since they admitted that: 'it is a very good and a charitable deed to pray for souls departed', but made no claim that such prayers were efficacious and even questioned whether purgatory existed at all. Finally, although they sanctioned images in churches, prayers for the dead, and the veneration of saints, the Ten Articles included a warning about the superstitious beliefs which sometimes lay behind them. The question of images in churches was further addressed by two sets of injunctions issued by Cromwell in 1536 and 1538, but even here the reforms did not go as far as some iconophobes would have liked, as they drew back from condemning all images and denounced only those that encouraged 'superstition and hypocrisy' and 'that most detestable sin of idolatry'. Nor was it clear from the 1538 injunctions whether the offending images should simply be removed or totally destroyed. Even after Cromwell had promoted the translation of the Bible into English and ordered that a copy be placed in every parish church in order that it could be read by the laity, William Tyndale's New Testament could not be circulated, as the author was still considered to be a heretic.

To religious conservatives, however, even these tentative and moderate reforms were undesirable and alarming. While men like Thomas Howard, Duke of Norfolk, and Stephen Gardiner, Bishop of Winchester, were prepared to accept the royal supremacy, they baulked at these evangelical reforms, which in their view smacked of heresy and threatened to lead England into the Lutheran camp. Their opportunity to discredit the reformers and gain influence with the king came in the late 1530s. The conservative rebellion known as the Pilgrimage of Grace and the threatened Franco-Imperial invasion of 1538–9 awakened Henry to the dangers of the evangelical reform programme, and he decided to call a halt to all further theological discussion and experimentation. In 1539, he supported, and perhaps even initiated, a parliamentary Bill which contained a Catholic statement on six central points of doctrine. These Six Articles affirmed royal support for the central Catholic doctrines of transubstantiation, communion in one kind for the laity, clerical celibacy, the inviolability of priestly vows of chastity, the validity of private masses, and the necessity of private auricular confession. The fall of Thomas Cromwell the following year helped to ensure that this conservative statement of faith remained in force until Henry's death. At the beginning of 1547, therefore, the doctrinal position of the English church was unequivocably orthodox. Henry's main religious innovations – the break with Rome, the dissolution of the monasteries, and the partial dissolution of the chantries – had been introduced for political and financial rather than theological reasons. Other reforms such as the vernacular translation of the Bible, the attack on idolatry, and the use of an English litany were not entirely incompatible with Catholicism, and their impact was deliberately limited in order to prevent any movement away from orthodoxy. Thus, a statute of 1543 condemned 'untrue' translations of the Bible and forbade the lower orders to read even those licensed by the government.

It was not until Edward VI's brief reign that the Protestant Reformation was brought to England. Between 1547 and 1552, a series of parliamentary statutes ushered in major doctrinal and liturgical change; restrictions on the reading of the scriptures were ended; the fifteenth-century heresy laws were rescinded; all remaining chantries were dissolved; and clerical marriage, communion in both kinds, and the use of a Protestant English Prayer Book were all authorized. In the event, this official reformation was both rapid and radical, but up until just a few weeks before Henry's death it had by no means been inevitable. On the contrary, it had only resulted from a number of complex and unforeseeable political developments at court. Despite the fall of Cromwell, the evangelicals had survived the attacks of the conservatives during the early 1540s and managed to maintain an important presence on both the council and the privy chamber. As a consequence, the last six years of Henry's reign had witnessed a long and bitter power struggle between the conservatives led by Gardiner and Norfolk, and the evangelicals led by Archbishop Thomas Cranmer, Sir Anthony Denny, and the Seymour uncles of Prince Edward. The outcome had remained finely poised until the last months of Henry's reign, when the conservative cause was seriously damaged by the actions of Norfolk's son, the Earl of Surrey. After foolishly drawing attention to his own royal blood, Surrey was arrested on a charge of treason, which was subsequently extended to his father. Two weeks later, Henry changed his will and excluded Gardiner from the regency council which had been appointed to rule during the minority of his son. On Henry's death, therefore, the evangelicals were dominant at court, and they further consolidated their position when Edward Seymour overturned the dead king's will and appointed himself Lord Protector Somerset. Somerset's arrest in 1549 did not, as many expected, return the conservatives to power, but rather led to the primacy of John Dudley, Duke of Northumberland, who in alliance with Archbishop Cranmer eliminated the remaining conservatives from the council. By this stage too, the young king, who was himself a committed Protestant, was beginning to exert his own personal influence.

Initially the religious innovations of Edward's reign reflected the Lutheran doctrines on salvation and the eucharist. The dissolution of the remaining chantries in 1547, for example, was justified on the Lutheran grounds that they encouraged 'vain opinions' concerning purgatory and intercessory masses and left people ignorant of 'their very true and perfect salvation through the death of Jesus Christ'. Similarly, the liturgy of the eucharist outlined in the 1549 Prayer Book was consistent with a belief in consubstantiation, although it is doubtful whether its author, Cranmer, either fully understood or shared Luther's eucharistic views. The new communion ceremony was designed to dispel the belief that each individual mass was a re-enactment of Christ's sacrifice, or that the bread and wine were physically changed as a result of their consecration by a priest. Yet, at the same time, the wording of the administration of the bread and wine, which referred to them as the 'body and blood' of Christ, implied the real presence so important in Luther's theology.

From 1552, however, official statements on doctrine and liturgy began to depart from this Lutheran standpoint, and to echo instead the theology of the Reformed Churches of Zurich, Strasbourg, and John Calvin's Geneva. The threat from the gathering forces of the counter-Reformation, and in particular the defeat of the German Protestants by Charles V at the battle of Muhlberg in 1547, had driven many European Protestants to take refuge in Edwardian England. These Protestant refugees set up 'stranger churches' in London, thus providing models of the ideal Reformed church, and also forged close links with influential English Protestants, such as John Hooper, the future Bishop of Gloucester. The leading Reformed émigrés – Martin Bucer of Strasbourg, the Italian Peter Martyr, and the Pole John à Lasco – provided theological leadership in the universities and offered advice to the English bishops. Their influence encouraged the assimilation of the Reformed theology of grace, salvation, and the eucharist into the new Edwardian Protestant Church.

The distinctive feature of this Reformed theology of salvation was its emphasis on the doctrines of predestination, assurance (or perseverance), and sanctification. Luther's solafidianism had implied the doctrine of predestination, but had not explicitly asserted it. Reformed theologians, however, and in particular John Calvin, emphasized that all men and women were predestined by God before their births either for election (salvation) or reprobation (damnation). As works or good deeds played absolutely no part in this process, the elect were assured that they could never fall from grace, and derived great comfort from this 'assurance'. They could not, however, simply rest on their laurels, for they were obliged to fulfil God's purpose by sanctifying themselves and doing his will on earth, both individually and collectively. It was also generally believed that, while good works could never of themselves merit salvation, the leading of a saintly life was both a consequence and a sign of one's elect status. While sanctification was essentially a work of God's grace rather than of the human will, it was believed that the process could be assisted by the discipline imposed by the church. This Reformed or Calvinist doctrine of grace and salvation was clearly reflected in Cranmer's Forty-Two Articles of Faith issued in 1553; Article Seventeen in particular declared: 'predestination to life is the everlasting purpose of God', and it went on to imply that individual salvation and damnation had been decreed at the beginning of creation, even before the Fall of Adam and Eve.

In the same way, the second Edwardian Prayer Book of 1552 conformed to the Reformed theology of the eucharist and denied both transubstantiation and consubstantiation. Any suggestion of a re-enactment of Christ's sacrifice or of a bodily presence in the bread and wine was now removed from the communion service. The word 'mass' was no longer used, vestments were forbidden, and the communion table was positioned east to west rather than altarwise. The wording of the administration no longer referred to the body and blood of Christ but emphasized instead the commemorative signifi-cance of the sacrament, the minister declaring: 'Take and eat this in remembrance that Christ died for thee, and feed on him in thy heart by faith with thanksgiving.' In addition, the Prayer Book included a communion rubric, known as the Black Rubric, which contained an explicit denial of the real presence; it stated that the bread and wine 'remain still in their very natural substances', and that kneeling to receive communion did not signify that 'any adoration is done or meant to be done'. Ironically, the close association between this new English Protestant church and the Reformed churches abroad was reinforced with the accession of Queen Mary in 1553. For while she returned her kingdom to full doctrinal and liturgical conformity with Rome, many English Protestant exiles fled their homeland and took up residence in Strasbourg, Zurich, Emden, Frankfurt, and Geneva, where they gained first-hand experience of the Zwinglian and Calvinist forms of Protestantism, and became fully immersed in the Calvinist theology of grace and salvation.

On Mary's death in 1558, it was by no means certain what form of religion the new queen, her sister Elizabeth, would adhere to. Some foreign observers, including Philip II of Spain, thought that England might remain doctrinally and liturgically Catholic, even if the royal supremacy were restored. Most English politicians, on the other hand, seemed confident that Elizabeth would attempt to introduce a Protestant form of worship, although they were unsure whether it would be based on the first or second Edwardian Prayer Book. Elizabeth's intentions in 1558 have been no more clear to historians than they were to contemporaries, and have been the subject of much debate and discussion. The oldest tradition, which goes back to the contemporary historian John Foxe, claims that the queen and her Protestant councillors had intended to introduce a settlement based on the 1552 Prayer Book, but were later forced to make some concessions in the Catholic direction because of the implacable opposition of the bishops and some of the lay peers in the House of Lords. During the 1950s, Sir John Neale[1] presented an alternative view, which dominated historical accounts for a generation, but which some now believe was based upon questionable assumptions. According to Neale, Elizabeth had originally wished to do no more than reintroduce her father's national church, but was pressured into a more radical programme by Protestants in the House of Commons, who insisted on the adoption of the 1552 Prayer Book. Neale's thesis was challenged in 1982 by Norman Jones,[2] who exposed a number of errors in his argument and demonstrated that the religious settlement which finally emerged in 1559 was the one that had been originally planned by the government. This account is now generally accepted, although some historians still suggest that Elizabeth herself would have preferred to have reintroduced the 1549 Prayer Book, had she been able to enlist any support for this move from her lay and clerical advisers at court.

In the event, the 1559 parliament restored the Henrician anti-papal statutes and the 1552 Prayer Book – albeit modified in a number of important respects – and in 1563 convocation drew up thirty-nine articles of faith, based substantially on Cranmer's Forty-Two Articles of 1553. This religious settlement has sometimes been described as a *via media* between Catholicism and Protestantism. In reality it was uncompromisingly Protestant in doctrine, although it did reflect both Lutheran and Reformed teachings, and was sometimes deliberately ambiguous in its theology. Thus, while Article Seventeen of the

Thirty-Nine Articles incorporated the Reformed doctrine of predestination, its comments about the reprobate and the absolute assurance of salvation were left vague. Similarly, the Prayer Book published in 1559 described the baptized child as 'a member of Christ, the child of God, and an inheritor of the kingdom', a form of words which seemed to discount the possibility that the infant might have been born reprobate. The eucharistic theology of the new Elizabethan church also hovered uneasily between the Lutheran and Reformed positions. Articles Twenty-Nine to Thirty-One of the Thirty-Nine Articles denied transubstantiation but were ambiguous about the real presence, while the 1559 Prayer Book combined the formula used in 1549 to imply a physical presence with that of 1552 which was meant to indicate commemoration only. Thus, the Elizabethan minister was enjoined to declare ambiguously: 'The blood of our Lord, Jesus Christ, which was shed for thee, preserve thy body and soul unto everlasting life. Drink this in remembrance that Christ's blood was shed for thee and be thankful.' While the doctrinal pronouncements remained inexact, the commemorative interpretation was encouraged by Elizabeth's injunctions of 1559, which ordered that communion be dispensed from a table placed in the middle of the chancel during services, rather than from an altar.

In the longer term, it was Reformed rather than Lutheran theology that came to dominate Elizabethan Protestantism. As early as 1566, the Earl of Sussex had pointed out that Calvinism was being preached throughout the country, and after 1570 it was difficult to hear or read any non-Calvinist theology. All the published sermons preached at St Paul's Cross in London from 1570 onwards took a firm Calvinist line on predestination, and the theology faculties at the universities dispensed doctrinal Calvinism to those training for the ministry; meanwhile the laity were provided with the Genevan Bible in 1560 and a Calvinist catechism in 1563. The Geneva version of the English Bible was extremely popular, and ran to at least thirty-nine editions between 1579 and 1615. Virtually all the leading Elizabethan churchmen were thoroughly imbued with predestinarian theology, and in 1595 nine leading English theologians, including John Whitgift, Archbishop of Canterbury, and Richard Fletcher, Bishop of London, approved the Lambeth Articles, an unequivocal assertion of the Reformed theology of grace and salvation. While a small number of individuals in Elizabethan England stood outside this Calvinist consensus, as Nicholas Tyacke[3] has commented: 'it is not an exaggeration to say that by the end of the sixteenth century the Church of England was largely Calvinist in doctrine.'

Some historians have argued that there was a deep theological divide within Elizabethan and early Stuart England, between so-called Anglicans on the one side and Calvinists or Puritans on the other. This, however, was clearly not the case, for the leading figures of the established church shared with their Presbyterian critics a common theological position, all of them being, in the historian Peter Lake's[4] phrase, 'credal' predestinarians. The orthodox clerics were distinguished from the Presbyterians and from those dubbed Puritans not by a differing theology of salvation, but rather by the fact that they did not share the intensified spirituality displayed by the latter two groups, a spirituality which Lake and R. T. Kendall[5] have labelled 'experimental' predestinarianism. Anxious to lead their lives in accordance with a strict and literal interpretation of predestination, experimental Calvinists sought to distance themselves both religiously and socially from the reprobate or ungodly. In their view, the practical separation of the elect and the damned was an essential prerequisite for the creation of the true church. Consequently, some experimental predestinarians would only associate with sub-groups of the elect within the established church, while others like William Bradshaw would have preferred to have limited communicant membership of the visible, national church solely to the elect. Such exclusivity was viewed with horror by mainstream credal Calvinists such as Whitgift, who saw in such elitism the seeds of a subversive and divisive separatism which might threaten the very existence of a national church. While, therefore, he accepted the idea of an invisible church of the elect, Whitgift rejected any suggestion that it should be synonymous with the visible church of this world, arguing that: 'We must walk in those ways that God hath appointed to bring them [the reprobate] to salvation which is to feed them continually and watch over them so long as they are in danger.'

Although both the credal and experimental forms of predestinarianism may now appear harsh and inflexible creeds, during the late sixteenth and early seventeenth centuries they accorded well with the political and social realities of life in England. The survival of Catholic recusancy and the existence of large numbers of ungodly and seemingly unregenerate vagrants and dissolutes gave credence to the idea of reprobation. In addition, the proffered certainties of Calvinism had great appeal for the many men and women who were suffering from the dislocation and anxiety produced by a period of unpredictable economic development and rapid social change. Not that even the staunchest of experimental Calvinists could allow the doctrine of assurance or perseverance to make them complacent about their own salvation. Indeed, many of them experienced agonies of self-doubt; all too aware of their inadequacies as Christians, they threw themselves headlong into acts of piety and charity in order to prove to themselves that they really were God's elect. Their insecurities were doubtless increased through reading theological works such as William Perkins' *Whether a Man*, published in 1589, which argued that a reprobate might attain temporary faith and 'seem both unto himself and to the Church of God to be a true professor of the Gospel, and yet indeed be none'. Only after many years of mental torment did some Calvinists achieve a certainty of conviction about their elect status, which helped them to cope with, and sometimes to change, the threatening and disturbing world that surrounded them.

While its theology was unmistakably Protestant, in ceremonials and externals the Elizabethan church retained many features which closely resembled those of the Catholic church. An Ornaments Rubric included in the 1559 Prayer Book ordered the use of vestments and the alb and cope during the communion service; and the 1559 injunctions required the clergy to wear the surplice during services, as well as their distinctive outdoor dress which set them apart from the laity. Communicants were allowed to kneel to receive the bread and wine, and the 1552 Black Rubric, which had declared that kneeling in no way implied a real presence, was deleted from the 1559 Prayer Book. The sign of the cross in baptism, the ring in marriage, crucifixes, candles, and other 'popish' remnants were also permitted. Initially, many believed that their retention would only be temporary; they failed to understand, however, that Elizabeth herself saw the 1559 settlement as final, and that she intended to resist all pressure from her councillors, divines, and MPs to purify or reform these ceremonials. As her reign progressed, the 1559 Prayer Book came to attract considerable support, both popular and intellectual; its most outspoken critics, meanwhile, diminished in number and influence, particularly as a consequence of Archbishop Whitgift's successful campaign against unorthodoxy during the 1590s.

During the final years of Elizabeth's reign, the unique form of Protestant church she had erected was given a more distinct theoretical and philosophical identity in the writings of Richard Hooker, an Oxford academic and master of the Temple church in London. During the late 1580s, Hooker became involved in a bitter theological dispute with the Presbyterian, Walter Travers, and as a result in the early 1590s he retired to a country living in Wiltshire to compose a literary *apologia* for the church which had been created in 1559. The various books of the resulting work, entitled *A Treatise on the*

Laws of Ecclesiastical Polity, justified the Elizabethan church as a *via media* between the extremes of Roman Catholicism and radical Puritanism, and defended its own particular ceremonial style and form of government. In his theology, however, Hooker was not simply a traditionalist; although he stood within the mainstream of the Calvinist consensus on the issue of predestination, he challenged many of the assumptions held by both credal and experimental Calvinists. His view of the visible church, for example, was much wider than that of even Whitgift, as he appeared to argue that since Christ had died for all, all men and women – including Roman Catholics – were potentially part of the visible church, and as such should be offered the sacrament of the eucharist, if they were prepared to receive it in good faith. He also put more emphasis on public worship, prayers, and the sacraments than most of his contemporaries, and played down the role of preaching as a means of edification; for these reasons, Hooker has been seen by some ecclesiastical historians such as Peter Lake[6] as 'close to the ideological origins of Arminianism'.

The death of Elizabeth in 1603 resulted in few immediate changes in the English church. The new Calvinist monarch, James I, retained all the most important doctrinal and liturgical features of the Elizabethan settlement, and his first Archbishop of Canterbury, Richard Bancroft, continued Whitgift's campaign to impose uniformity and eliminate irregularity. As part of this policy, Bancroft issued a new set of ecclesiastical canons in 1604. With regard to liturgy, these canons demanded the retention of a number of procedures which had come under attack from Puritans, such as the use of the surplice, kneeling to receive communion, and the inclusion of the sign of the cross and godparents in the baptism ceremony. Doctrinally, the canons were undeniably Calvinist in outlook; yet at the same time they expressed some ambivalence over the doctrine of predestination, and hinted at a recognition of the potentially damaging consequences of it being inadequately or incorrectly explained to the laity. One canon stipulated that the parish clergy were to avoid discussing predestination in their sermons, and leave the topic to bishops, deacons, and 'learned men', who would approach it 'moderately and modestly by way of use and application rather than by way of positive doctrine, as being [more] fitted for schools and universities than simple auditors'. The inclusion of this statement suggests that, while the theology faculties of Oxford and Cambridge universities remained firmly committed to the doctrines of predestination and assurance, some other Jacobeans, including perhaps James I himself, believed that the more extreme implications of these beliefs needed to be played down in order to make them more palatable to the laity.

During the latter half of James's reign, the existence of such doctrinal contradictions within the English church was cleverly exploited by a small group of conservative clerics who were firmly opposed to predestinarian Calvinist theology and subscribed instead to the theories of the Dutch theologian, Jacobus Arminius. Although Arminius, who had taught theology at the University of Leyden, was in most respects an orthodox Protestant, on the question of salvation he had turned his back on a century of Reformed theology by arguing against the extreme predestinarian theology of Calvin's successor at Geneva, Theodore Beza. While Arminius had not explicitly denied predestination, he had claimed that God's grace could be resisted by the individual, that salvation was open to all men and women, and that it depended not only on faith but also on the individual's conduct while on earth. Many of the most committed Calvinists, who had wrestled for lengthy periods with the doctrine of predestination before finally convincing themselves of the assuredness of their salvation, reacted with fury and outrage to Arminius's teachings, and in the United Provinces the resulting theological controversy provoked a major political crisis, culminating in the defeat of the Arminians at the Synod of Dort in 1618.

In England, Arminius's theological opinions proved attractive to a small group of influential churchmen, including Lancelot Andrewes, Richard Neile, Richard Montagu, William Laud, and John Cosin. As well as accepting the Dutch theologian's views on salvation, these English Arminians, or Laudians, exhibited a number of other conservative theological and liturgical positions, which were not to be found in continental Arminianism. They were suspicious of preaching and the personal interpretation of scripture by the laity, and placed great stress on the sacraments as sources of grace. They argued that episcopacy was divinely instituted, and emphasized the divine sanction behind royal authority and the duty upon all subjects to obey monarchs without question. While accepting that Roman Catholicism contained many errors and abuses, they denied that the pope was the Antichrist and that it was impossible for Catholics to attain salvation. Some Arminians were even accused of attempting to disseminate views on the eucharist that were suspiciously similar to transubstantiation. Others rejected the Calvinist insistence on an uninterrupted round of religious duties on Sundays and advocated a far less austere observance of the sabbath, encouraging the laity to indulge in a range of sporting and leisure activities. Above all, however, the Laudians disliked the asceticism and astringency of Calvinism, and desired a return to what Laud called 'the beauty of holiness'. This involved the embellishment of church interiors through the use of the visual arts; the incorporation of more music into church services; and an emphasis on the need for greater reverence and respect in worship.

Although James I may have begun to experience some doubts about the validity of the doctrine of predestination during the last months of his life, earlier in his reign he had given little if any encouragement to the Arminian caucus within his Calvinist church. His son, Charles I, however, who possessed both a highly developed aesthetic sense and a strong attachment to decorum and order, found the ceremonialism and sacramentalism of the Arminians extremely appealing. Consequently, following his accession to the throne in 1625, he took every opportunity to advance the ecclesiastical careers of the Arminians, and by 1633 when William Laud succeeded George Abbot as Archbishop of Canterbury, they had gained control of virtually all the most important high offices in the English church. As a result of their advancement, marked alterations to the official theological outlook of the church were introduced. In 1628, William Laud persuaded Charles I to issue a declaration prohibiting all theological disputation and ordering that the Thirty-Nine Articles should be adhered to in their full and literal sense. By the late 1620s, it was impossible to obtain a licence to publish any theological books containing predestinarian opinions. Attempts were also made to purge the theology departments of the two universities of all Calvinist influences, and any who dared to criticize the new orthodoxy were prosecuted with the full vigour of the ecclesiastical courts.

The impact of the rise of the English Arminians and the scale of their departure from pre-1625 theological norms has been the subject of some considerable historical debate over the last few years. In an article published in the early 1970s, Nicholas Tyacke[7] argued that during the period from 1560 to 1625 there was a common predestinarian Calvinist heritage within the English church, shared by both prelates and Presbyterians alike, against which Laud and his supporters firmly set their faces in the 1630s. In the early 1980s, this view was attacked by Peter White[8] in a controversial article which questioned whether the Elizabethan church was ever fully predestinarian, and went on to claim that the apparently religious conflicts within England in the late 1620s were in fact primarily caused by the pressures of international power politics rather than by theological differences. White further asserted that a basic theological harmony was restored in the 1630s after England's withdrawal from the Thirty Years' War, and concluded by declaring that the so-called rise of Arminianism was merely 'a puritan alibi for repeated failures to impose rigid predestinarian doctrine on the Church of England'.

In 1987, Tyacke[9] vigorously restated his original position in his book *Anti-Calvinists: The rise of English Arminianism c. 1590–1640*, only to be turned on once more by his critics. In an article published the same year, Kevin Sharpe[10] questioned whether it was entirely accurate to label Laud as an Arminian, stressing that the archbishop saw as his main task not the propagation of a new theology but the prevention of divisive doctrinal debate. More recently, George Bernard[11] has also attempted to refute the contention that the church established by Elizabeth was predominantly predestinarian. Claiming that Tyacke has paid too much attention to the academic debates of the university teachers and too little to the realities of parochial life, he asserted that throughout the period from 1529 to 1640 the English church was in essence a monarchical church whose leaders were primarily concerned to maintain stability by restricting controversy. According to Bernard, as there was a long and well-established tradition of acceptability of anti-predestinarian theology going back to 1559 and beyond, the events of the 1630s did not represent any sea-change in the doctrinal position of the English church.

Tyacke's critics are right to point out that he and other historians have been too preoccupied with the theological disputes within the academic communities of pre-civil war England. It must never be forgotten that the great majority of the English people had only a passing interest in the niceties of academic theology, and that outside the bishops' palaces and the two universities such issues remained relatively unimportant. Furthermore, it is almost certainly true that the great majority of the English laity did not share the intellectuals' and higher clergy's attachment to the doctrine of predestination, but retained instead a residual loyalty to the idea that all could potentially achieve salvation. The work of these revisionists has also done much to advance our knowledge of the intricacies of sixteenth- and seventeenth-century theology. None the less, the attention they have rightly drawn to parochial religion and to non-predestinarian elements within the church should not be allowed to obscure the fact that during the period from 1560 to 1625 credal predestinarianism claimed the allegiance of the great majority of Elizabethan and Jacobean churchmen, or that during the 1630s this creed came under a concerted and unprecedented attack from the ecclesiastical authorities.

What White and Bernard also omit to make clear is that, while the great majority of the ordinary members of the church may well have been largely indifferent to theological issues, many of them were at the same time both outraged and alarmed by a number of alien liturgical practices, which were a unique and highly visible feature of English Arminianism. In line with their wish to introduce greater solemnity into worship, the Arminian bishops insisted that the parish clergy should incorporate into their church services a number of ritualistic features regarded by ministers and parishioners alike as 'popish'; these included bowing at the name of Jesus, genuflection, kneeling to receive communion, and the insistence that women should wear veils while being churched following childbirth. Particularly divisive at a parochial level was the stress placed by the bishops on the need for a greater reverence in the communion rite, and their determination that the portable communion tables, which had been used since Elizabethan times, should be replaced by altars permanently positioned at the east end of the chancel and separated from the body of the church by altar rails. These innovations, which were much more obvious and immediate than any doctrinal changes, struck at the very root of Reformed religious beliefs, and in the popular imagination closely equated Arminianism with popery. As a consequence, they elicited a widespread and determined opposition, an opposition consistently down-played in the work of Sharpe, White, and Bernard.

Despite their growing unpopularity, the Laudian bishops continued to pursue their objectives with great vigour throughout the 1630s. In 1637 Laud attempted to impose his sacramental and ceremonial brand of English Protestantism on the rigidly Calvinist Scots, a move that precipitated both the Bishops' War and a profound political crisis in England. Yet, even as this crisis came to a head, the bishops remained unrepentant. In the summer of 1640, they pressured convocation into publishing a new set of conservative canons, which both confirmed the innovations of the previous decade and demanded that the clergy swear an oath not to support any alteration to the government of the church 'by archbishops, bishops, deans, archdeacons, etcetera'. The imposition of this notorious 'etcetera oath' was, however, a tacit acknowledgement that their policies had proved unpopular and had brought the office of bishop into serious disrepute. There can be little doubt that the liturgical policies of these Arminian prelates engendered very deep frustrations, fuelled anxieties about a Catholic insurrection, and produced an increase in support for the alternative, non-episcopalian, Presbyterian system of church government. In so doing, they probably constituted the most important single cause of the subsequent civil war and revolution.

In the confused political and religious climate of the 1640s and 1650s, a wide range of doctrinal and liturgical practice was displayed by the various different religious groups which now had the freedom to worship openly. Throughout the period of the civil war and Interregnum, successive parliamentary and military regimes presided over a church establishment which remained staunchly Calvinist in outlook, and accepted the full, literal interpretation of the doctrine of predestination. However, many ordinary men and women came to find this undiluted predestinarian Calvinism uncongenial and repressive. John Morrill has recently suggested, in an as yet unpublished paper, that the religious history of the period 1640 to 1660 can be usefully viewed as a revolt by large numbers of the English people against the more rigid applications of the doctrines of predestination and perseverance. One thrust of this revolt displayed itself in a widespread attachment to the established church of the pre-1625 period, with its more relaxed doctrinal approach that was able to accommodate the beliefs of Richard Hooker as well as those of the compilers of the Lambeth Articles; the other took the form of the 'left-wing Arminianism' of radical groups such as the General Baptists and Quakers, who rejected the rigidities of predestination in favour of the belief that all could attain salvation, and who, it is argued, won much popular support as a consequence. During these same revolutionary years, others took advantage of the breakdown of press censorship to publicize doctrinal positions which were far more unorthodox. In the tract *Man's Mortalitie*, published in 1644, the Leveller Richard Overton expressed his belief in mortalism, the heretical idea that the soul dies with the body at death to be reborn with it at the Second Coming. In the late 1640s and early 1650s, radicals like William Walwyn and Gerrard Winstanley began to express doubts about the doctrine of hell, while the Ranters went so far as to deny the existence of sin, and some early English Unitarians, such as John Bidle, attacked the doctrine of the trinity and denied Christ's divinity.

A similar wide disparity in liturgical practice was evident during these decades. Between 1645 and 1660, the official liturgy of the state church was that outlined in the Presbyterian Directory of Public Worship, which contained shortened and simplified versions of most of the pre-1640 Prayer Book ceremonies, purged of the features that the Puritans had found so offensive. The new baptismal ceremony, for example, dispensed with the sign of the cross and godparents, the infant being now presented by its own parents, while the marriage service no longer included the use of the ring or the husband's promise to worship his bride with his body. The Directory failed, however, to gain much popular support; many parishes neglected to purchase a copy, and large numbers of conservative clergymen continued to conduct services based predominantly on the Elizabethan Book of Common Prayer. Throughout the Interregnum, there is evidence of a strong popular attachment to the old Prayer Book liturgy, particularly with respect to the traditional rites of passage. Despite the exclusion from the Directory of any ceremony of thanksgiving following childbirth, many women continued to be churched during the 1650s. There was also a widespread attachment to the Book of Common Prayer burial service, and when in 1653 Barebone's Parliament abolished church weddings, hundreds of couples refused to accept the new civil ceremony and continued to be married by the clergy. In contrast, a wide range of new and often revolutionary liturgical practices were adopted by the various radical sects of the 1650s. The Quakers, for example, dispensed with a professional ministry altogether and held completely unstructured meetings, at which both male and female members of the congregation could testify as and when the spirit moved them; they also developed their own simple marriage and burial services.

With the restoration of the monarchy and established church in 1660, this doctrinal and liturgical Babel was brought to an abrupt end. Those who had hoped to see the return of a comprehensive church encompassing a wide spectrum of opinion were disappointed, for the restored Anglican church of the 1660s possessed a narrow, virtually Laudian theological base. As Charles II's reign progressed, more and more Anglican theologians turned their backs on the rigid predestinarian Calvinism so prevalent in the pre-1660 period in favour of a modifed version of the Arminian position on salvation. The restored liturgy was also broadly Laudian. Following the failure of leading Anglican and Presbyterian divines to devise a compromise Prayer Book during the debates at the Savoy Conference in 1661, a new Book of Common Prayer was drawn up by convocation. This 1662 Prayer Book retained a number of highly contentious features, such as vestments, the sign of the cross in baptism, kneeling at communion, and the ring in marriage, and its preface dismissed the Puritan objections to such practices as 'either of dangerous consequence . . . or else of no consequence at all but utterly frivolous and vain'. The compilers of the new Prayer Book talked of priests rather than ministers, and even incorporated sections of Laud's 1637

Scottish Prayer Book into the communion rite. Altars were once more to be railed off at the east end of parish churches. The Act of Uniformity passed by the Cavalier Parliament in 1662 demanded that the clergy accept every one of the Thirty-Nine Articles and every detail of the Prayer Book. This narrow Restoration orthodoxy remained the doctrinal and liturgical basis of the Anglican church for the next half-century, and the many hundreds of men and women who were unable to accept it were forced to leave the established church and join the ranks of the nonconformists.

Throughout the seventeenth century, therefore, the English church was wracked by a series of bitter and divisive doctrinal and liturgical conflicts. During most of this same period, however, there existed within Anglicanism another more liberal and conciliatory tradition, which drew inspiration from the work of Richard Hooker and sought to minimize controversy by advocating a wide measure of toleration on questions of dogma and ceremony. In the pre-civil war period, one group of clerics and laymen who shared this approach and who thus opposed the confrontational policies of Laud and his followers, began to meet at the house of Lucius Cary, Lord Falkland, at Great Tew in Oxfordshire. As well as Falkland himself, the 'Great Tew Group' included individuals like John Hales and William Chillingworth, who were opposed to rigid dogma and argued that the laity had the right to interpret scripture for themselves 'in the light of private Reason'. These conciliatory figures were profoundly disturbed by the bitter armed conflict of the 1640s, and the Royalist Falkland appears to have committed virtual suicide on the battlefield at Newbury in 1643. None the less, even in the climate of intense religious controversy which existed during the civil war and Interregnum, this moderate strain survived. During the 1650s, the Cambridge Platonists, a group of academics centred on Emmanuel College, Cambridge, who included within their number Henry More, Ralph Cudworth, and Benjamin Whichcote, continued to advocate a non-dogmatic, liberal, and rationalistic version of Anglicanism, and sought to bring about greater unity among English Protestants by emphasizing the core of belief upon which all could agree.

Although in the immediate post-Restoration period the religious climate proved uncongenial to such ideas, by the later decades of the seventeenth century churchmen schooled in this tradition began to gain some real influence within established Anglican circles. In a recent article, the historian John Spurr[12] has suggested that the name 'Latitudinarianism', which has traditionally been given to this movement, is inappropriate. He has argued that historians who have sought to identify a Latitudinarian party within the church have been chasing a chimera, as the label was merely a vague, derogatory term devised by embittered contemporary Puritans who felt betrayed by the abandonment of predestinarian theology. It none the less remains true that there existed within the late seventeenth-century church a group of churchmen who adopted a tolerant approach towards dissent, were willing to respond to the discoveries of the early natural scientists, and were interested in the relationship between religious belief and reason. Spurr concedes that the influence of this group grew steadily between 1660 and 1688, and that by the 1690s, when one of their number, John Tillotson, was appointed Archbishop of Canterbury, they had become the dominant Anglican theological school. However they should be labelled, these men represented a modernist strain within the late seventeenth-century church and anticipated many elements of the religious and intellectual climate of the eighteenth century.

NOTES

1 Sir John Neale, *Elizabeth I and her Parliaments* (London, 1953).
2 Norman Jones, *Faith by Statute: Parliament and the settlement of religion 1559* (London, 1982).
3 Nicholas Tyacke, *Anti-Calvinists: The rise of English Arminianism* c. *1590–1640* (Oxford, 1987).
4 Peter Lake, 'Calvinism and the English church 1570–1635', *Past and Present* 114 (1987).
5 R. T. Kendall, *Calvin and English Calvinism to 1649* (Oxford, 1979).
6 Lake, 'Calvinism and the English church'.
7 Nicholas Tyacke, 'Puritanism, Arminianism and counter-revolution', in Conrad Russell (ed.), *The Origins of the English Civil War* (London, 1973).
8 Peter White, 'The rise of Arminianism reconsidered', *Past and Present* 101 (1983).
9 Tyacke, *Anti-Calvinists*.
10 Kevin Sharpe, 'Archbishop Laud', *History Today* 33 (1987).
11 George Bernard, 'The Church of England, *c.* 1579–*c.* 1642', *History* 75 (1990).
12 John Spurr, '"Latitudinarianism" and the Restoration church', *Historical Journal* 31 (1988).

SUGGESTIONS FOR FURTHER READING

An excellent introduction to the first half of the period is Horton Davies, *Worship and Theology in England from Cranmer to Hooker 1534–1603* (New Jersey, 1970). For sixteenth-century debates on the eucharist, see C. W. Dugmore, *The Mass and the English Reformers* (London, 1958);

and P. N. Brooks, *Thomas Cranmer's Doctrine of the Eucharist* (London, 1965). On the theology of predestinarianism in the sixteenth and early seventeenth centuries, see R. T. Kendall, *Calvin and English Calvinism to 1649* (Oxford, 1979); Dewey D. Wallace, *Puritans and Predestination: Grace in English Protestant theology, 1525–1695* (Chapel Hill, N.C., 1982); and P. Lake, 'Calvinism and the English church, 1570–1635', *Past and Present* 114 (1987).

The pressures for evangelical reform in Henry VIII's reign are discussed by Maria Dowling in 'Anne Boleyn and reform', *Journal of Ecclesiastical History* 36 (1985); and in 'The gospel and the court: reformation under Henry VIII', in P. Lake and M. Dowling (eds), *Protestantism and the National Church in Sixteenth-century England* (London, 1987). Conservative pressures are analysed in G. Redworth, 'A study in the formulation of policy: the genesis and evolution of the Act of Six Articles', *Journal of Ecclesiastical History* 37 (1986). For the influence of Lutheranism in England, see B. Hall, 'The early rise and gradual decline of Lutheranism in England', in D. Baker (ed.), *Reform and Reformation: England and the Continent* c. *1500–c. 1750*, Studies in Church History, Subsidia 2 (Oxford, 1979).

Sir John Neale's views on the Elizabethan Settlement are included in *Elizabeth I and her Parliaments* (London, 1953). There are several more recent important studies of the Elizabethan church settlement; W. S. Hudson, *The Cambridge Connection and the Elizabethan Settlement of 1559* (Durham, N.C., 1980), Norman Jones, *Faith by Statute: Parliament and the settlement of religion 1559* (London, 1982); and N. M. Sutherland, 'The Marian exiles and the establishment of the Elizabethan regime', *Archiv für Reformationsgeschichte* 78 (1987).

The theological positions of Whitgift and Hooker are examined in detail in an excellent, but difficult book by Peter Lake, *Anglicans and Puritans? Presbyterianism and English conformist thought from Whitgift to Hooker* (London, 1988). Bancroft's theology can be found in S. B. Babbage, *Puritanism and Richard Bancroft* (London, 1962). For differing views on the rise of Arminianism, see Nicholas Tyacke, 'Puritanism, Arminianism and counter-revolution', in Conrad Russell (ed.), *The Origins of the English Civil War* (London, 1973), and Nicholas Tyacke, *Anti-Calvinists: The rise of English Arminianism* c. *1590–1640* (Oxford, 1987); P. White, 'The rise of Arminianism reconsidered', *Past and Present* 101 (1983), and the subsequent debate between White and Tyacke in *Past and Present* 115 (1987); Kevin Sharpe, 'Archbishop Laud', *History Today* 33 (1987); and G. W. Bernard, 'The Church of England c. 1529–c. 1642', *History* 75 (1990). The best account of the rise of Arminianism in England remains Tyacke's *Anti-Calvinists*.

For the theological and liturgical diversity during the Interregnum, see John Morrill, 'The church in England 1642–9', in John Morrill (ed.), *Reactions to the English Civil War 1642–9* (London, 1982); Christopher Hill, *The World Turned Upside Down: Radical ideas during the English revolution* (London, 1972); and Claire Cross, 'The church in England 1646–60', in G. Aylmer, *The Interregnum: The quest for settlement* (London, 1972).

For the post-Restoration church, see I. M. Green, *The Re-establishment of the Church of England 1660–1663* (Oxford, 1978). The new Prayer Book of 1662 is discussed in Ronald Hutton, *The Restoration: A political and religious history of England and Wales 1658–1667* (Oxford, 1985); and F. Proctor and W. H. Frere, *A New History of the Book of Common Prayer* (London, 1902). 'Latitudinarianism' is considered by John Spurr in '"Latitudinarianism" and the Restoration church', *Historical Journal* 31 (1988).

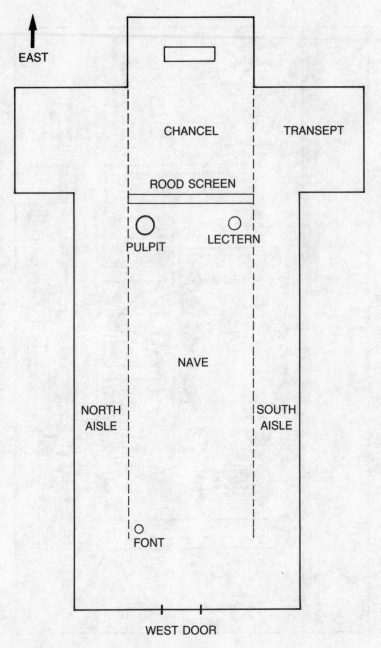

Figure 1 Plan of a church interior.

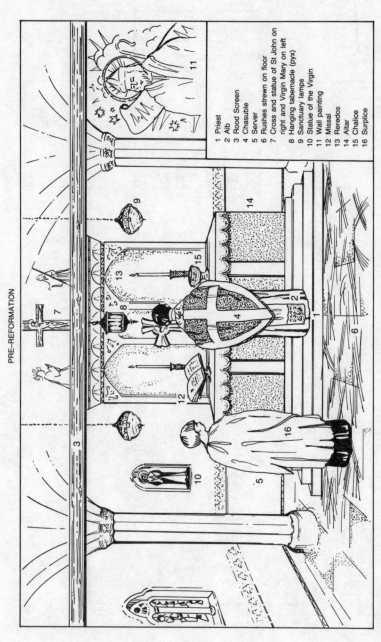

PRE-REFORMATION

1 Priest
2 Alb
3 Rood Screen
4 Chasuble
5 Server
6 Rushes strewn on floor
7 Cross and statue of St John on right and Virgin Mary on left
8 Hanging tabernacle (pyx)
9 Sanctuary lamps
10 Statue of the Virgin
11 Wall painting
12 Missal
13 Reredos
14 Altar
15 Chalice
16 Surplice

Figures 2a and *2b* Changes in church interior and clerical dress as a result of the Reformation.

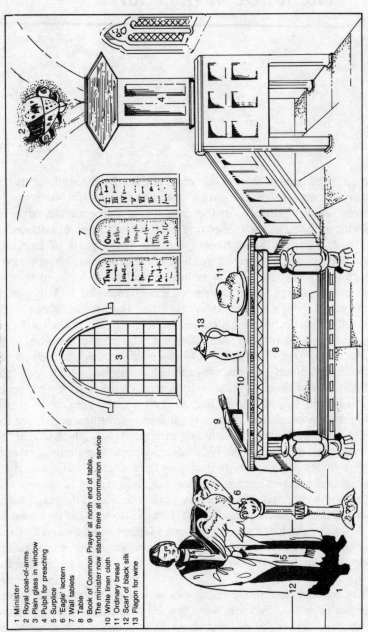

POST-REFORMATION

1 Minister
2 Royal coat-of-arms
3 Plain glass in window
4 Pulpit for preaching
5 Surplice
6 'Eagle' lectern
7 Wall tablets
8 Table
9 Book of Common Prayer at north end of table.
  The minister now stands there at communion service
10 White linen cloth
11 Ordinary bread
12 Scarf of black silk
13 Flagon for wine

2b

3   The fabric of the church

During the course of the fifteenth and early sixteenth centuries over 60 per cent of the parish churches in England were extensively rebuilt, normally in the magnificent Perpendicular style of Gothic architecture first employed in the construction of Gloucester Cathedral during the thirteenth century. In all parts of England, but particularly in the rich wool-producing regions, church naves were enlarged, new aisles were added, and stone replaced by vast expanses of stained glass. This work was financed by the laity – both patrons of livings and parishioners, large numbers of whom made contributions during their lifetimes and left bequests in their wills for the refurbishing of their local churches. During the period 1370 to 1532, 95 per cent of testators in Norwich left bequests to their parish churches. Similarly, on the eve of the Reformation, over 90 per cent of testators in three of the archdeaconries of the diocese of Lincoln were leaving bequests to cathedrals, and over 80 per cent to parish churches. A number of distinct but linked motivations accounted for this high level of support, including a personal piety which sought the glorification of God, a deeply-felt anxiety about the attaining of personal salvation, and a desire to display their wealth and express their communal pride in impressive local buildings. Often, of course, all these motives coexisted, as they did in the erection of the magnificent Holy Trinity Church at Long Melford in Suffolk. Built as a rival to the parish church at Lavenham, Long Melford was financed by local parishioners, some of whose names were carved in stone around the clerestory in an inscription which called for prayers to be said for their souls.

By contrast, during the century or so which separated the Reformation from the civil war, very few English parish churches were built or substantially renovated. Only one major new church, St Giles, Cripplegate, London, was constructed during the last years

Plate 1
Holy Trinity
Church, Long
Melford, Suffolk.
The names of
the donors
are inscribed
above the upper
windows. (The
Hulton–Deutsch
Collection)

of Henry VIII's reign. During Elizabeth's long reign a mere nineteen churches or chapels were built, and only a handful more, including Fulmer and Bletchley in Buckinghamshire, Groomsbridge and St Nicholas, Rochester, in Kent, and St John Briggate in Leeds, were completed under the early Stuarts. Given the widespread destruction of church interiors during the post-Reformation period and the relentless removal of 'superstitious' objects, it is hardly surprising that the parishioners of the mid- and late sixteenth century were unwilling to finance new ecclesiastical building or furnishing. Furthermore, the new Protestant theology did little to encourage donation, since solafidianism removed much of the potential advantage to benefactors, and the emphasis upon the Word reduced the importance of beautifying the church interior. The laity, therefore, became reluctant to invest in their local churches, while an impoverished ecclesiastical establishment had few resources to spare for its buildings.

The small number of new Elizabethan and Jacobean churches that were constructed were built in the Perpendicular style, and, in order to assert the continuity of medieval and Reformed churches, they retained the compartmentalized lay-out of the Gothic buildings. The post-Reformation additions to existing churches were also Gothic, with one notable exception – the Renaissance-style porch added to St Nicholas church at Sunningwell in Berkshire in 1562. The porch was commissioned by Bishop John Jewel, and its design may have been influenced by the neo-classical architecture to which Jewel had been exposed during his years of exile in Mary's reign. Although a more general move away from the indigenous Gothic style of architecture and church design only began in earnest a century later after the Restoration, the trend was signalled as early as the 1630s with the construction of St Paul's, Covent Garden. St Paul's was the first important example of the new 'auditory' churches which were to become increasingly common in the later seventeenth and eighteenth centuries. Architecturally, these churches reflected the impact of the Renaissance, and their internal lay-out gave physical expression to the doctrinal and liturgical changes of the Reformation. Unlike Catholic churches, which had been primarily places of sacrifice, Protestant churches were essentially arenas for the exposition of scripture, and the new auditory style was more appropriate for services dominated by preaching and the reading of the Word. In commissioning St Paul's, Covent Garden, the Earl of Bedford is reputed to have told his architect, Inigo Jones, that he wished the building to resemble a barn, and the interior of the church was indeed extremely simple, consisting only of a chancel and a nave without arcades. Its exterior was, however, more elaborate, built to a Palladian design and fronted by an impressive classical portico.

Prior to the introduction of these purpose-built auditory churches, existing Gothic church interiors were adapted for Protestant use by the cheapest and most convenient means possible. Although some Protestants, such as Bishop Hooper, argued that a single-roomed effect was more appropriate to the new Protestant liturgy and the doctine of the priesthood of all believers, the compartmental interior of the church with a separate nave and chancel divided by a huge rood screen was usually left unaltered, and in many parishes ministers chose to use different parts of the church for distinct types of corporate worship: the nave for matins and evensong, the side chapels for weekday services, and the chancel and sanctuary for Holy Communion. Theological change, however, rendered some alterations to the fabric of parish churches unavoidable. The most significant of these was the substitution of a wooden table for a stone altar, a move that gave a visual emphasis to the Protestant belief that the eucharist was not the re-enactment of Christ's sacrifice on Calvary but a remembrance of the Last Supper. As even Calvinists were not opposed to all ornamentation, the new communion tables were not entirely without detail. Some indeed were heavily decorated; at Hedenham in Cambridgeshire the table had seven legs, while at Townstall in Devon the bulbous-shaped legs were carved into the forms of allegorical beasts.

The position of the communion table was also changed by the Reformation. Protestants found it theologically unacceptable to separate the table from the laity in the nave, and to place it on high in the position of an altar at the east end of the church. The 1559 Elizabethan injunctions had specified that, while not in use, the holy table should be 'set in the place where the altar stood', but that during the communion service it should be moved down 'in good sort within the chancel' so that the minister could be more clearly heard. Some parishes followed this peripatetic approach, using a trestle table to facilitate mobility; others, however, preferred to keep the table permanently in the middle of the chancel, sometimes surrounding it with rails to protect it from dogs. In these latter churches, the minister would conduct the main part of the communion service in the nave with the screens closed, and then take communicants through to the chancel to receive the eucharist, an arrangement that inevitably invested the sacrament with a sense of mystery. A number of other Catholic accessories to the mass disappeared along with the altar after 1559. With no elevation of the host there was no need for the pyx, and now that the notion of sacrifice had been denied, censers too were redundant. Communion in both kinds also rendered the existing small chalices inadequate, and many were melted down to make new cups large enough to hold sufficent wine for all the lay communicants.

Further changes to the interior of parish churches resulted from the new emphasis upon the importance of the sermon, although here implementation was only gradual. As a great many parishes had invested in new pulpits and lecterns during the fifteenth century, few were erected during Elizabeth's reign, but following the issuing in 1604 of new ecclesiastical canons which ordered that 'a comely and decent pulpit' should be kept in every church, the reign of James I saw a notable upsurge in pulpit-building. Some of these new Jacobean pulpits were raised to a great height and topped by impressive sounding-boards in order both to emphasize the importance of the sermon and to make the preacher visible above the rows of high-backed pews. Pews were also modified in a number of ways in the post-Reformation period. To satisfy the demands of wealthier parishioners for more comfort during the often lengthy sermons, pews with cushions began to proliferate. Many were also given lockable doors to preserve privacy, and curtains to prevent draughts; indeed, some became so elaborate that during the 1630s the Bishop of Norwich, Richard Corbett, was led to remark wryly that they lacked 'nothing but beds to hear the word of God on'. The pews all faced the pulpit and reading-desk, and were usually arranged so that the most prosperous and socially elevated parishioners were positioned nearest the front. These seating arrangements thus provided a visual reflection and reinforcement of the social divisions within the parish; when Richard Gough set out at the end of the seventeenth century to write the history of his parish of Myddle in Shropshire, he decided that the most natural way to organize his account was to consider in turn the occupants of each pew in Myddle church.

The most noticeable and dramatic changes, however, in the fabric of post-Reformation English churches were those resulting from iconoclasm – the widespread destruction of 'popish' images and ornamentation during the reigns of Edward and Elizabeth. During the second half of the sixteenth century, hundreds of medieval sculptures and carved images of saints were destroyed or removed, the colourful wall-paintings which had decorated most churches were whitewashed, stained glass was shattered or taken away, and the rood lofts which had held up the great crucifixes and figures of the Virgin Mary and St John were pulled down. The motive for this destruction and its impact upon contemporaries was well described by the Protestant, Bernard Gilpin, who wrote in 1552:

> They [Catholics] come to the church to feede their eyes, and not their soules: they are not taught, that no visible thing is to be worshipped. And for because they see not in the church the shining pompe and pleasant variety (as they thought it) of painted clothes, candlesticks, images, altars, lampes, tapers, they say, as good to go into the barne.

Iconoclasm was from the outset inspired by the government. It began during Henry VIII's reign with the Cromwellian injunctions of 1536 and 1538, which singled out for destruction superstitious images attracting pilgrimages and offerings. At this stage, however, the vast majority of churches remained unaffected, and it was not until Edward's reign that images were removed and destroyed wholesale. In response to the government's condemnation of images in July 1547 and February 1548, commissioners roamed the country, either chivying churchwardens into taking action, or on occasions, as at Hull, smashing the images themselves. At the same time, the royal visitors checked that rood screens had been demolished, wall paintings covered with white lime, and stained glass windows reglazed with white glass. While initially the work of these Edwardian commissioners was motivated primarily by religious conviction, later in the reign churches began to be looted purely for profit. Hard-pressed financially, the government, headed by the Duke of Northumberland, ordered the commissioners to confiscate all remaining church treasures, in the form of plate, jewels, vestments, and even the bronze of the bells, to meet royal debts.

Many ecclesiastical objects of great value and craftsmanship were thus lost during Edward's reign, but a large number of others managed to escape detection and destruction. The high cost of substituting plain white for stained glass deterred some churchwardens from complying with the government's orders, while many others were motivated to hide and preserve sacred objects by an enduring spirit of Catholic piety. Roger Martyn, churchwarden of Long Melford in Suffolk, for example, kept the reredos, organ, clocks, and bells of Holy Trinity Church in his own home, in the hope that his heirs would be able to restore them to the church sometime in the future. After Mary's accession in 1553, considerable numbers of images, vestments, chalices, and crucifixes did indeed reappear in parish churches throughout the country, but only a few years later many of them were to fall foul of renewed attacks on images at the beginning of Elizabeth's reign. In some parts of the country Elizabeth's accession was greeted with spontaneous outbursts of iconoclastic activity, and shortly afterwards a new set of royal visitors began systematically to pull down, smash, or burn any remaining images. As a result, the interiors of Elizabethan churches were barer, plainer, and far less colourful than those of the early sixteenth century. Yet, once again, although devastating in places, the destruction was far from complete. In some of the more remote parishes, sculptures and carvings escaped the attentions of the iconoclasts, and elsewhere ornamental features such as carved fonts were boarded over and plastered to protect them from the commissioners. Nor did the widespread destruction of the vestments, stained glass, and crucifixes, which many Calvinists found so objectionable, meet with the approval of Elizabeth herself. As a result, many ornamental objects once again survived, if only to become the focus for the activities of Puritan iconoclasts during the civil war.

Only two kinds of ornamentation were allowed by the Elizabethan church: painted boards and family memorials. The former depicted the royal coat of arms, texts from the scriptures, the Creed, or the Lord's Prayer. The royal arms, which symbolized the supremacy of the crown over the church, were generally placed over the tympanum where the rood had previously stood. The painted texts, which emphasized the importance of the Word, were intended as an aid to devotion, and were more readily seen than the Bibles, which were also on display in every church. These texts were often inscribed on woodwork which had formed part of the old rood screens, reredoses, and triptychs; this was the case at Binham Priory in Norfolk, where the medieval paintings of saints are now showing through the worn whitewash and black-letter Protestant text.

The second vehicle for ornamentation allowed by the Elizabethan church was the family tomb. While the superstitious veneration of the saints had been swept away by the reformers, the worldly vanity of elaborate family memorials was permitted and grew ever more popular. Indeed, it became almost *de rigueur* for a man of substance to put aside a considerable sum for his funeral monument, the £600 spent on the third Earl of Sussex's memorial being fairly typical. Even the godly were not averse to the outward display of a funeral monument, as the tomb at St Bartholomew's, London, of Sir Walter Mildmay who endowed Emmanuel College, Cambridge, for the education of godly preachers well illustrates. Many of the godly liked to portray themselves and their families kneeling in prayer on their tombs. For the most part, however, Elizabethans preferred to be remembered for their ancestry and achievements rather than for their piety, and in order to impress succeeding generations of parishioners, they incorporated into their monuments inscriptions, heraldic devices, and portraits of themselves in their lavish official robes. Funeral monuments continued to be erected in parish churches in all parts of the country throughout the seventeenth century. By this stage, many of them reflected the growing importance of the classical movement, depicting their subjects in classical settings, surrounded by symbolic fruits, flowers, and urns. During the later years of the century, it was also common to show the deceased dressed in Roman costume. Among the best surviving examples of seventeenth-century monuments are Lady Elizabeth Carey's at Stowe-Nine-Churches in Northamptonshire, Sir Thomas Lucy's at Charlecote in Warwickshire, Edward St John's at Lydiard Tregoze in Wiltshire, Sir Edward Spencer's at Great Broughton in Northamptonshire, and Edward Marshall's bust of William Harvey at Hempstead in Essex.

Despite these minor concessions towards decoration, between 1560 and 1625 the great majority of English churches remained without any significant internal ornamentation. With the accession of Charles I, however, and the subsequent rise to prominence of the Arminian party, the situation was to change dramatically. Charles and his leading ecclesiastical adviser, William Laud, agreed with Roman Catholics about the efficacy of the visual arts as aids to devotion, and thus made the revival of what they called 'the beauty of holiness' one of their chief religious priorities. This campaign to reincorporate the visual arts into religious devotion had a particular appeal for Charles I, who was one of the foremost art collectors of his day. During the 1630s, the king and his Arminian bishops encouraged both laity and clergy to fill their parish churches with lavish decorations and furnishings, in the form of new altars, chalices, pictures, and stained glass, thus provoking a bitter conflict with those who preferred the plainness of the pre-1625 church interiors and who continued to regard decoration as popish and idolatrous.

Several bishops, in particular Laud himself and Richard Neile, were responsible for important changes in the decoration of their cathedrals. At Durham, Neile installed a new marble altar at the east end of the cathedral, and he subsequently introduced similar changes to the interiors of Winchester Cathedral and York Minster. Laud altered the internal lay-out of Gloucester Cathedral while dean of that diocese, and as Bishop of London he launched a nationwide appeal in the late 1620s for the repair of St Paul's Cathedral in

London, which was on the point of collapse, entrusting major restoration work to the classical architect, Inigo Jones. Altars were also erected in Bristol, Exeter, Salisbury, and Worcester Cathedrals. The interiors of a number of parish churches were similarly transformed as the Laudian bishops campaigned vigorously for the erection of altars positioned permanently at the east end of the chancel and railed off from the nave. Parishes such as St John's, Beverley, in Yorkshire, All Saints, Maidstone, in Kent, and St Thomas-in-the-Cliffe, Lewes, in Sussex, responded quickly to episcopal pressure and introduced the new altars and rails.

In some churches the importance of the Laudian altar was further emphasized by the addition of an elaborate new reredos. At Wigan, a reredos depicting the death of Ananias, which had been woven in the Mortlake tapestry works, was placed behind the altar of the parish church, and at Nicholas Ferrar's parish church at Little Gidding in Cambridgeshire, a reredos consisting of three brass plates inscribed with the Ten Commandments, the Creed, and the Lord's Prayer was erected. The Commandments were also written in gold above the altar of St Peter's, Wolverhampton. Several churches were structurally redesigned along Arminian lines during the 1630s; the Arminian cleric and poet, George Herbert, supervised the restoration of the ruined church at Leighton Bromswold near Huntingdon, and Abbey Dore church in Herefordshire was restored by a local landowner, Viscount Scudamore, who commissioned a new oak roof and screen.

Elsewhere, however, the Arminian initiatives were widely resisted. In the late 1620s, some Calvinists attempted to obstruct the collection of money for the repair of St Paul's, and throughout the 1630s large numbers of churchwardens were summoned to appear before the ecclesiastical authorities for failing to introduce the required changes to the lay-out of their churches. In 1635, the churchwardens of Beckington in Somerset were excommunicated and imprisoned for defying the authorities; yet the following year William Piers, Bishop of Bath and Wells, admitted that fewer than a third of the parishes in his diocese had converted their communion tables into altars. A similar widespread refusal to co-operate was encountered in the diocese of Peterborough, where parishes such as Pattishall and All Saints', Northampton, witnessed prolonged battles between the churchwardens and the episcopal visitors over the position of the communion table. In East Anglia, the efforts of the Bishop of Norwich, Matthew Wren, to enforce the new orders caused great resentment and led to the publication of the highly critical, anonymous tract, *Newes from Ipswich*. Even some of the most socially elevated paid a heavy price for opposing the policy. In the mid-1630s, John Williams, who as Bishop of Lincoln was one of the few remaining non-Laudian prelates, made public his opposition to his colleagues' initiative; he became involved in a heated literary battle on the subject with the staunch Arminian, Peter Heylyn, and following the publication of his work *The Holy Table Name and Thing*, he was thrown into prison. Charles I's government gave the bishops its firm backing on this issue; when the parishioners of St Gregory's in London appealed to the Court of Arches against a directive from the dean and chapter of St Paul's Cathedral concerning the position of their communion table, no less a body than the privy council itself intervened with an order in favour of the ecclesiastical authorities.

With the coming of war and revolution in the 1640s, the interiors of many churches were once more substantially altered. Within weeks of their meeting in November 1640, the MPs of the Long Parliament launched a full-scale attack upon Laud and his Arminian innovations, and throughout the country those who had objected to the physical changes introduced during the previous decade began to destroy altars, rails, and stained glass. The next two years saw frequent attacks on churches, leading to considerable loss and damage. In 1643, parliament gave retrospective official approval to this iconoclasm by passing an ordinance for the dismantling and destruction of 'all crucifixes, crosses and all images and pictures of any one or more persons of the Trinity, or of the Virgin Mary, and all other images and pictures of saints or superstitious inscriptions'. Zealous Calvinists, like Sir Robert Harley and William Dowsing, received specific commissions to oversee the destruction of images; Dowsing, who kept a journal of his activities, personally visited nearly sixty churches in East Anglia. Among the hundreds of churches that suffered attack during the 1640s, particularly badly affected were the parish churches of Shrivenham in Oxfordshire, Compton Wynyates in Warwickshire, and Harley's own church at Brampton Bryan in Herefordshire. Perhaps surprisingly, however, a great many funeral monuments survived the destruction of the civil war period, and indeed new tombs and mounuments continued to be commissioned and placed in parish churches throughout the 1640s and 1650s.

The English cathedrals also paid heavily for their association with Arminianism, as image-breakers inflicted considerable damage on them during the civil war. At the beginning of the war, parliament seized the remainder of the money which Laud had collected for the repair of old St Paul's, and the MPs later gave the scaffolding being used to repair the tower to one of its army regiments in lieu of pay. Carlisle Cathedral suffered badly from the attentions of garrisons between 1645 and 1652, and York Minster only avoided serious damage through the personal intervention of the New Model Army commander, Sir Thomas Fairfax. The period following the parliamentary victory saw a number of proposals for the demolition or conversion to secular use of the English cathedrals. In 1651, the Rump Parliament debated a suggestion that all twenty-six should be demolished and their stonework and furnishings sold to provide funds for the poor. Yarmouth corporation argued that Norwich Cathedral should be pulled down and its stone used for the construction of a workhouse, and in 1657 it was proposed that Rochester Cathedral should be sold and the proceeds used to pay the arrears owed to disabled sailors. At Lichfield, demolition work was actually started; some lead was removed from the roof and the great bell was broken up. While the threat of wholesale destruction failed to materialize, the cathedrals were turned over to a variety of secular uses. The portico of St Paul's in London was let out to shopkeepers, and the main body of the church became a cavalry stables. At St Asaph, a wine-shop was set up in the cathedral and the font was used as a trough for animals. At Exeter, the bishop's palace was used as a bakery and the cathedral became a centre for preaching, a wall being built to divide the building in two so that Presbyterians and Independents could worship separately. Other cathedrals functioned as barracks and prisons.

Many important and beautiful works of art were undoubtedly lost as a result of the image-breaking of both the Reformation and civil war, and succeeding generations have rightly regretted the serious cultural impoverishment which has resulted. Indeed, iconoclasm has frequently been portrayed as little more than mindless vandalism perpetrated by Philistine bigots. It is, none the less, important to remember that such activity was by no means simply destruction for destruction's sake. For those who carried out the purges of the English cathedrals and parish churches during the sixteenth and seventeenth centuries, the artistic objects they destroyed were synonymous with paganism and superstition, and were thus the antithesis of true religion. Puritans like Harley and Dowsing regarded altars, statues, paintings, and stained glass not as aids to religious devotion, but as positive dangers to men's souls, and they reacted to them rather as a modern-day Jew might do to a beautifully sculpted or painted swastika. Justifiable regrets, therefore, about the effect of the iconoclasts' activities on the nation's ecclesiastical heritage should not be allowed to blind us to the sincerity of their motives.

In the midst of all this destruction of ecclesiastical property, the decision of one individual to build an entirely new church assumed considerable political importance. The only completely new church to be constructed in England during the Interregnum was built at Staunton Harold in Leicestershire by the staunch Anglican and Royalist, Sir Robert Shirley. It was constructed to a traditional Perpendicular Gothic design, and despite the official proscription of Anglicanism, its internal lay-out and furnishings incorporated a number of obvious Laudian features. The commissioning of such an overtly Anglican church was seen by the authorities as a deliberately provocative gesture, and when Shirley shortly afterwards refused to contribute towards the military defence of the Cromwellian state, he was imprisoned in the Tower of London, where he later died.

In the immediate aftermath of the Restoration, the newly restored bishops made the rebuilding and renovating of their cathedrals one of their chief priorities, and by 1662 all except Lichfield and Rochester were once more in a good state of repair. The most important development in English ecclesiastical architecture, however, during the post-Restoration period came about not through any new religious initiative, but as a result of the ever-present danger of fire. In early September 1666, the old city of London was devastated by the Great Fire, which as well as destroying thousands of secular buildings left old St Paul's with severe structural damage, and no fewer than eighty-seven of the capital's parish churches gutted or in ruins. In the aftermath of the disaster, the rebuilding of London's churches was entrusted to the brilliant young architect, Christopher Wren, who set to work almost immediately, and over the next few years completely transformed the ecclesiastical architecture of the capital.

Wren designed fifty new churches, most of which were constructed during the 1670s. Although he consistently employed classical conventions in his designs, he also incorporated features reminiscent of the older indigenous style of English ecclesiastical architecture, and he was careful to make each church unique. The churches were built to two basic designs – the traditional format of nave and aisles, and the newer auditory lay-out of a rectangular space decorated with varying arrangements of columns and vaulting. Of particular importance to his designs was the great variety of individual spires, steeples, and towers which he employed; again, while some of these, such as at St Vedast, Foster Lane, and St James, Garlickhithe, echoed the earlier

English Gothic style, others were classical in influence. Among the best examples of Wren's parish churches are St Stephen's, Walbrook, St Magnus Martyr, St Martin's, Ludgate, St Bene't's, Paul's Wharf, and St Margaret Lothbury. Before long, new parish churches in other parts of the country began to reflect Wren's innovations, one early example being Willen parish church in Buckinghamshire, built in 1680.

The centrepiece of Wren's work in London was, of course, the construction of his imposing new cathedral, a project that occupied much of his working life from the submission of his earliest plans in 1669 and the beginning of construction work in 1675, to the eventual completion of the building in 1710. As we have seen, old St Paul's had been in a very poor state of repair even before 1640, and had suffered further damage as a result of the events of the 1640s before being fatally weakened by the Great Fire. The justly famous building that replaced it once more illustrated Wren's genius for combining classical and Gothic themes. The lay-out was traditional and mirrored that of the old medieval cathedral, but both exterior and interior were lavishly decorated with classical arches and columns, and the whole building was dominated by a vast classical dome, which rose almost to the height of the spire of Salisbury Cathedral, one of the tallest Gothic buildings in Europe. Wren's thrusting and dynamic cathedral reflected the pride and confidence of what was by now one of the foremost cities and commercial centres in Europe, and symbolized the growing assertiveness and patriotism of an emergent imperial power. It was an arena perfectly adapted to pomp and circumstance and was to witness many subsequent celebrations of the successes of the English nation as it grew to become a dominant world power.

Following the passing of the 1689 Toleration Act, which gave Presbyterians, Baptists, Quakers, and other dissenters from the Anglican church the right to worship in public, new nonconformist meeting-houses began to be constructed throughout England. While these buildings often shared with Wren's London churches a basic classical design, they fundamentally differed from them both in their smaller scale and greater simplicity. The dissenters who met in these new places of worship belonged to a Puritan tradition which disapproved of the decoration of churches, and the interiors of meeting-houses were thus kept bare and plain. Many, none the less, displayed an ordered and simple beauty. Among the best early examples are 'Old Meeting' in Norwich, Flowergate Unitarian Chapel at Whitby, Friar Street Chapel, Ipswich, and Churchgate Street Chapel, Bury St Edmunds. The earliest Quaker meeting-houses, such as Jordans

Plate 2
St Paul's
Cathedral,
London, and
some of Wren's
parish churches.
(The Hulton–
Deutsch
Collection)

Plate 3
Jordan's Quaker
meeting-house,
Buckinghamshire.
(The Hulton–
Deutsch
Collection)

in Buckinghamshire, Colthouse in Lancashire, Skipton in Yorkshire, and Marazion in Cornwall, were built in the vernacular style of the late seventeenth century and closely resembled the farm buildings which had been used for Quaker services prior to 1688. Hidden away in a secluded Chilterns valley, Jordans meeting-house has the appearance of a small farmhouse with sparse internal furnishings, and represents a clear visual symbol of the self-effacement and exclusivity of nonconformity. There is perhaps no better way to appreciate the chasm which was to grow up between the established Anglican church of the eighteenth and nineteenth centuries with its close links to the powerful secular state and English nonconformity with its tenacity and separateness, than to contrast the pride and grandeur of Wren's St Paul's with the humbleness and lack of pretension of Jordans meeting-house.

SUGGESTIONS FOR FURTHER READING

The influence of doctrine on the fabric of the church can best be approached through Horton Davies, *Worship and Theology in England from Cranmer to Hooker 1534–1603* (New Jersey, 1970); and Nicholas Tyacke, *Anti-Calvinists: The rise of English Arminianism* c. *1590–1640* (Oxford, 1987).

Descriptions of individual cathedrals and parish churches, as well as information on general architectural developments, can be found in J. Bowyer, *The Evolution of Church Building* (London, 1977); A. Clifton-Taylor, *The Cathedrals of England* (London, 1967); O. Cook, G. Hutton, and E. Smith, *English Parish Churches* (London, 1976); J. H. Cox, *The Parish Churches of England* (Woking, 1950); K. Lindley, *Chapels and Meeting Houses* (London, 1969); and K. H. Southall, *Our Quaker Heritage: Early meeting houses* (York, 1974).

The arguments of the iconoclasts and the progress of iconoclasm are the subjects of J. Phillips, *The Reformation of Images: The destruction of art in England, 1335–1660* (London, 1973); and Margaret Aston, *England's Iconoclasts* (Oxford, 1988). The impact of iconoclasm is further discussed by Ronald Hutton, 'The local impact of the Tudor reformations', in Christopher Haigh (ed.), *The English Reformation Revised* (Cambridge, 1987); John Morrill, 'The church in England 1642–9', in John Morrill (ed.), *Reactions to the English Civil War 1642–9* (London, 1982); and G. B. Tatham, *The Puritans in Power* (Cambridge, 1913). For a highly subjective vent of spleen against the Puritan iconoclasts of the seventeenth century, see A. L. Rowse, *Reflections on the Puritan Revolution* (London, 1986).

4 The church in England and churches abroad

During the late medieval period, the English Catholic church was extremely wealthy and enjoyed many privileges. On the other hand, its independence was seriously curtailed and its affairs were firmly controlled by the monarchy; fifteenth-century English kings appointed their own bishops, regularly taxed the clergy, and used parliamentary legislation to limit clerical immunities. The English church was thus an essentially Erastian church, and by 1500 the English crown had few reasons to complain about the otherwise privileged position that it had acquired within the realm. Certain sections of the English laity, however, were clearly much more hostile. Common lawyers detested the right of benefit of clergy, and made strenuous efforts to legislate against the practice in the parliaments of 1512 and 1515. Many town corporations resented the rival jurisdiction of ecclesiastical institutions, and on occasions their officers became embroiled in unseemly disputes with the heads of cathedrals and monastic houses; in 1506, for example, the sheriff and gaol-keeper of Norwich became involved in a brawl with the prior of the city's Benedictine cathedral priory, who was seeking to rescue one of his servants recently arrested by municipal officers. While some historians have dismissed such jurisdictional conflicts as routine and insignificant, others have argued convincingly that they were signs of a well-established corporate anti-clericalism. A. G. Dickens,[1] in particular, has consistently maintained that the anti-clerical tracts of lawyers such as Simon Fish and Christopher St German were not merely isolated examples of lay hostility to the church, totally unrepresentative of public opinion, but on the contrary part of a long tradition of anti-clericalism among the literate classes, and most especially London merchants, common lawyers, parliamentarians, and royal officials.

However, while some real tensions existed between the church and a number of vested interest groups within England, no such animosity appears to have clouded relations between the English state and the papacy. By the eve of the Reformation, the English monarchy had firmly subordinated papal authority to its own secular power, and relations between crown and papacy were on the whole productive and harmonious. Papal influence over the English church had been significantly eroded during the course of the fifteenth century, partly as a consequence of late fourteenth-century legislation, such as the statutes of Provisors and Praemunire, and partly as a consequence of the international political situation. From the 1480s onwards, the papacy needed the diplomatic support of the early Tudor monarchs in order to strengthen its political hold over the Papal States and to mount a crusade against the Turks, who had captured Constantinople in 1453. In return for their help, individual popes were prepared to accede to the political requests of the early Tudor kings, even at the cost of the loss of their plenitude of power. Compliance sometimes caused no hardship; Innocent VIII, for example, issued a bull of excommunication against claimants to Henry VII's throne, granted Henry a dispensation to marry Elizabeth of York, and later validated the marriage between his son, Prince Henry, and Henry's brother's widow, Catherine of Aragon. Other concessions, however, were more serious; both Henry VII and Henry VIII were allowed to nominate at will to the English episcopal bench, to translate bishops from see to see, and to obstruct the collection of papal taxes. Henry VII even received papal support for the reduction of the important clerical immunities of right of sanctuary and benefit of clergy.

There would also appear to have been relatively little popular hostility towards papal authority. The financial demands made by Rome were in no way oppressive, for in an average year the early Tudor kings were exacting two-and-a-half times as much money from the English church as was the pope. In addition, far from questioning the spiritual supremacy of the pope, large numbers of the English laity regularly applied to Rome for indulgences and dispensations from the requirements of canon law. Indeed, so popular were indulgences that during 1498 and 1499 an estimated 2000 English priests were obliged to request plenary indulgences from the pope on behalf of their lay parishioners.

Given this tranquil climate, few contemporary observers could have predicted that by the late 1520s the English crown and the papacy would be locked in a bitter jurisdictional conflict which would eventually end in schism. The issue which brought Henry VIII into dispute with Pope Clement VII was the question of the annulment of his marriage to Catherine of Aragon. By the spring of 1527, Henry had convinced himself that his marriage to Catherine of Aragon was contrary to divine law and canonically invalid, and had resolved to put Catherine aside and to marry Anne Boleyn. As his determination to change his wife was motivated not only by his infatuation with Anne but also by the pressing need to produce a legitimate male heir to the throne, the papal stamp of approval for an annulment and remarriage was essential. Henry, therefore, asked Clement to establish a decretal commission, authorizing the cardinal and papal legate, Thomas Wolsey, to make a judgment on the case in England, where he could most easily influence the outcome.

Although the case for an annulment was weak in terms of canon law, it was politically expedient for the pope to concede and few believed that the request would be denied. Henry, however, was extremely unfortunate in his timing, for his agents arrived in Rome just when his wife's nephew, the Holy Roman Emperor Charles V, was winning important military victories in Italy; in May 1527 imperial troops sacked Rome, and the following year Charles forced Clement to promise that he would not find against Catherine of Aragon in the annulment case. Neither Henry's pre-existing contacts in Rome nor the special envoys sent out from England were able to improve or circumvent this adverse diplomatic situation. Despite engaging in extended negotiations lasting two years, Henry's representatives failed to persuade the pope that the case should be heard by Wolsey in England, with no right of appeal to Rome against the verdict. In May 1529, Henry decided to wait no longer and arranged for Wolsey to hear the case under his own legatine authority at a court at Blackfriars in London. His hope was that the pope would allow the decision reached there to stand; the plan, however, misfired for soon after the court's opening the case was revoked to Rome, and Henry was left with little hope of a satisfactory verdict.

None the less, Henry did not rush headlong down the road to schism. Initially, he attempted to browbeat the pope into judging the case in his favour or handing it back to an English ecclesiastical court. In order to intimidate Clement, he brought a charge of praemunire against Wolsey, and orchestrated the attacks on the clergy by the MPs of the 1529 parliament. When the London Mercers' Company presented a petition attacking clerical malpractice to the first session of that parliament, Henry allowed it to be transformed into three statutes, which curbed abuses in the areas of pluralism and non-residence, and in the exaction of probate and mortuary fees. Although these measures were not especially radical in themselves, the Act against pluralism did infringe ecclesiastical immunity from secular jurisdiction, as offenders were to be prosecuted in royal rather than ecclesiastical courts. Consequently it was bitterly opposed by some of the bishops. Henry's backing for this parliamentary assault on the church was also intended to demonstrate to both the pope and Catherine's supporters among the bishops how much the church needed the protection of the crown against the anti-clerical elements in parliament, and how this royal safeguard would be jeopardized by a papal refusal to grant the annulment. When the pope nevertheless steadfastly refused to give way, Henry intensified his attack on the church; in the summer of 1530 he issued a charge of praemunire against fifteen clerics, including the four bishops who had supported Catherine, on the grounds that they had aided Wolsey in the exercise of his legatine authority and thereby given support to papal jurisdiction within his realm.

During these same months, Henry was also pursuing an alternative strategy to obtain the annulment by sending his agents to rifle through archives in England and on the continent in the hope of uncovering precedents to support his claim that the pope had no right of judgment over his marriage. These researchers soon went beyond this narrow brief, and their study of the Bible and various other historical sources led them to formulate many of the theories which were later embodied in the royal supremacy. Two of these scholars, Edward Foxe and Thomas Cranmer, who were both members of Anne Boleyn's faction at court, were responsible for drawing up a document called the *Collectanea satis copiosa*, in which they advanced a claim of imperial sovereignty for the English monarchy. They argued that, as Henry was answerable to no earthly superior, neither he nor his subjects could appeal to or be cited in any court outside his realm. Such an assertion was not entirely novel; as early as 1515 Henry had declared that: 'By the ordinance and sufferance of God, we are king of England, and kings of England in time past have never had any superior but God only.' However, the fact that the royal scholars had found conservative rather than revolutionary arguments to support their case only added to their appeal, and Henry read the *Collectanea* with interest and approval in the late summer of 1530.

Somewhat before this he had been introduced, probably by Anne Boleyn, to some rather more revolutionary reading matter: *The Obedience of a Christian Man*, written by the suspected heretic William Tyndale. Tyndale's claim that 'God hath made the king in every realm judge over all' also made a favourable impression on Henry, and he subsequently declared: 'This book is for me and all kings to read.' In the event, Tyndale's unorthodox beliefs and his lack of support for the annulment prevented him from having any direct impact on royal policy. The *Collectanea*, on the other hand, almost certainly influenced both the tone and direction of Henry's statements on the subject, for unlike Tyndale its authors were not calling for Henry to seize new powers in order to reform the church, but were merely insisting that he was already head of the church and only needed to exercise a pre-existing authority.

From late 1530 onwards, Henry became even more determined not only that his matrimonial case should be heard in England, but also that he should reassert his imperial status which had been usurped by the papacy. He followed up his earlier limited charge of praemunire against selected churchmen with a similar charge against the whole of the English clergy, accusing them of exercising a spiritual jurisdiction that conflicted with their duty as his subjects. Pardoning them in return for a fine of £18,840, he initially demanded that in the prologue to the official grant of pardon he should be styled 'sole protector and supreme head of the English Church and clergy'. However, after impassioned protests from Bishop John Fisher, he agreed to the less contentious formula: 'especial protector and as far as the law of Christ allows even supreme head.' In 1532, he again revealed the drift of his thinking by informing parliament that the clergy's oath of allegiance to the pope was 'clean contrary to the oath that they make to us'. Over the next two years the powers of the papacy were gradually whittled away by successive parliamentary statutes; all papal financial exactions were withheld; papal dispensations were invalidated; and papal consecration of bishops and the right of appeal to Rome were both declared unnecessary. The same legislation which stripped the pope of his control over the English church gave a range of new powers to Henry, authorizing him to reform the church, supervise canon law, lay down doctrine, and conduct visitations of monastic houses. Ecclesiastical canons now required royal sanction, all proceeds from the taxes of annates and tenths were annexed to the crown, and final appeals against judgments in the ecclesiastical courts were to be made to the king in the court of Chancery. By the end of 1534, papal jurisdiction was confined only to the investigation of cases of suspected heresy, and this last vestige of authority was to disappear in 1536.

It is difficult to state with any certainty the exact date at which Henry finally decided on a full breach with Rome. He may have come to this decision in 1531 or 1532 and then proceeded cautiously because of the fear of opposition both at home and abroad. Alternatively, he may have devised the anti-clerical legislation of the period 1529 to 1533 as a weapon to bludgeon the pope into granting the annulment, only to resort to the supremacy as an emergency measure when Anne Boleyn became pregnant in 1533. Though admittedly inconclusive, the evidence suggests that the annulment was uppermost in Henry's mind until early 1532, but was then overtaken by thoughts of the supremacy. Between 1532 and 1534, the passing of each individual piece of legislation was closely followed by the appearance of official government propaganda justifying it and anticipating the next move, a fact that suggests that a coherent policy was unfolding by this stage. Furthermore, although Anne's pregnancy may well have determined the exact timing of the Act of Appeals, the statute's assertion that England was an empire was by then well-established government policy and echoed arguments formulated several years earlier.

Throughout the remainder of the 1530s, royal propagandists were systematically employed to justify and publicize Henry's claim to supremacy over the English church. Their arguments were deliberately couched in language which played down the revolutionary implications of the legislation and was designed to convince doubters that no changes of any real significance were taking place. But while it was certainly true that there were precedents for government policy towards the church in the 1530s, and that earlier monarchs had acted on the assumption that they had no superior within their realm, the Henrician supremacy was none the less unquestionably revolutionary. As a result of the royal actions of the 1530s, the church's institutions were weakened, much of its wealth was confiscated, and the right of the state to interfere in its affairs was dramatically extended. By the Submission of the Clergy of 1532, convocation surrendered its position as an independent legislative body for the church, and agreed both that all existing canons should be reviewed by a royal commission composed of both lay and clerical members and that in the future ecclesiastical laws would be subject to royal assent. Direct royal involvement in ecclesiastical affairs intensified from the middle years of the decade. After 1534, Henry began to issue ecclesiastical injunctions on his own authority; in 1535 his secretary of state, Thomas Cromwell, who had already played a major role in engineering the break with Rome, was appointed vicegerent or vicar-general of the church. In 1536 and 1539, Henry and Cromwell dissolved the English monasteries and confiscated their wealth and property. Taken together, these changes represented a decisive shift in favour of the secular power.

Furthermore, Henry was not content with investing himself with merely an administrative and political imperium, but also claimed a spiritual supremacy, arguing that the monarch was the vicar of God. Although he did not assume priestly powers, he did act as a 'lay bishop' with the right to define articles of faith. Thus, the Act of Appeals of 1533 empowered him to punish heretics and hinted that he possessed the additional authority to determine what constituted heresy. Similarly, the Act of Six Articles of 1539 laid down the penalties for disobedience to the prescribed articles of faith, and left it to him as supreme head to pronounce upon their doctrinal content. Henry also felt able to authorize a new translation of the Bible and to insist that it be made available to the laity. No king before him had ever assumed so complete a spiritual leadership of the English church.

In the mistaken opinion that the only obstacle to a reconciliation between Henry and the pope was the annulment issue, many observers initially believed that the rupture with Rome would be temporary. Their hopes for a reconciliation were especially high after the death of Catherine of Aragon in January 1536 and the execution of Anne Boleyn several months later. In reality, however, such expectations were entirely unfounded, for by now neither Henry nor Thomas Cromwell had any great desire to mend the breach, or at least not on terms that would undermine the newly promulgated royal supremacy. Both had become convinced that papal jurisdiction had been wrongful, and now wished to make use of the supremacy to strengthen the monarchy. Their true intentions were revealed by their promotion of the 1536 Act Extinguishing the Authority of the Bishop of Rome; by their dissolution of the smaller monasteries; and by their execution of prominent opponents of their policy, such as Sir Thomas More, Bishop John Fisher, and the London Carthusians. These moves convinced Pope Paul III that Henry's disobedience was serious, and in an attempt to activate an earlier bull of excommunication against the king, he lent his support to the Northern rebels during the Pilgrimage of Grace.

Henry's anti-papalism was based on the belief that the pope had wrongfully usurped the spiritual and temporal power which had traditionally belonged to the kings of England, and while he therefore rejected the pope's claim to jurisdiction in England, he was prepared to regard him as the rightful Bishop of Rome. Others, however, including Cromwell and Archbishop Thomas Cranmer, were much more vehement in their condemnation of the papacy; attracted by the new ideas and reforming zeal of the continental Protestants, they argued that the papacy had falsified the word of

God and distorted true religion. Cranmer indeed went so far as to claim that: 'where the word of God was adversary and against his authority, pomp, covetousness, idolatry and superstitious doctrine, he [the pope], spying this, became adversary unto the word of God, falsifying it, extorting it out of the true sense.' During the later years of Henry's reign, a number of radical Protestants, such as John Bale, took such comments to their logical conclusion by arguing in a series of historical and theological works that the pope and the Roman church should be seen as the Antichrist – the powerful antithesis of Christ and the fount of all evil whose downfall was a necessary forerunner of the second coming of Christ. By the reign of Edward VI this identification of the papacy with the Antichrist had emerged into the mainstream of religious opinion.

During the succession crisis of 1553, Edward's Roman Catholic sister Mary studiously declined to make any public statement about the possibility of a restoration of papal authority in England. None the less, the supporters of the Duke of Northumberland lost no opportunity to represent her as a staunch papist, and attempted to make use of anti-papal fears to win support for their rival candidate for the throne, Jane Grey. A proclamation issued by the ill-fated Queen Jane announced that Mary wanted to bring 'this noble, free realm into the tyranny and servitude of the Bishop of Rome', and the letters which the council sent out to the provinces declared that Mary's accession would have resulted in 'the bondage of this Realme to the old servitude of the Antichriste of Rome'. That there was, none the less, some considerable support for Mary's successful bid for the throne must be attributed to the widespread distrust of the duke and respect for the rights of legitimate succession, rather than to any general desire for a return to the papal fold. Undoubtedly, many members of the English political nation viewed the prospect of a reunion with Rome with grave misgivings, and when it became reality it was far from popular. The anti-papal propaganda of the preceding twenty years had not been without effect, but more importantly there remained considerable anxiety about the new queen's plans for the vast amount of ecclesiastical land which had been acquired by the laity. Thus, although Mary's first House of Commons readily accepted the restoration of Catholic doctrine and liturgy, it initially refused to repeal the Henrician anti-papal legislation, and it delayed the reconciliation with Rome until Pope Julius III had secured the future of secularized ecclesiastical property by guaranteeing the rights of existing lay holders.

Parliament eventually agreed to rescind the royal supremacy in November 1554, but fears that the papacy might renege on the land settlement persisted. These anxieties were heightened afer 1555 by the election of Pope Paul IV. Far from possessing the tact and sensitivity required to construct a harmonious relationship with the English church and restore Mary's subjects' confidence in the papacy, Paul was a rigid, inflexible pontiff who could hardly have been less suited to the task of cementing the reunion of England and Rome. Given his hard-line views – in particular his anti-Spanish outlook, his personal hostility to Mary's chief religious adviser, Cardinal Pole, and his inflexibility over the issue of ecclesiastical property – it was only a matter of time before relations between England and the Holy See foundered. Indeed, one of Paul's first actions was to issue a bull denouncing the alienation of ecclesiastical property, and it was only the considerable diplomatic efforts of Pole that eventually persuaded him to exempt England from its provisions. Knowledge of the bull overshadowed the discussions in the 1555 English parliament on the Bill restoring annates and tenths to Rome, contributing to the strength of anti-papal sentiment and forcing the government to redraft the measure so that these taxes would remain in the hands of the English church rather than accrue to the pope.

During the next two years, although Anglo–papal relations continued to be strained by a number of minor irritations, further serious disturbance was avoided. In 1557, however, Paul once again took action which severely tested the relationship. After breaking off diplomatic relations with Mary's husband, Philip II of Spain, he revoked Pole's legatine commission and proceeded to order the arrest of Cardinal Morone, a close friend of Pole and the representative of English interests at the papal court. Finally, he summoned Pole himself to Rome to answer 'certain religious suspicions'. Mary was outraged by these measures, and resisted Pole's recall by forbidding him to leave the country, and refusing to receive either the papal nuncio bearing the letters of revocation or any replacement for the cardinal. She further declared that any charges of heresy against Pole would be heard in England, announcing in words ironically reminiscent of her father's that: 'she would in observance of the laws and privileges of her realm, refer them [the charges] to the cognisance and decision of her own ecclesiastical courts.' Despite endless negotiations and a subsequent improvement in the international situation, the quarrel was never resolved. Mary died in November 1558 in union with Rome, but at loggerheads with the pope. She was followed just a few hours later by Pole who, like Wolsey before him, had remained to the end torn between his allegiance to his monarch and his obedience to his spiritual lord.

Following Mary's death, observers at home and abroad realized that the papal connection with England would once more be severed by her successor. Elizabeth's legitimacy as Anne Boleyn's daughter depended upon the validity of her father's divorce, and the new government was also propelled in an anti-papal direction by the crown's need for money and by the general uneasiness about the papal attitude to expropriated church property. The immediate appointment of Protestant ministers and the introduction of a Supremacy Bill in the 1559 parliament was therefore widely predicted, but despite Elizabeth's concession in changing her title from 'Supreme Head' to 'Supreme Governor', the move was none the less fiercely contested by the Marian bishops in the House of Lords. Although primarily designed to win over Catholic waverers, the new title was also preferred by some Protestant zealots who argued that only Jesus Christ could be the head of the church, as well as by those who believed that Elizabeth's gender debarred her from assuming a quasi-episcopal role. The queen herself was quite ready to concede that her area of responsibility was confined to the administration and jurisdiction of the church and did not extend to defining 'any article or point of the Christian faith and religion'. In practice, however, although she was powerless to prevent some of the religious changes she disliked – such as the introduction of clerical marriage, the use of bread rather than unleavened wafers at communion, and the removal of crucifixes and roods from the interiors of churches – she frequently intervened personally in religious matters and had an important influence on the nature of the English church established during her reign. In January 1565, she ordered Archbishop Parker of Canterbury to impose uniformity of clerical dress and ceremonials on those radicals who were disobeying her regulations. In 1576, she insisted that her new Archbishop of Canterbury, Edmund Grindal, should suppress prophesyings, and when he disobeyed and challenged her right as supreme governor to decide on the matter, she suspended him from office. In 1595, she even refused to allow the publication of the predestinarian Lambeth Articles, although they had been approved by her favoured archbishop, John Whitgift.

Although the Act of Supremacy was passed shortly after her accession in 1559, papal condemnation of Elizabeth was postponed for over a decade. The delay was partly the result of the intervention of Philip II of Spain, who had no desire to see the English queen deposed in favour of the Catholic but pro-French claimant, Mary Queen of Scots. In addition, until 1568 there seemed a good chance that Elizabeth might have married Philip's cousin, Charles of Austria, and have thereby returned England both to the Catholic church and the Hapsburg interest. Although Anglo-Spanish relations deteriorated after 1568 and Philip's protective mantle gradually began to slip away, the Spanish king still declined to involve himself in plots and conspiracies to overthrow Elizabeth. Pope Pius V, on the other hand, was from the late 1560s prepared to give his support to Catholic activists in England who were plotting against Elizabeth. Assured by his agents that disaffection was widespread in England and that the Catholic Northern rising of 1569 would win extensive support, Pius responded to the appeals of the rebels by signing in February 1570 the bull *Regnans in Excelsis*, excommunicating Elizabeth and releasing her subjects from their allegiance to her. This bull did irreparable harm to the Catholic cause in England; coming too late to assist the Northern rising, which had already collapsed by the time it was issued, in the long term it equated Catholicism closely with treason and made the recusant community the object of deepening fear and suspicion. Papal implication in subsequent plotting against Elizabeth and financial support for the Spanish Armada only served to confirm this equation, and as a consequence Elizabeth was unable to withstand the growing pressure from her Protestant subjects for the introduction of harsher recusancy laws and civil disabilities for Catholics. Given this international climate, it is not surprising that the Catholic missionary priests, who began to arrive in England from continental seminaries during the 1570s and 1580s, were viewed as papal spies and fifth columnists, and if captured were dealt with accordingly. By the end of Elizabeth's reign, the pope was regarded by an increasingly patriotic English people not only as the Antichrist but also as their sworn national enemy, a view that was deeply embedded in, and reinforced by, John Foxe's highly popular *Acts and Monuments*, better known as the *Book of Martyrs*.

The initial Lutheran challenge to papal authority in 1517 had ushered in an age in which Europe would be divided into hostile confessional camps, but, despite the fact that he himself had dispensed with papal authority within his own realm, Henry VIII had been extremely reluctant to accept this reality. He had continued instead to think in terms of a united Christendom organized into national churches, 'compacted and united together to make and constitute but one Catholic Church or body'. Considering himself throughout a true Catholic, Henry had been reluctant to enter into close association with foreign Protestant states, and when political necessity had induced him to consider allying with the German Lutheran princes in the 1530s, he had adamantly refused to accept their confession of faith or to view them as co-religionists. During Edward's short reign, England had grown much closer to continental Protestantism and had begun to embrace the nascent Protestant internationalism being fostered by Calvin at Geneva. Indeed, in the aftermath of Charles V's victory over the Protestants at the battle of Muhlberg in 1547, Edward's England had become the refuge for a number of important refugees, including Peter Martyr and Martin Bucer. These men had taken up influential posts at the universities and advised the government on the introduction of Protestantism into England. All such links between the English church and the Protestant churches in Europe had quickly disappeared, of course, once Mary had come to the throne in 1553 and had set about reuniting England to Rome.

Like her father before her, Elizabeth I was also reluctant to accept a split in Europe along religious lines or to identify herself too closely with international Protestantism. Preferring détente to confrontation, she resisted the pressure from some of her advisers to enter into an offensive alliance with her co-religionists, and in general her policies were conditioned more by political pragmatism than religious zeal. In the late 1560s, for example, she considered a marriage alliance with the Catholic Hapsburgs as protection against the French, while in the different circumstances of the 1570s she contemplated marriage to a French Catholic prince as a defence against Spain. Only in the mid-1580s, when the Catholic powers in France had allied with Philip II, was she reluctantly forced into offering active help to the French Huguenots and the Calvinist rebels in the Netherlands.

A number of English Protestants were, however, more ideologically motivated than their queen and campaigned vigorously for the adoption of an offensive Protestant alliance, with the aim not simply of protecting English security, but also of furthering the gospel and destroying the forces of Antichrist. These individuals were in regular communication with co-religionists abroad, gave help to religious refugees in England, and raised money at home for beleaguered Calvinist communities on the continent. During 1582 and 1583, for example, they organized a public collection for the city of Geneva, which was under threat from attack by the Duke of Savoy, raising nearly £6,000. Yet, although the English people were prepared to contribute such large sums at times of real emergency, for most of the time the international Calvinist cause had little real appeal outside a small coterie of radical Protestants, who had important connections at court, but who, as Patrick Collinson[2] has put it, remained 'somewhat estranged from the generality of society'. On the other hand, anti-papalism and anti-Catholicism had struck deep roots within Elizabethan society, and when England was threatened by Spain in the late 1580s the war that followed was viewed by many in England as a glorious life or death struggle for national and religious survival against the evil forces of the counter-Reformation. None the less, the English Protestant outlook remained essentially parochial and chauvinist, and the ideology of international Calvinism made few converts.

As in much of the previous century, during the early seventeenth century the English church was obliged to define itself in relation to the rival religious power blocs within continental Europe. Despite the fact that the war with Spain was brought to an end in 1604, the great majority of the English clergy and laity continued to view Roman Catholicism with the same mixture of deep loathing and suspicion as had their Elizabethan predecessors, regarding it as a serious threat to both their national security and the well-being of their souls. Their pathological hatred of the Roman church continued to be fuelled by the deeply entrenched belief that the pope was the Antichrist, a conviction that was by now accepted without question by conservative bishops and godly Puritans alike. James I's reign saw the publication of an extensive literature devoted to illustrating that the pope was the Antichristian 'Beast' referred to in the Book of the Apocalypse. Among the titles that appeared were *The Mysterie of Iniquity*, written by the French Huguenot theorist, Philip Du Plessis-Mornay, and translated into English in 1612; and *Antichrist the Pope of Rome*, the work of Oliver Cromwell's schoolmaster Thomas Beard, which appeared in 1625. No less a figure than James I himself also published several works on the subject. Indeed, so fundamental to the outlook of Jacobean Protestants was this identification of the pope with Antichrist that one contemporary went so far as to define a Protestant as one who 'can swear the Pope is antichrist and that flesh is good on Friday'.

If most early seventeenth-century English Protestants regarded Roman Catholics as their arch-enemies, a good many also saw their fellow Protestants within continental Europe as natural friends and allies. An insistence on international support and co-operation had been a central feature of missionary Calvinism from its inception, and during the early seventeenth century it was regarded as essential to the survival of the Reformed faith in the face of the threat from a resurgent counter-Reformation Catholicism. James, who journeyed down from Scotland in 1603 to take up his new positions as English monarch and supreme governor of the English church, was firmly committed to Calvinist theology and was to take a very active interest in the ecclesiastical affairs of his new kingdom. However, his appreciation of the dangers from militant continental Catholicism did not blind him to the threat from the more radical varieties of Protestantism at home, and as Kenneth Fincham and Peter Lake[3] have commented: 'it is difficult not to be impressed by the skill with which he handled both anti-Puritan and anti-papal stereotypes to create the ideological space within which the royal will could maneuver and policy be formulated.'

The maintaining of links with co-religionists played a significant role in the formulation of James's foreign policy. In 1613, for example, the king married his daughter Elizabeth to Frederick of the Palatinate, one of the leading figures of European Calvinism; similarly, in 1618 four representatives of the English church attended the Synod of Dort, the conference called to resolve the bitter dispute which had been raging in the United Provinces over the doctrine of predestination. At the same time, however, like Elizabeth before him, James kept the English commitment to the 'Protestant international' within strict limits. Not only did he share his predecessor's misgivings about aiding any rebels, Calvinist or otherwise, he also had a strong temperamental dislike of all conflict. Seeing himself as the peacemaker among his fellow monarchs, and adopting as his motto *Beati Pacifici* (Blessed are the Peacemakers), he repeatedly refused to commit himself wholeheartedly to the Protestant cause. When in 1618 the Protestant nobles of Bohemia renounced their allegiance to their Catholic Hapsburg monarch, Ferdinand of Styria, and offered the vacant throne to Frederick of the Palatinate, James advised his son-in-law to decline. Frederick's rejection of this sensible advice and subsequent acceptance of the Bohemian crown sparked off a series of events which culminated in the Thirty Years' War. However, even though Frederick and Elizabeth were subsequently expelled from both Bohemia and the Palatinate, James resisted the clamour for war from his later parliaments and resolutely refused to agree to military intervention on behalf of his family and faith. Furthermore, in order to balance out his marriage alliance with the Calvinist Palatinate, he alarmed and antagonized many of his subjects by conducting protracted negotiations with Madrid over the possibility of a marriage between his son, Charles, and the Spanish Infanta.

Following James's death in 1625, the relationship between the English church and the major religious factions in Europe was to be markedly changed by the accession of Charles I and the subsequent rise to power of William Laud and the English Arminians.

Of great importance in this context was the Arminian re-evaluation of the intrinsic merits of English Protestantism. During the period from 1560 to 1625, many contemporaries, both inside and outside England, had regarded the English church as a pragmatic, if rather unsatisfactory compromise between two purer denominations. By the early 1630s, however, some Arminians had begun to argue that the English *via media* was in fact superior both to Roman Catholicism and the more extreme varieties of continental Protestantism. Such an outlook is particularly well illustrated by the literary work of the Arminian clergyman, George Herbert. His poem *The British Church*, for example, displays its author's deep devotion to the English church of the 1630s, which is described as a 'dearest mother'. He refers to its 'fine aspect in fit array' and 'perfect lineaments and hue both sweet and bright'. At the same time he denounces both the 'painted' Roman church for its wanton attachment to ritual and relics, and the 'undressed' Calvinism of Geneva which, he claimed, excluded all decency and decorum from religious observance. For Herbert and his fellow Arminians, therefore, the 'mean' way of English Protestantism was its 'praise and glory', which enabled it to avoid all the worst excesses of its rivals.

As a result of this growing self-confidence among the English hierarchy and of the widening doctrinal gulf between European Calvinism and English Arminianism, Charles's church severed most of its links with the international Protestant cause. During the early years of his reign Charles did intervene actively in the Thirty Years' War by leading England into another war against Spain. His decision to do so, however, appears to have been motivated more by his belief that he had been personally insulted by the Spanish during the earlier marriage negotiations and by a romantic desire to restore his sister and brother-in-law to their inheritance than by any wish to display solidarity with the Protestant cause, which was crumbling away before the seemingly irresistible progress of the Hapsburg armies. English intervention was anyway short-lived, for by 1630 the threat of imminent financial disaster at home had forced Charles to withdraw from the European conflict. Thereafter, relations between the English church and Protestant churches abroad continued to deteriorate. William Laud, who along with the king directed ecclesiastical policy throughout the 1630s, had little interest in the struggles of his beleaguered co-religionists on the continent, and was far more concerned that money be raised for the repair of St Paul's Cathedral in London than for the relief of Calvinist refugees from the Palatinate. The only 'foreign' Protestant churches in which

Laud took any real interest were those in Charles's other kingdoms of Scotland and Ireland, and those that served the American colonists and the English émigrés in Holland. In the event, his attempt to impose his new conservative orthodoxy upon these churches was to cause disturbance and resistance abroad, and ultimately civil war and revolution at home.

Sharing George Herbert's view of the intrinsic superiority of Anglicanism over both Catholicism and Calvinism, William Laud was opposed to any attempt to draw the English church closer to Rome. However, despite Laud's personal antipathy towards the papacy, the 1630s did see a growth in the influence of Catholicism over the English government and an improvement in relations between Charles's court and the papal curia, and for the large numbers of English Protestants who were unable to distinguish between Arminianism and popery and who regarded Laud as little more than an agent of Rome, there could be no doubt that the archbishop was to blame. In reality, these developments came about largely through the influence of Charles's Catholic wife, Henrietta Maria. From the late 1620s onwards, a significant number of courtiers had begun to attend mass at the queen's chapel and a steady stream of them subsequently became converts to Roman Catholicism. By the mid-1630s, prominent members of the privy council, such as Francis Windebank, Francis Lord Cottington, and Sir Richard Weston, were either openly Catholic or secretly sympathetic. Most significantly, and as far as most English observers were concerned most ominously, diplomatic relations with Rome which had been broken off at the Reformation were now restored. An initial mission by Gregorio Panzani in 1634 was followed by the arrival in 1636 of a fully accredited papal envoy, George Con, whose considerable charm and diplomatic skill did much to further the Catholic cause. Most committed English Calvinists viewed these developments with growing anxiety and alarm, and by the late 1630s some, like John Pym, had become convinced that Con, Laud, the queen, and possibly even the king, were party to a conspiracy to return England to Rome, if necessary by force. This paranoid fear of a Catholic insurrection was heightened in 1641 by the news that the Catholic Irish of Ulster had risen up in armed rebellion against the Protestant settlers of that province, and it subsequently became one of the most powerful influences motivating those who took up arms against Charles I in the civil war.

During much of the civil war and Interregnum, the English church was far too preoccupied with its own internal convulsions to concern itself with its relations with Catholic and Protestant communities abroad. This did not, however, prevent representatives of both these opposed confessional camps becoming embroiled in England's religious conflicts. Following the signing of the Cessation Treaty between Charles and the Irish rebels in September 1643, large numbers of Irish Catholics crossed to England to join Charles's royalist army, despite the fact that they faced summary execution if captured by parliament. In the same year the English parliament agreed a 'Solemn League and Covenant' with the Presbyterian Scots Covenanters, and in early 1644 a Scottish army crossed into England to bring much needed military assistance to parliament's northern forces. The Scots' intervention was motivated almost entirely by religion, the price for their help being a commitment by parliament to introduce a Scottish-style Presbyterian church system into England at the earliest opportunity. When the subsequent rise to power of the Independent New Model Army in the period following the end of the war prevented the English Presbyterians from delivering this promise, the Scots promptly looked elsewhere. In the late 1640s and early 1650s, they lent their military support first to Charles and then to his son, the future Charles II, on condition that once the throne had been regained a Presbyterian church would be imposed upon the English.

Many of those who witnessed the execution of Charles I and the founding of an English republic in 1649 must have anticipated that the foreign policy of the new staunchly Protestant state would have a strong religious orientation. There were indeed many influential soldiers and civilians who believed that the victorious New Model Army should now seek to export its religious revolution, and who in their more ecstatic moods talked of marching on Rome and of setting Cromwell's chaplain, Hugh Peter, upon the throne of St Peter. One of the earliest military initiatives of the new state – the raising of an expeditionary force to suppress the Irish rebellion – was partly motivated both by security considerations and by the prospect of financial gain, but was also widely seen as a religious crusade; this fact was clearly demonstrated in the autumn of 1649, when Cromwell's soldiers attacked the Catholic inhabitants of Drogheda and Wexford with a savagery which only religious conflict can engender. Cromwell returned from Ireland in 1650 to lead the English resistance to the threat from the Scots, and by his subsequent victories at the battles of Dunbar and Worcester he thwarted not only those who wished to see the return of the house of Stuart, but also those who sought to impose a Presbyterian church on the English people.

While the English army remained preoccupied during the early 1650s with these military campaigns against the Irish and Scots, the Rump of the Long Parliament was able to pursue a foreign policy motivated primarily by commercial considerations, leading England into a naval war with her principal trading rival, Protestant Holland. Following the appointment of Oliver Cromwell as Lord Protector in 1653, religious considerations once more came to the fore, although whether they ever took precedence over the more secular impulses behind foreign policy is doubtful. Disturbed that the English were at odds with a nation that should have been one of its natural religious allies, Cromwell brought about a rapid end to the Dutch War, and during the peace negotiations he even proposed that in the interests of their common religion the English and Dutch republics should merge to form one united Protestant state. When these overtures were spurned by the pragmatic Dutch leaders, Cromwell transferred his more messianic aspirations to the Swedes, and for a while dreamed of joining with Queen Christina, daughter of the legendary Protestant hero Gustavus Adolphus, in a religious crusade against popery. When in turn these fantasies foundered on Christina's subsequent defection to Rome and her successor's preoccupation with challenging his Protestant neighbours for supremacy in the Baltic, Cromwell resorted to the popular policy of war against England's traditional enemy, Spain. As well as fulfilling the role of religious crusade, this conflict offered possibilities for commercial gain through encroachments into the lucrative Spanish colonies in Central and South America.

In the half-century that followed the restoration of the Stuart monarchy in 1660, the English church and state displayed in turn two very different attitudes towards the rival religious groupings within continental Europe. During the period from 1660 to 1688, the main orientation of English foreign policy was towards maintaining close relations with the leading European Catholic power, France. Although Charles II had been restored to the leadership of the Anglican church as well as the English state, his own personal religious preference was for Roman Catholicism, and he was thus keen to maintain friendly relations with the dominant Catholic monarch in Europe, Louis XIV. Consistently ignoring the many Protestant MPs who advised him to lend his support to the various coalitions which grew up to curb Louis's pretensions, Charles remained a close ally of the French king throughout his reign. By the terms of the secret Treaty of Dover of 1670, he even agreed to announce his conversion to Catholicism and to accept French military assistance if his parliament offered any resistance to his policies. Two years later, he joined Louis in a war against Holland, which came close to destroying the Protestant republic. Louis also gave valuable financial assistance to Charles during the Exclusion crisis which erupted in

1679, assisting the English king to prevent an attempt by a powerful group of Protestant MPs to bar his Catholic brother James, Duke of York, from the succession. When James did succeed to the throne in 1685, the pro-Catholic and pro-French orientation of foreign policy was naturally maintained, and the new king made strenuous efforts both to return England to the papal fold and to realign her fully with the international Catholic axis.

Throughout the same twenty-eight years, however, a large body of both lay and clerical opinion within England remained deeply suspicious of the papacy and firmly attached to the international Protestant cause. In 1666, many saw the Fire of London as the work of Catholic conspirators, and a decade later the revelation of an alleged 'Popish Plot' to assassinate Charles II was readily accepted as further evidence of the seriousness of the threat posed to the English state and church by international Catholic plotting. Protestant commentators were very aware that the papacy retained the right to depose excommunicated rulers, and took little comfort from the fact that many English recusants had taken a special oath of allegiance to the crown. When the Oxford academic Henry Foulis declared in 1671 that 'Treason [is] the sign of the true Roman religion', he was expressing an opinion that the great majority of his contemporaries still accepted without question. In reality this perceived threat from the papacy was greatly exaggerated, for as John Miller[4] has commented, there was by now 'little sign of the satanic, all-pervading fixity of purpose, the dedication to the extirpation of Protestantism, or the Machiavellian unscrupulousness which English Protestants traditionally attributed to it'. By the 1660s, Rome had given up all thoughts of the forcible deposition of the English Protestant monarchy; indeed, in the 1670s its cautious and reluctant response to the proposed marriage of the heir to the throne James and the Catholic noblewoman Mary of Modena threatened to block the best route for a peaceful end to the English schism, and Rome continued to offer only lukewarm support to James both before and after 1685.

Unaware that the papacy had lost much of its earlier counter-Reformation vigour and that relations between Rome and Paris were far from harmonious, many English Protestants remained convinced that their church was increasingly at risk from the growing ambition of Louis XIV, and made strenuous efforts to divert Charles and James from their pro-Catholic paths. In 1674, the pressure exerted in parliament by Protestant MPs forced Charles to withdraw prematurely from the war against the Dutch. A decade later England became the home for many of the Huguenot refugees who fled from France in the wake of Louis's revocation of the Edict of Nantes in 1685. During 1686 and 1687, it was once again representatives of this English Protestant opinion who made overtures to the leading political champion of European Protestantism, the Dutch stadtholder William of Orange, for help in opposing the Catholic policies of James II. In 1688, William responded to these requests by invading England on behalf of the Protestant cause, and subsequently replaced James on the English throne. In so doing, he wholeheartedly committed the English nation to the military struggle against Catholic France and inaugurated an important new phase in the international relations of both state and church. By the early eighteenth century, the Jacobite supporters of the deposed king had become closely associated with popery, and the English church and state had assumed the role of a full and active member of the international Protestant alliance, a role which radical Protestants at home had been unsuccessfully urging on them throughout the previous century and a half.

NOTES

1 A. G. Dickens, 'The shape of anti-clericalism and the English Reformation', in E. I. Kouri and T. S. Scott (eds), *Politics and Society in Reformation Europe* (Basingstoke, 1987).
2 Patrick Collinson, 'England and international Calvinism 1558–1640', in M. Prestwich (ed.), *International Calvinism* (Oxford, 1985).
3 Kenneth Fincham and Peter Lake, 'The ecclesiastical policy of King James I', *Journal of British Studies* 24 (1985).
4 John Miller, *Popery and Politics in England 1660–1688* (Cambridge, 1973).

SUGGESTIONS FOR FURTHER READING

For Dickens' views on anti-clericalism see A. G. Dickens, 'The shape of anti-clericalism and the English Reformation', in E. I. Kouri and T. S. Scott (eds), *Politics and Society in Reformation Europe* (Basingstoke, 1987). England's relations with Rome throughout this period are explored in a number of useful essays in J. Aveling, D. Loades, and H. McAdoo (eds), *Rome and the Anglicans* (New York, 1982). For relations with the papacy on the eve of the Reformation, see W. E. Lunt, *The Financial Relations of the Papacy with England, 1327–1534* (Cambridge, Mass., 1962); W. E. Wilkie, *The Cardinal Protectors of England: Rome and the Tudors before the Reformation* (Cambridge, 1974); and J. A. F. Thomson, 'The Well of Grace: Englishmen and Rome in the fifteenth century', in R. B. Dobson (ed.), *The Church, Politics and Patronage in the Fifteenth Century* (Gloucester, 1984). The intellectual origins of the royal supremacy are analysed by John Guy in a number of essays in A. Fox and J. Guy (eds), *Reassessing the Henrician Age: Humanism, politics and reform, 1500–1550* (Oxford, 1986).

Also interesting is an article by W. Ullmann, 'This realm of England is an Empire', *Journal of Ecclesiastical History* 30 (1979).

Henry VIII's policy towards the church is discussed in many books and articles. Among the most important are J. J. Scarisbrick, *Henry VIII* (London, 1968); John Guy, *Tudor England* (Oxford, 1990); J. A. Guy, 'Henry VIII and the *praemunire* manoeuvres of 1530–1531', *English Historical Review* 97 (1982); G. Redworth, 'Whatever happened to the English Reformation?', *History Today* 37 (1987); and Maria Dowling, 'The gospel and the court: Reformation under Henry VIII', in Peter Lake and Maria Dowling (eds), *Protestantism and the National Church in Sixteenth-century England* (London, 1987).

For anti-papalism in Mary's reign, see J. Loach, *Parliament and the Crown in the Reign of Mary Tudor* (Oxford, 1986). The significance of Elizabeth's title of Supreme Governor and the working of the royal supremacy in her reign is the subject of M. C. Cross, *The Royal Supremacy in the Elizabethan Church* (London, 1969). For the pope as Antichrist, see K. R. Firth, *The Apocalyptic Tradition in Reformation Britain 1530–1645* (Oxford, 1979); Christopher Hill, *Antichrist in Seventeenth-century England* (Oxford, 1971); P. Lake 'The significance of the Elizabethan identification of the Pope as Antichrist', *Journal of Ecclesiastical History* 31 (1980); and Peter Lake, 'Anti-popery: the structure of a prejudice', in Richard Cust and Anne Hughes (eds), *Conflict in Early Stuart England* (London, 1989). For the influence of Protestant ideology in England's foreign policy there is an unpublished thesis which should soon be converted into a book on foreign policy: S. L. Adams, 'The Protestant cause: religious alliance with the West European Calvinist communities as a political issue in England, 1585–1630', unpublished Oxford D. Phil. thesis (1973). Another perspective on England's relations with Calvinist communities abroad is provided in P. Collinson, 'England and international Calvinism 1558–1640', in M. Prestwich (ed.), *International Calvinism* (Oxford, 1985).

For James I as supreme governor, see Kenneth Fincham and Peter Lake, 'The ecclesiastical policy of King James I', *Journal of British Studies* 24 (1985). Charles I's and Archbishop Laud's attitude and policies towards the Roman church can be found in H. R. Trevor-Roper, *Archbishop Laud* (London, 1965 edn); Nicholas Tyacke, *Anti-Calvinists: The rise of English Arminianism* c. *1590–1640* (Oxford, 1987); and E. S. Cope, *Politics Without Parliaments* (London, 1987).

For the post-Restoration period, see John Miller, *Popery and Politics in England 1660–1688* (Cambridge, 1973); W. Speck, *Reluctant Revolutionaries* (Oxford, 1988); and Jonathan Scott, 'England's troubles: exhuming the Popish plot', in T. Harris, P. Seaward, and M. Goldie (eds), *The Politics of Religion in Restoration England* (Oxford, 1990). Relations between Rome and the English recusant community are discussed in John Bossy, *The English Catholic Community 1570–1850* (London, 1975); and J. C. H. Aveling, *The Handle and the Axe* (London, 1976).

5 Religion and popular belief

Many aspects of the religious beliefs and practices of the early modern English laity are notoriously difficult to anatomize, and historians need to employ great care and sensitivity when attempting to dissect them. The sources that allow us access to the lower orders are scarce, incomplete, and open to varying interpretations. In addition, what can easily be dismissed as paradox, inconsistency, or even hypocrisy may none the less represent some form of genuine religious commitment. How, for example, does one categorize the piety of an individual like the Restoration diarist, Samuel Pepys, who frequently attended several churches on a Sunday, but spent much of the time surveying the attractive women in the congregation; and who regularly supervised the daily prayers of his household, but often in a state of extreme inebriation?

Although the early modern period was a time of profound religious and cultural upheaval in England, certain important features of popular belief and religious practice remained largely unchanged throughout the sixteenth and seventeenth centuries. During this whole period, conventional Christianity continued to occupy a central position in the lives of the great majority of English men and women of all ranks, except perhaps the vagrants and beggars at the very bottom of the social order. There is little evidence that the conflicts between Protestants and Catholics produced any disenchantment with religion, or that the speed and frequency of the changes provoked a widespread scepticism or agnosticism. Nor do the advances in scientific knowledge, which began in Elizabeth's reign and multiplied during the Stuart period, appear to have caused any appreciable weakening of the Christian belief of intellectuals, or to have created a new elite group of educated non-believers. On the contrary, the researches of historians such as Margaret Spufford[1] and Martin Ingram[2] have revealed that in both rural and urban areas orthodox Christianity enjoyed an unchallenged predominance throughout these two centuries.

Another feature of popular belief which was consistent throughout the period under discussion was the wide variation in levels of personal piety and individual preoccupation with religion. At one extreme, some of the more staunch believers, Catholic and Protestant alike, were obsessed with religious questions to a degree which most twentieth-century observers would consider neurotic and obsessional; in contrast, at the other end of the spectrum, there existed a minority of lay men and women who consistently ignored their legal obligation to attend regular Sunday services and remained extraordinarily ignorant of even the most basic tenets of Christianity. While the exact size of this latter group is unclear, Peter Clark[3] has estimated that as many as one fifth of the population of Kent regularly stayed away from church in the later sixteenth century, and the situation may well have been worse in the peripheral 'dark corners of the land' to the north and west. Of those that did turn up at their parish churches, a good number behaved in a manner that was anything but reverential: talking, joking, spitting, arguing, and catching up on lost sleep. The minister Nicholas Breton, for example, noted in 1603 that his parishioners 'came to service more for fashion than devotion', while the preacher John Angier of Denton in Lancashire believed that his parishioners came 'for no other purpose but to sleep, as if the sabbath were made only to recover that sleep they have lost in the week'.

Some historians have argued that the period following the Reformation saw a marked increase in both absenteeism and non-attentiveness, as the replacement of the colourful Catholic ritual with long, erudite Protestant sermons reduced the congregation's sense of reverence and awe, and at the same time increased its boredom and restlessness. Such a view, however, is questionable on several counts. Absenteeism and lack of reverence in church had been far from unknown before the Reformation; indeed such charges were the most frequent cause of appearances before the Suffolk ecclesiastical courts in the fifteenth century. Furthermore, many absences from services in the post-Reformation period were occasioned not by apathy or reluctance to forgo a morning's work or relaxation, but rather by ill-health or family commitments; when William Kirke of Stow-cum-Quy in Cambridgeshire, for example, was hauled before the church courts for absenteeism, he informed them that at the time his wife had been 'lying in childbed and also his children wanted succour'. Finally, there is a growing body of evidence which suggests that regular attendance at church and annual participation at communion were actually increasing in the late Elizabethan and Jacobean periods. Ingram[4] has found that in many parts of southern England the levels of these practices were much higher in the 1620s and 1630s than they had been in the middle years of Elizabeth's reign; and Jeremy Boulton[5] has discovered that between 80 and 98 per cent of all the potential communicants of two large suburban parishes in London were receiving annual communion during the late Elizabethan and Jacobean periods – a very high proportion by any standards.

Few historians would now wish to dissent from the view that the vast majority of the laity of fifteenth-century England were deeply attached to the beliefs and practices of the Roman Catholic church, or to deny that that church exercised an unrivalled influence over the shaping of late medieval popular mentality. Central to both Catholic doctrinal belief and the public life of the local community was the regular weekly mass, attendance at which was both a legal and religious obligation upon all the laity. Mass was usually celebrated by the priest alone; taking no active part in the service, the laity viewed proceedings from behind the rood screen, which separated the nave from the chancel. None the less, despite this lack of lay involvement there is considerable evidence that the institution was very popular on the eve of the Reformation. In early sixteenth-century London it was customary for the most pious lay people to rush from church to church in order to be present at as many elevations of the host as possible in a single day. On the feast of Corpus Christi, crowds lined the streets to catch a glimpse of the consecrated host in procession. Moreover, in addition to attending these public celebrations of the sacrament, wealthy individuals, guilds, and lay fraternities frequently held masses in their own chapels or on portable altars, and numerous chantry priests celebrated thousands of private masses for the souls of the faithful departed.

Many other features of late medieval Catholicism exercised a similarly strong hold over the popular mind. Holy objects, relics, and talismans, such as the Agnus Dei – a small piece of wax containing an image of the lamb and flag – were widely believed to provide supernatural help during times of crisis; and holy bells, holy water, and candles were thought to give protection against diabolical spirits. The company of the saints in heaven was considered an additional potent source of assistance; individual saints were identified as especially efficacious for particular problems – there was even a saint of hopeless causes (St Jude) – and large numbers of men and women undertook long and sometimes hazardous pilgrimages to sites associated with them. Furthermore, the Catholic church involved itself fully both in the important rites of passage, such as baptism, marriage, and the last rites, that marked an individual's progress from the cradle to the grave, and also in the annual round of celebrations which marked out the changing seasons. Catholic ritual was, of course, a central element of the major liturgical feasts of Easter and Christmas, but the church also gave its blessing to the festivities associated with other religious and civic holidays; in Canterbury, for example, these included the Corpus Christi processions, the celebration of the translation of the relics of St Thomas à Becket, and the St George's Day procession, which was headed by the mayor and aldermen of the town. In many other towns, feasts such as Corpus Christi were marked by processions and the staging of mystery plays, the latter providing both highly popular entertainment and an extremely effective means of disseminating the fundamentals of Christian belief to the illiterate. All these seasonal rituals had important social functions too; they helped to affirm the unity of the civic community, to create good fellowship, and to channel youthful deviant behaviour into socially acceptable misrule.

To the Protestant reformers of the early sixteenth century, many features of this popular Catholicism were hugely offensive. One of their central objections was that Catholic piety incorporated elements of paganism and rendered religion little more than magic or sorcery. 'If a man will take a view of all Popery', wrote the late sixteenth-century Calvinist theologian William Perkins, 'he shall easily see that a great part of it is mere magic.' Protestant reformers were strongly opposed to practices such as the wearing of relics and talismans, and the sprinkling of homes and fields with holy water to ward off evil spirits. Moreover, they equated popery with magic at a more fundamental level, regarding the central doctrinal tenets of Catholicism as blasphemous, superstitious, anti-scriptural, and inherently evil. Of particular offence to many Protestants was the widespread popular belief in the power of the Catholic priesthood to intercede with God, to exorcise the devil at baptism, and to transform the elements of bread and wine into the body and blood of Christ during the mass.

As a consequence, following Henry VIII's break with Rome and more particularly after the accession of the Protestant Edward VI, the traditional beliefs and devotional practices of the English laity came under fierce attack from the reformers. The Protestant Prayer Books of 1552 and 1559 divested the parish clergy of their sacramental powers; the new communion service bore no resemblance to the central, sacramental miracle of the mass, and the reformed baptismal ceremony omitted the exorcism and the anointing with chrism. A whole range of intercessory objects was also outlawed, as were prayers to the saints, pilgrimages, and requiem masses. Shrines, chantries, and reliquaries were plundered or demolished, and the interiors of churches were denuded of their images, which were now regarded as idolatrous. Many liturgical festivities were banished from the churchyard as pagan or blasphemous, and most of the mystery plays were suppressed on the grounds that they wrongly mixed 'scurrilitie with divinity'. The reformers' wish to separate the sacred from the profane also led to the repression of many of the popular ballads of the day, which combined a godly lyric with a well-known tune. There is considerable evidence to suggest that Catholic devotional practices remained extremely popular right up until the time they were banned, and there can be little doubt that, following their suppression, many lay people initially felt an acute sense of loss and found the new Protestant liturgy an uncongenial and inadequate substitute for their traditional customs and beliefs.

Certain aspects of the Protestant assault on popular religious culture did meet with a limited degree of success. Governmental orders forbidding images, chantries, saint worship, and requiem masses, for example, seem to have had an immediate impact on expressions of personal piety. The researches of Robert Whiting[6] into the impact of the official reformation on the people of Devon and Cornwall have revealed that even in this conservative part of the country, where attachment to Catholic ritual had been particularly strong, statues of the saints began to disappear from churches soon after their condemnation by the Henrician injunctions, and within a short space of time the wills of the laity contained fewer references to images or intercessory masses. According to Whiting, much of this initial conformity was occasioned either by a fear of and respect for authority, or by the reluctance of testators to throw away their assets on objects and practices which were now proscribed. As time went by, however, Protestant propaganda did begin to loosen the laity's commitment to saint worship and the other Catholic means of intercession. When Mary reintroduced Catholicism into England in the 1550s, few of her subjects undertook pilgrimages to the newly restored shrines, and lack of demand prevented the publication of any new editions of the lives of the saints. Similarly, comparatively few chantries were re-established by pious benefactors, and endowments for masses failed to recover to their pre-Reformation level.

By contrast, the Protestant attack on traditional religious festivals was far less successful. Mary's reign witnessed a spontaneous renewal of enthusiasm for the local celebrations banned under Edward, and Corpus Christi processions, Whitsun ales, May games, and the decking of churches once more became as common as they had been in the last years of Henry's reign. This popular attachment to church festivities persisted well into Elizabeth's reign, the laity demonstrating their affection for them by vociferously opposing the efforts of godly ministers or town corporations to suppress them. Such protests were quite common and sometimes led to disorder and affrays. In 1588, several inhabitants of Shrewsbury were imprisoned after physically resisting the attempts of the magistrates to pull down a maypole, and the following year the Mayor of Canterbury was confronted with a protest morris dance outside his house when he forbade maypole dancing in the town. So popular were the proscribed celebrations that it proved quite impossible to eradicate them completely. The godly had some success in severing their connection with the church by banishing them from the churchyard, but the old festal calendar survived and the activities associated with it – mumming at New Year, dancing at Candlemas, football and other games at Shrovetide, and maypole dancing on Mayday – were relocated in and around the village ale-house. While, therefore, the efforts of successive reforming governments gradually weaned the common people from their attachment to Catholic views on images and intercession, throughout the Tudor and early Stuart periods all interference from local preachers and magistrates in the folk culture of the lower orders continued to be widely and successfully resisted.

Protestant endeavours to extinguish popular superstitions and the widespread belief in magical remedies also proved largely futile. The emphasis that Calvinists placed upon the majesty of God led them to condemn as blasphemous any attempts to tinker with the supernatural, and thus their reaction to calamities was to accept them as part of God's inscrutable purpose – the working out of a divine providence which governed all human affairs. Personal misfortune was regarded either as a test of faith which had to be patiently endured, or as a punishment for past transgressions requiring deep repentance. In some circumstances adversity was even thought to be a desirable proof of God's favour, as in the cases of the Old Testament heroes, Job and Jeremiah. More commonly, however, Calvinists viewed natural disasters as signs of divine anger, requiring appeasement through prayer and public fasting; during the famine of 1586, for example, the Bishop of London commented in a letter: 'for appeasing His wrath it is convenient that we fall to earnest repentance, prayers, fasting and other deeds of charity.'

The diaries, memoirs, and letters that have survived from the post-Reformation period reveal that many Protestants found their trust in divine providence to be a source of great comfort and solace during times of public or private affliction. For a great many others, however, particularly those who made up the largely illiterate and religiously unsophisticated rural masses, it brought insufficient comfort and left them feeling powerless in the face of disaster. At a time when so many natural phenomena remained both inexplicable and uncontrollable, and when medical knowledge was more often a force for harm than good, many individuals continued to feel a pressing need for supernatural assistance, and to seek it indiscriminately through both Christian prayers and magical charms. Bereft of the supernatural assistance previously offered by the Catholic priest and unwilling to rely solely on the petitionary prayers favoured by Protestants, they resorted to time-honoured magical charms and remedies to cure sickness, improve the weather, or ward off evil spirits. Large numbers regularly resorted to 'cunning women', who offered to heal both their physical and psychological ills by magical means. Indeed, in the eyes of some, the clergyman and the wizard continued to represent little more than alternative conduits of a much needed protective magic.

Nor were more educated Protestants totally impervious to the pull of the supernatural. The great majority of sixteenth- and seventeenth-century English men and women, intellectuals as well as illiterates, were addicted to reports of astrological predictions and rumours of prodigious happenings, such as monstrous births. Horoscopes were also extremely popular and frequently drawn up for Protestant clergy and laity; even Queen Elizabeth, the head of the English church, consulted her astrologer before deciding on a date for her coronation. Indeed, the advent of Protestantism gave rise to a number of new superstitious practices, such as the opening of the Bible at random in an attempt to secure divine guidance in the face of problems or dilemmas, a practice that was widespread even among Puritans.

Another more sinister aspect of this predisposition towards magic was the belief in the existence of witchcraft, which once again was accepted without question by educated Protestant zealots as well as illiterate country folk. From the mid-sixteenth century onwards, a succession of suspects, mainly old and unsightly women, were hauled before the courts and found guilty of practising black magic. New legislation against witches was introduced in 1563, largely through the influence of returning Marian exiles who had absorbed the continental belief that witches were the agents of the devil. During the subsequent forty years, witchcraft prosecutions reached unprecedented heights; in Essex, where there was an unusually high incidence of trials, as many as 163 women were indicted between 1560 and 1600, with roughly half of them being convicted and burnt. It seems likely that the Reformation may have contributed to this dramatic rise in prosecutions – which some historians have labelled a 'witch-craze' – both because the new climate of religious strife led to a general heightening of fears and suspicions, and because without the protective magic of Catholicism, many individuals felt themselves more vulnerable in the face of malevolent forces, and thus more impelled to take action against them.

Throughout the early modern period, therefore, English Protestantism was obliged to coexist alongside a wide range of magical beliefs and practices which retained a strong hold over the popular mind. For most of this period too, between these two apparently opposed ideological systems there existed a substantial penumbra, within which habits of thought from both overlapped. Only towards the very end of the seventeenth century, as the new explanations of mechanistic science began to gain ground, did religion and magic begin significantly to diverge from each other.

If Protestant zealots were only partially successful in their attempt to sweep away the supernatural aura which had surrounded late medieval religion, their efforts to give the common people some grounding in knowledge of the gospels and a basic understanding of the Reformed theology of grace and salvation also met with only limited success. Educated Protestants were all too aware of the popular ignorance of the basics of theology. Thomas Cartwright, the Elizabethan Presbyterian, declared on one occasion that 'heaps' of his contemporaries had cast aside the old religion without discovering the new, and the minister Josias Nichols complained in 1602 that only one in ten of the inhabitants of a Kentish parish with 400 communicants knew the basics of Protestant doctrine. In 1606, Nicholas Bownde commented that many people were still more knowledgeable about Robin Hood than the Bible. Such widespread ignorance is not difficult to explain, since during the middle decades of the sixteenth century there was an acute shortage of ministers to undertake the uphill task of disseminating the new and intellectually demanding beliefs.

In contrast to the colourful processions, plays, paintings, and sculptures which were employed as teaching aids by Catholics, Protestant evangelists sought to spread their message through sermons, lectures, devotional books, catechisms, and Bible reading. They were to discover, however, that a barely literate populace found the abstract word far more difficult to absorb than more concrete visual images, for as one Henrician reformer had earlier noted: 'into the common people things sooner enter by the eyes than by the ears.' Until the 1580s, Protestant propagandists were generally prepared to use illustrations to convey their message, and this device was used to particularly good effect by John Foxe in his *Book of Martyrs*. Thereafter, however, most refused to countenance the use of any pictorial assistance. Bibles ceased to have illustrations to enliven their text, and the small number of mystery plays, which had been allowed to continue at centres such as Coventry, Chester, Wakefield, and York, were suppressed. In essence, Protestantism was a religion of the literate, and although educational opportunities continued to expand during the course of the sixteenth and early seventeenth centuries, illiteracy, which was commonplace throughout the country and particularly evident in rural areas and among women, continued to exclude the majority of the laity from a full understanding of their new faith.

None the less, while standards of religious zeal and knowledge of the rudiments of the faith continued to fall well short of the aspirations of the most committed reformers, by 1603 England was undoubtedly a Protestant nation. From the 1570s onwards, even in the conservative south-west of the country, statements by testators which indicate a belief in solafidianism appeared regularly in the preambles of large numbers of wills, although the comments which the same testators made when leaving bequests to charities suggest that many still found it difficult to appreciate that good works could play absolutely no part in their salvation. From about the same time onwards, Catholic books and pious objects began to be used more sparingly – or at least more discreetly – in most parts of the country. Anti-papalism was also by now endemic, and a strong link had been forged in people's minds between Protestantism and English nationalism. Church sermons and public preaching had brought about many conversions, and catechisms had proved useful in inculcating Protestant beliefs. Most important of all, however, in creating a greater understanding of and attachment to the Protestant message was the regular use of the Elizabethan Prayer Book, which appears to have experienced a gradual increase in popularity as its ceremonies grew in familiarity over the course of the queen's reign.

One of Elizabeth I's primary objectives in devising the religious settlement of 1559 was the creation of a broad Protestant consensus which would be acceptable to the great majority of her subjects. Her efforts met with a large measure of success; nonconformity was restricted – in numerical terms at least – to a relatively insignificant role, and the overwhelming majority of English men and women remained members of the established state church. During the period 1560 to 1640, virtually all these conformist English Protestants shared a set of common doctrinal beliefs, but in terms both of liturgical preference and intensity of commitment it is possible to divide them into two broad and fluid categories: a mainstream Protestant majority which was relatively content with the hybrid character of the Elizabethan church; and a minority, labelled 'Puritan' by their contemporaries, which aspired to bring about further reform of that church in the direction of continental Protestantism.

The Puritans – who have sometimes been given the useful alternative title 'the hotter sort of Protestants' and are now increasingly referred to by historians as 'the godly' – did not necessarily uphold different beliefs from the moderates, but their religious activities generally occupied a far greater proportion of their time and energy. At the core of their religious experience was a deep attachment to the rigours of Calvinist theology, and in particular to the doctrine of predestination. Many of them had had to wrestle for years with their consciences and suffer agonies of anxiety and insecurity before they could finally convince themselves that they were included within the elect group of saints which was predestined for heaven. Once this conviction had been acquired, however, it became almost impossible to dislodge it, and they came to see themselves as an elite, chosen people permanently set apart from the majority of their unregenerate contemporaries. Many Puritans were given to extreme introspection, and regularly committed their innermost thoughts to paper in the diaries and memoirs which they used as spiritual account books. Other central features of their religious outlook were a deep loathing of Roman Catholicism and the papacy, which they viewed as the epitome of all evil; a millenarian belief that the end of the world was imminent; and a tendency to interpret contemporary experiences in the light of biblical history. In the later 1650s, for example, Oliver Cromwell came to see himself as a second Moses who, having led his people out of the Egyptian slavery of Laudianism and through the Red Sea of civil war, was now struggling to bring them towards the Promised Land.

Puritans believed that their distinctive religious outlook should inform every aspect of their lives. A lifestyle involving hard work, charity, abstinence from drink, strict morality, and thrift was deemed absolutely essential, as it was not only insisted on in the Bible, but was also seen as a sign of an individual's elect status. Rather than being confined to the church, therefore, Puritan religious life also focused on the household and various voluntary forms of public worship. At home, Puritans surrendered themselves to study, self-examination, and prayer; they taught the catechism to their children, pored over Foxe's *Book of Martyrs*, and read devotional manuals for guidance in the formulation of private, *ex tempore* prayers. On Sundays, they attended several church services as well as private meetings for prayer, Bible reading, and the singing of the psalms. On week-days, they listened to lectures in local churches, and on market days travelled to hear sermons in nearby towns. Sometimes they journeyed alone, sometimes in groups, singing psalms as they walked. Periodically they would devote an entire day to a communal fast, praying, reading aloud from the Bible, attending several sermons, and sharing a simple communal meal in the evening before returning to their homes. Their religious lives thus combined an internalized and private spirituality with the warmth and conviviality of good fellowship, or as they themselves called it, 'holy sympathy with the godly'.

Puritans found a number of the liturgical features of the established church, such as bowing at the name of Jesus and the sign of the cross in baptism, highly offensive. They preferred sparse and unadorned church interiors, and objected to pictures and statues on the grounds that they encouraged the worship of images. The repugnance they felt towards more decorated churches occasionally erupted into violent bouts of iconoclasm. In addition, from their position on the moral high ground, they repeatedly denounced many of the leisure pursuits of their neighbours, such as drinking, dancing, and theatre-going, which they regarded as occasions of sin and distractions from religious devotion. Indulgence in such recreational activities on Sunday was especially scandalous to Puritans. As a result of their ascetic lifestyle and their verbal assaults on their less godly neighbours, they were frequently subjected to ridicule and abuse at the hands of their contemporaries. As a result, many undoubtedly experienced deep feelings of isolation and alienation, and came to see themselves as prophets in the wilderness or pilgrims journeying through hostile territory. Richard Baxter, for example, recalled in later life a vivid childhood memory of seeing his father reviled by his neighbours for his strict observance of the Lord's Day, and for 'reproving drunkards or swearers'.

Puritans also believed it to be their pressing duty to agitate for the introduction of godly reforms into the church. Some organized petitions which urged parliament to initiate reform, while most employed their money and influence to promote godliness. Many left bequests to educational establishments 'to the maintenance of Christ's holy gospel'; others gave financial support, either during their lifetimes or through their wills, for the endowment of lectureships or the payment of stipends to preachers. In some areas they were able to further the cause of reform through their positions on the bench of justices. During Elizabeth's reign, the magistrates of Nottingham, for example, not only provided for a town preacher but, in order that 'God's glory [be] set forth and the people brought into good obedience', they also held a weekly assembly of ministers and lay justices for the correction of blasphemy, whoredom, drunkenness, and other ungodly behaviour. Similarly, the town council of Leicester ordered that at least one member of every household should attend sermons twice a week.

Despite their distinctive lifestyle, Puritans do not appear to have shared any distinctive social philosophy or consistent political outlook. Few historians today would argue that there was a close link between Calvinism and the rise of capitalism, or between Puritanism and a parliamentary 'opposition' to the crown during the reigns of Elizabeth and James. Nor did Puritans belong to any one socioeconomic group. Included within the ranks of those who 'gadded to sermons' and aspired to a higher spiritual plain were peers, gentlemen, clothworkers, cobblers, and humble villagers; according to the Jesuit William Weston, Puritan meetings on the Isle of Ely were attended by 'men, women, girls, rustics, labourers, and idiots'. They may, however, have contained within their ranks a higher than average representation of women, and historians have recently begun to recognize the importance of mothers as transmitters of Puritan values from one generation to the next. In addition, while they were not restricted to any one social class, they did develop a clear sense of identity, fostered by a number of distinctive badges, such as their preference for Christian names of an Old Testament origin or of their own elaborate and didactic construction, such as Sin-deny, Be-Thankful, Praise-God, and Sure-Trust.

The majority of the other group of mainstream Protestants, so frequently castigated by these Puritans, held fast to an alternative religious outlook which, if perhaps more relaxed, was often no less valid or deeply felt. Although they too nominally subscribed to Calvinist theology, it seems unlikely that the doctrine of predestination ever made more than the most superficial inroads into their collective consciousness. Recognizing the complexities and psychological dangers of this awesome doctrine, most non-Puritan clergy played down the Calvinist theory of salvation to such an extent that many of their parishioners were able to continue to believe that their conduct could influence their destination after death. Thus, when Josias Nichols asked the parishioners of one parish in Kent 'whether it were possible for a man to live so uprightly that by well doing he might win heaven', virtually all of them thought that this was so.

For many of these more moderate members of the Church of England the ritual and ceremonial elements of its liturgy, which were so offensive to Puritans, were a source of great comfort and spiritual solace. There was undoubtedly considerable attachment, particularly among the rural lower orders, to the Elizabethan Book of Common Prayer and to its ceremonies marking both the stages of the agricultural year and the important milestones in the life of the individual. The celebration of feasts such as Easter, Christmas, Whitsuntide, Rogationtide, and the Harvest Thanksgiving gave the local community a much needed opportunity for a collective expression of its religious values. Similarly, the regular church-ales – boisterous forerunners of the modern church fete – fulfilled an important role in the social life of the late sixteenth- and early seventeenth-century parish. Many individuals also displayed a strong attachment to the Prayer-Book ceremonies associated with rites of passage: baptism, churching, marriage, and the burial of the dead. Baptism was considered an important initiation ceremony, and continued to involve godparents and a number of 'popish' rituals, such as the signing of the cross on the infant's forehead. While marriage was no longer a sacrament, it remained 'holy matrimony', and involved the reading of banns in church and the use of the ring. Those close to death were no longer anointed with holy oil, but a special service was held in their homes and they could make a private confession and receive absolution and communion. After their demise, the Prayer-Book funeral service provided an opportunity for communal mourning of their passing. While, therefore, the first generation of English Protestants had found the new Protestant liturgy a pale shadow of earlier Catholic ceremonial, there is every indication that by the end of the sixteenth and beginning of the seventeenth centuries their children and grandchildren had become firmly wedded to the Protestant services of the Prayer Book.

Puritan polemicists frequently scoffed at what they saw as the uninformed nature of this mainstream spirituality. In his *A Brief Discourse of . . . the Countrie Divinitie*, published in 1581, the Elizabethan

Puritan, George Gifford, poured scorn on an uneducated countryman for his lack of theological knowledge. Similarly, in *Micro-
cosmography*, which appeared in 1627, John Earle declared that
the typical rural Englishman was 'a Good Christian to his power,
that is, he goes to church in his best clothes and sits there with
his neighbours where he is capable only of two prayers, for rain
or fairweather'. It is important, however, that historians should
avoid displaying the kind of intellectual condescension which lay
behind such contemporary statements; the weather was after all
a major factor in the success or failure of the harvest, and thus
for many English men and women at this time was not far short
of a life and death issue. George Gifford's ignorant peasant also
made some valid points in his defence; at one point, for example,
he declared: 'I know men which are no scripture men which serve
God as well as the best of them'; and he added: 'is it not enough
for plain countrymen, ploughmen, tailors and such others, for to
have their ten Commandments, the Lord's Prayer and the belief?'
Moreover, there is evidence to suggest that by the seventeenth
century both literacy and Bible reading were on the increase; in
the parish of Keevil in Wiltshire, for example, only 4 per cent
of testators who died during the decades between 1590 and 1630
appear to have possessed a Bible, whereas during the course of
the 1630s and 1640s the proportion rose to 18 per cent. A similar
increase in Bible ownership can also be observed in other parts of
the country.

   For much of the eighty-year period which separated the Elizabethan
church settlement from the civil war, the leaders of the English church
made strenuous efforts to accommodate these two very different religious outlooks within its deliberately broad boundaries. However,
as the Puritan and moderate positions were in many ways mutually
antagonistic, some towns and villages inevitably witnessed acrimonious and protracted disputes over the character of local worship and
divergent attitudes towards what some historians have labelled 'maypole culture'. The existence of such conflicts had been acknowledged
and deplored as early as the 1580s by George Gifford's non-Puritan
countryman, who had commented: 'I know towns myself which are
divided one part against another since they had a preacher, which
was not so before . . . whereas before they loved each other, now
there is dissension sown among them.' As Patrick Collinson[7] has
remarked, such communities became polarized between 'those who
gadded to sermons and those who gadded to dances, sports and other
pastimes'. Believing that private meetings were potentially a greater

threat to order than public gatherings for recreation, in 1618 James I's government intervened in these cultural conflicts by publishing the *Book of Sports*, which enjoined the laity to participate in a range of sporting and leisure activities on Sundays. Fifteen years later in 1633, James's son Charles, who disliked the Puritans' insistence upon sabbatarianism, reprinted the book and ordered that it be read in parish churches throughout the country.

One community which seems to have experienced a particularly acute polarization along these lines was the village of Terling in Essex. The researches of Keith Wrightson and David Levine[8] have revealed that Terling was socially and culturally divided between, on the one hand, a godly elite of 'the better sort' – yeomen, substantial husbandmen, and craftsmen – who attempted to bring about a reformation of manners through their control of local offices; and on the other, an illiterate 'multitude' with little or no religious commitment. Similar divisions existed at Bruen Stapleford in Cheshire, where on one occasion the local Puritan landowner, John Bruen, instructed his servants to pull down a maypole which had been erected on the village green. Such Puritan zealots and their minor moral crusades were cruelly satirized in the work of the Jacobean playwright, Ben Jonson, and particularly in the character of Zeal-of-the-Land Busy, who appeared in *Bartholomew Fair*. However, while cultural and religious conflict was far from uncommon, it is important to point out that many village communities of England managed to avoid the damaging conflicts which existed at Terling and elsewhere. From his study of several village communities in Wiltshire, for example, Ingram[9] has found that the great majority of villagers did not belong to polarized extremes, but rather adhered to a conventional mainstream Protestantism; furthermore, Ingram believes it was the youth of the parish, rather than the least well-off, who were the most indifferent to religion and most impervious to moral discipline.

After 1640, these religious and cultural conflicts, which had become endemic within some local communities, were subsumed within the wider struggle of the English civil war. From his investigations into the divisions that the fighting produced within the village communities of Wiltshire, Somerset, and Devon, David Underdown[10] concluded that 'the distribution of support for the two sides in the western counties shows how strongly Church and King were associated with the old festive culture'. By the end of the war this culture had been defeated, and the victorious Puritans and their nonconformist allies who had gained control of the reins of central government believed they now had an opportunity to impose on the whole nation the same moral reforms that prior to 1640 they had struggled to instigate piecemeal at a local level. Accordingly, they set about the task of reforming the religious and cultural life of the English localities with a vengeance. In the late 1640s, the pre-civil war church was officially proscribed, and its liturgical ceremonies were replaced by the starker services of the Presbyterian Directory of Public Worship. The well-established and popular rites of the 1559 Prayer Book were either shortened and simplified, as was the case with baptism and marriage, or abolished altogether, as with the churching ceremony after childbirth. The London theatres, which had for so long been a particular thorn in the side of Puritan moralists such as William Prynne, were closed down at the outbreak of the civil war and remained shut until the Restoration. From the mid-1640s, the celebration of Christmas was forbidden, Puritans arguing both that the festival was pagan in origin and also that it gave licence to 'carnal and sensual delights'. During the seven-year period 1642 to 1649, parliament also designated the last Wednesday of each month as a solemn day of 'fasting and humiliation', which was to be observed by abstinence from food and drink and attendance at a day-long round of religious exercises aimed at producing both personal and national reformation.

Governmental efforts to bring about what amounted to a cultural revolution intensified in the 1650s, when England came under the control of army leaders such as Oliver Cromwell who considered the reform of the nation's morality one of their chief priorities. Throughout the 1650s, extreme restrictions were placed upon the activities of individuals on Sundays; a strict Puritan sabbath was imposed, and all working, sports, and non-essential travel were made illegal. Puritans also viewed breaches of traditional, Christian sexual morality in a serious light; in 1650, the Rump Parliament passed an Adultery Act, which sought to punish those convicted of fornication with three months' imprisonment, and those found guilty of adultery with death. In 1653, church weddings were outlawed, and replaced by a short, secular marriage service conducted by a justice of the peace. The campaign for moral reform intensified during 1655 and 1656, when the country was placed under the control of Cromwellian major-generals. Some of these, such as Charles Worsley who controlled the north-west of the country, paid special attention to their moral duties and were untiring in their efforts to close down brothels, gaming-houses, and unlicensed ale-houses, and to prevent a whole range of popular recreations, including horse-racing, cock-fighting, and bear-baiting.

However, despite this frontal Puritan assault, the popular religious culture of the pre-war period survived. The Elizabethan Book of Common Prayer continued to be used in many parishes throughout the Interregnum; parents continued to choose godparents for their children, and mothers continued to be churched following childbirth. Hundreds of couples ignored the new secular ceremony instituted by the 1653 Marriage Act and sought out clergymen to conduct clandestine church weddings for them. Christmas also proved too durable for its opponents. Some attended secret Christmas Day church services, while many more continued to celebrate the day with traditional feasting and merriment. The monthly days of fasting and humiliation were widely disliked and ignored. Most frustrating of all for the Puritan reformers was the consistent failure of the justices of the peace to prosecute vigorously those who transgressed the new moral legislation of the Interregnum period. By the end of the 1650s, the Puritan attempt to build a Calvinist Zion in England had foundered on the rock of the nation's preference for its traditional religious and cultural life.

The restoration of the monarchy in 1660 brought about both the return of the traditional festivities of the church year, and an immediate and decisive revival of maypole culture. There can be little doubt that the great majority of the population were ready to accept the return of Anglicanism and eager to participate in the services outlined in the revised Prayer Book of 1662. The church was once more fully involved in the traditional festive culture of the people, for the old ceremonies associated with Christmas, Easter, Whitsun, Shrovetide, and Maytide were quickly resumed in all parts of the country and proved as popular as ever. Indeed, David Underdown has argued that rural sports and recreations became more common after 1660 than ever before. Unsurprisingly, Puritan opinion found these developments extremely distasteful; one Newcastle Puritan remarked shortly after the Restoration that 'the reins of liberty are set loose . . . maypoles and players and jugglers . . . now pass current'. By now, however, such Puritans – or 'fanatics' as they were generally labelled by their mainstream critics – were once more a powerless minority. As Charles II's reign progressed, they were gradually to give up their earlier hopes of remodelling the established church into a closer conformity to European Protestantism, and to lend their support instead to the nonconformist struggle for the right to worship outside its boundaries. After basic religious toleration was conceded in 1689, the dissenters turned their back once and for all on Anglicanism and went on to develop the distinctive spirituality which was to play so dynamic a role in the revolutionary social and economic changes of the next century. The great majority of the laity, meanwhile, continued to reject the approach of the fanatics, and remained deeply attached to the conservative liturgy of the Prayer Book. As a result, by the end of the seventeenth century popular Anglicanism was enmeshed more closely than ever within the social fabric of the English countryside.

NOTES

1 Margaret Spufford, *Contrasting Communities: English villagers in the sixteenth and seventeenth centuries* (Cambridge, 1984).
2 Martin Ingram, *Church Courts, Sex and Marriage in England, 1570–1640* (Cambridge, 1987).
3 Peter Clark, *English Provincial Society from the Reformation to the Revolution: Religion, politics and society in Kent, 1500–1640* (Sussex, 1977).
4 Ingram, *Church Courts*.
5 Jeremy Boulton, 'The limits of formal religion: the administration of Holy Communion in late Elizabethan and early Stuart London', *London Journal* 10 (1984).
6 Robert Whiting, *The Blind Devotion of the People: Popular religion and the English Reformation* (Cambridge, 1989).
7 Patrick Collinson, *The Religion of Protestants* (Oxford, 1982).
8 Keith Wrightson and David Levine, *Poverty and Piety in an English Village: Terling 1525–1700* (New York, 1979).
9 Ingram, *Church Courts*.
10 David Underdown, *Revel, Riot and Rebellion: Popular politics and culture in England 1603–1660* (Oxford, 1985).

SUGGESTIONS FOR FURTHER READING

A good introduction to late medieval Catholic piety and the impact of the Reformation can be found in J. J. Scarisbrick, *The Reformation and the English People* (Oxford, 1984), but the reader needs to be aware of the author's pro-Catholic bias. The impact of Protestantism on popular religion and culture has been brilliantly surveyed by Patrick Collinson in *The Religion of Protestants* (Oxford, 1982); and also in *The Birthpangs of Protestant England: Religious and cultural change in the sixteenth and seventeenth centuries* (London, 1988). The emergence of a new Protestant popular culture is also charted in David Cressy, *Bells and Bonfires: National memory and the Protestant calendar in Elizabethan and Stuart England* (London, 1989). Also useful are the essays by I. Luxton and W. J. Sheils, in F. Heal and R. O'Day (eds), *Church and Society in England from Henry VIII to James I* (London, 1977). For the seventeenth century, see Barry Reay, 'Popular religion', in Barry Reay (ed.), *Popular Culture in Seventeenth-century England* (Beckenham, 1985); and David Underdown, *Revel, Riot and Rebellion: Popular politics and culture in England 1603–1660* (Oxford, 1985).

Professor Collinson is the best authority on the godly in this period;

particularly useful are *The Elizabethan Puritan Movement* (London, 1967); and *Godly People: Essays on English Protestantism and Puritanism* (London, 1983). For more specific aspects of Puritan beliefs and behaviour in the Elizabethan period, see C. J. Kitching, 'Prayers fit for the time: fasting and prayer in response to national crises in the reign of Elizabeth', in W. Sheils (ed.), *Monks, Hermits and the Ascetic Tradition*, Studies in Church History, vol. 22 (Oxford, 1985); and Nicholas Tyacke, 'Popular Puritan mentality in late Elizabethan England', in P. Clark, A. G. R. Smith, and N. Tyacke (eds), *The English Commonwealth 1547–1640* (Leicester, 1979). Useful studies on aspects of seventeenth-century Puritanism are T. G. Barnes, 'County politics and a Puritan cause célèbre: Somerset church-ales 1633', *Transactions of the Royal Historical Society*, Fifth Series, vol. 9 (1959); and Chris Durston, 'Lords of misrule: The Puritan war on Christmas', *History Today* 35 (1985).

Among the many local studies of popular religion during this period are Robert Whiting, *The Blind Devotion of the People: Popular religion and the English Reformation* (Cambridge, 1989); S. Brigden, *London and the English Reformation* (Oxford, 1990); Peter Clark, *English Provincial Society from the Reformation to the Revolution: Religion, politics and society in Kent 1500–1640* (Sussex, 1977); Martin Ingram, *Church Courts, Sex and Marriage in England 1570–1620* (Cambridge, 1987); M. E. James, *Family, Lineage and Civil Society; A study of society, politics and mentality in the Durham region 1500–1640* (London, 1974); W. J. Sheils, *The Puritans in the Diocese of Peterborough 1558–1610* (Northampton, 1979); M. Spufford, *Contrasting Communities: English villagers in the sixteenth and seventeenth centuries* (Cambridge, 1974); and K. Wrightson and D. Levine, *Poverty and Piety in an English Village: Terling 1525–1700* (New York, 1979). Research into attendance rates at communion in London has been published by Jeremy Boulton in 'The limits of formal religion: the administration of Holy Communion in late Elizabethan and early Stuart London', *London Journal* 10 (1984).

The best introductions to magic and witchcraft are Keith Thomas, *Religion and the Decline of Magic: Studies in popular beliefs in sixteenth and seventeenth-century England* (London, 1971); and Alan Macfarlane, *Witchcraft in Tudor and Stuart England* (London, 1970). Chris Durston examines the belief in wonders and portents in the 1640s and 1650s in 'Signs and wonders and the English civil war', *History Today* 37 (1987).

Evidence of the growing commitment of mainstream Protestants to the Elizabethan Prayer Book and its ceremonies can be found in Horton Davies, *Worship and Theology in England from Cranmer to Hooker 1534–1603* (New Jersey, 1970); John Morrill, 'The church in England 1642–9', in John Morrill (ed.), *Reactions to the English Civil War 1642–9* (London, 1982); and Chris Durston, '"Unhallowed wedlocks": The regulation of marriage during the English Revolution', *Historical Journal* 31 (1988).

For a European perspective, see Natalie Zemon Davis, *Society and Culture in Early Modern France* (London, 1975); Robin Briggs, *Communities of Belief* (Oxford, 1989); Peter Burke, *Popular Culture in Early Modern Europe* (London, 1978); and C. Larner, *Witchcraft and Religion: The politics of popular belief* (Oxford, 1984).

6 Heresy and dissent

For much of the medieval period England was remarkably free from heresy; serious trouble emerged only in the mid-fourteenth century when an Oxford theologian, John Wyclif, denied the real presence in the mass, called for the disendowment of the church, and strongly criticized the pope. By the time he was condemned as a heretic in 1382, Wyclif had attracted many followers, who came together to form an organized movement labelled by its enemies Lollardy (from an old word meaning to mumble). In the late fourteenth century, the ranks of the Lollards included clerics, knights, merchants, and artisans, but during the course of the 1400s the movement lost its influential support, declined in popularity, and went underground to escape episcopal persecution. No longer a broadly based social movement, it retained its strength only as a proscribed household religion, evident in parts of Essex, Kent, the Chilterns, London, Bristol, and Coventry. Nor was there much direct liaison between these disparate communities, although some contact was maintained through a group known as the Christian Brotherhood, which from a base in London published and distributed Lollard books to various parts of the country. Intellectually too the movement had lost vibrancy; no new Lollard text appears to have been composed after 1420, while Wyclif's original ideas became diluted with other deviant beliefs – some merely anti-clerical, some frankly bizarre. These later characteristics have led Jack Scarisbrick[1] to write off Lollardy as 'upland semi-paganism'. This, however, is an over-harsh verdict, which ignores the fact that many of the men and women condemned as Lollards in the early sixteenth century were wealthy and literate citizens, who continued to attend official church services, as well as Lollard meetings, where they heard readings from their outlawed English Bible.

This indigenous English heresy was injected with new life in the early 1520s when the ideas of the German and Swiss Reformers, especially those of Martin Luther, began to trickle into the country. Experienced in dealing with Lollardy, the English Catholic church was quick to appreciate the new danger and took speedy action. Soon after Luther's teachings had been condemned by the pope in 1521, his works were publicly burnt in Oxford, Cambridge, and at St Paul's Cross, London. English academics also set about refuting his theology in a series of sermons and polemical tracts. None the less, Lutheran books and William Tyndale's translation of the Bible into English continued to be smuggled into the country by foreign traders and disseminated by the Christian Brotherhood. In London, the port areas and nearby law courts seethed with underground Lutheran groups. Some young members of the Inns of Court became ardent and lifetime proselytizers of Lutheran views, and only a few, like Sir Thomas More's son-in-law William Roper, were to be persuaded out of their heresy by argument and prayer. Elsewhere, it was the two universities which were most affected. At Oxford, a group of scholars met at Cardinal College (later Christ Church) in the mid-1520s to read and discuss the reformers' theology, while at Cambridge scholars and preachers gathered informally at the White Horse Tavern to exchange ideas about biblical texts and the new doctrines coming out of Germany. The names of the participants at these sessions, as recorded by the martyrologist John Foxe, read like a roll-call of future English Protestants: included among them were Miles Coverdale, Hugh Latimer, Nicholas Ridley, Thomas Bilney, William Tyndale, Robert Barnes, John Bale, Matthew Parker, and possibly Thomas Cranmer. At this stage, however, most had not yet formulated their mature beliefs. They were young men attracted to, rather than convinced by, the advanced ideas gaining ground on the continent, and the White Horse Tavern should thus be seen less as a den of heretics than as a meeting place for study, where radical ideas were aired and future Protestant leaders nurtured.

Links soon began to be forged between these few English Lutheran pioneers and the remaining underground Lollard cells. In 1526, for example, representatives of the Essex Lollards came to London to meet Robert Barnes, and they purchased from him a copy of Tyndale's translation of the New Testament. The new reformers also sought out Lollards; Thomas Bilney preached in Lollard areas of East Anglia, while Robert Forman, one-time President of Queens' College, Cambridge, distributed Lutheran books and Tyndale's New Testament to Lollard cells. Far from resenting the intrusion of Lutheranism, many Lollards on the contrary welcomed the opportunity to obtain new translations of the Bible in 'more cleaner English', and some may have had hopes that the time for a true reformation had at last arrived. For their part, the new reformers quickly recognized the practical and propaganda value of the Lollards; on the practical level, the pre-existing underground movement could disseminate their literature and provide safe havens for their preachers, while for propaganda purposes the English Lollards could be claimed as the spiritual antecedents of the Lutherans.

For all their commitment and energy, prior to the breach with Rome the English Lutherans remained very few in number and as a threat to the church, easily containable. Intellectuals tainted with Lutheranism had no possibility of advancement in royal service, as Henry VIII himself and the conservative humanists who held sway over his court were violently hostile to the German reformer. Indeed, fear of Luther's pernicious influence inspired a new round of heresy trials which all but succeeded in suffocating the infant reform movement. Bishop Longland of Lincoln scattered the Oxford Lutheran scholars in 1526, and after 1529 a heresy hunt initiated by Sir Thomas More effectively silenced the most outspoken radicals in London. The Cambridge group was similarly intimidated when Wolsey interrogated and imprisoned Thomas Bilney and Robert Barnes in the late 1520s. Thus, without the issue of the king's marriage and the resultant break with Rome, it is difficult to see how Lutheranism could have made effective inroads into England.

It was the schism which brought heretics some immediate respite from persecution and allowed the further spread of radical ideas. Some radical intellectuals, like Hugh Latimer, were now protected by the king from the ecclesiastical authorities, because of their readiness to support the annulment; at the same time, many of the most outspoken and active enemies of Lutheranism provoked Henry's rage by their support for Queen Catherine and opposition to the supremacy. Thus, John Fisher, Bishop of Rochester, and Sir Thomas More, who had been the most prominent of the English opponents of Luther, were equally the most famous victims of Henry's annulment and break with Rome. After 1530, the new men and women with most influence at court were evangelical in outlook – sympathetic to plans for reform of the church, but prepared to work within the confines of royal policy. They patronized reformers, even heretics, who questioned Catholic doctrines, provided that they held their tongues in check. Through Anne Boleyn's influence,

Hugh Latimer and Nicholas Shaxton were promoted to the bishoprics of Worcester and Salisbury respectively; and Thomas Cromwell employed the Lutherans John Bale, Robert Barnes, and Richard Taverner to produce anti-papal polemics and translations of the works of foreign Protestants. Other radical ideas were spread through the influence of foreign heretics, many of whom were anabaptists from the Netherlands, who fled to England in their hundreds, possibly even thousands, to escape from less tolerant regimes at home. This period of relative freedom was brought to an abrupt end in 1540 with the fall of Thomas Cromwell, who was charged with 'damnable' heresies. Cromwell's execution proved a serious blow for the radicals, for it ushered in a period in which the religious conservatives were once again in the ascendant. The early and mid-1540s witnessed a number of heresy trials, and while some Protestants like Shaxton decided to recant, others like Anne Askew chose to die. None the less, heresy was far from extirpated during these years, chiefly because whenever possible Archbishop Cranmer and a number of other evangelicals who were still in favour with the king used their influence to protect radicals who were in trouble with the authorities.

The Henrician radicals drew their inspiration from a variety of sources: Lollard, Lutheran, Swiss Reformed, even anabaptist. The eclectic nature of their beliefs makes them difficult to categorize, for they differed as much among themselves as from Catholics. Some believed in the real presence in the eucharist, others denied it; some accepted saint worship, others abhorred it. It is also impossible to estimate with any precision the exact numbers of these religious radicals, for there is no source which bears any resemblance to a census of early Protestants. Court records, themselves incomplete, simply reveal those heretics who were caught. Wills provide some clues, for their preambles frequently contained a statement about the testator's last thoughts on religion and these can be classified theologically. Thus, according to some historians, those testators who called upon the intercession of the Virgin Mary, the saints, and the 'holy company of heaven', can be presumed to be Catholic; those, on the other hand, who stressed their inherent sinfulness and sole reliance on the mercy of Christ for their salvation were most probably Protestant.

Unfortunately, however, there are serious problems in interpreting wills in this way. It is often unclear whether the opinions expressed in the preamble were those of the testator himself or of the scribe who drew up the will. Again, it is questionable whether any statistical analysis of a series of wills can reliably reveal religious trends; any sample, no matter how large, will inevitably be unrepresentative of the laity as a whole, for it will be biased towards men, the sick and elderly, and those with some property to bequeath. Furthermore, from the 1540s onwards an increasing number of wills were theologically neutral, omitting any reference to Mary or the saints but also avoiding any assertion of solafidianism. While these omissions might have reflected a dissatisfaction with traditional Catholicism, they might equally well have been the result of a natural caution in uncertain times. A number of testators also seem to have been theologically confused; some combined both Protestant and Catholic formulas in their preambles, while others made a Protestant statement of faith yet provided for masses and obits in their bequests.

Partly because of these difficulties, there is considerable scope for disagreement between historians about the significance of the evidence from wills, and consequently about the extent of the spread of Protestantism during the period of the early Reformation. Although there is a general consensus that the new religion made little headway before 1545 outside London, parts of Kent, and a few isolated towns mainly in the south-east, differences have arisen, particularly between A. G. Dickens and Christopher Haigh,[2] over the extent of Protestantization in the reign of Edward VI. Whereas Haigh has argued that Protestantism only took root in most parts of England fairly late on in the reign of Elizabeth I, Dickens believes that by 1553 it had already gained a strong hold in the 'great crescent' of south-east England stretching from Norwich to Hove, taking in East Anglia, London, and Kent, and extending up the Thames Valley and the Chilterns to the outlying centres of Newbury, Bristol, and Gloucester. Thus, according to Dickens: 'by 1553 Protestantism had already become a formidable and seemingly ineradicable phenomenon in fairly large and very populous areas of marked political importance.'

Wills, court records, and anecdotal evidence all suggest that the new religious beliefs had indeed made some significant headway in the more populous, southern regions of the country by 1553. None the less, the burden of the evidence would seem to support Haigh's contention that even in its heartlands of East Anglia, the south-east, and the Thames Valley, Protestantism remained a minority religion at the time of Edward's death. Historians have discovered, for example, that in Colchester – a town described as 'a harbourer of heretics' – only 10 per cent of wills from the period from 1538 to 1553 contained an identifiably Protestant preamble. Similarly, even in Kent where 81 per cent of the wills written during the period up to 1550 had departed from the traditional Catholic forms, only 7 per cent were unmistakably Protestant. It would seem, therefore, that at this stage Protestant evangelists still had a great deal of work to do before England could justly be described as a Protestant country. On the other hand, it would be a serious mistake to underplay the importance of the influential minority who became Protestants before 1553, or to underestimate the extent to which traditional patterns of Catholic religious life had been undermined by the activities of the Edwardian reformers. After 1553, Edward's successor Mary encountered some difficulties in her attempt to revitalize English Catholicism, and in the next decade Elizabeth was able to construct her new church on the Protestant foundations laid down during her brother's reign.

Although Haigh and Dickens remain fundamentally divided on the question of Protestantism's inherent popularity, the researches of other historians into the spread of the Reformation in a number of local areas have revealed some findings which both are prepared to accept. There is now general agreement, for example, about the social background of those who embraced the new Protestant beliefs. Converts were often young, many were women, and they spanned almost all social groups: aristocracy, gentry, yeomanry, merchants, traders, artisans (especially clothworkers and shoemakers), lawyers, schoolmasters, and clergy. It is also now accepted that it is extremely difficult to identify the precise circumstances or character traits that encouraged these conversions. As relatively few autobiographies of either Catholics or Protestants have survived from the period, historians can only speculate about the influences that led individuals to become Protestants, though spiritual thirst, an anti-authoritarian temperament, or a discontent with the religious or political status quo may all have played a part. Most historians now agree that the reaction of the English people to the new religion varied greatly from region to region. While some counties, such as Essex and Kent, soon possessed significant numbers of Protestants, others, like Lancashire, Cornwall, and Lincolnshire, were hardly touched by the religious changes. This geographical variation should not be viewed as a simple divide between a Protestant south and east, and a Catholic north and west, for Protestantism did well in the northern and western towns of Leeds, Manchester, and Bristol, while Catholicism remained strong in the west of Sussex. Indeed, variation frequently occurred within the same county; in Suffolk, for example, the Stour Valley was a centre of Protestant fervour, while the fenlands and sheep-growing areas north of Bury St Edmunds remained impervious to religious change. Towns, too, could contain both Protestants and Catholics, as the Protestant Thomas Hancock found to his cost when his preaching raised a religious storm in Salisbury and Poole in 1548.

The reasons for this regional diversity may be somewhat easier to identify than the influences on individual conversions. Geographically isolated places, like the remoter parts of Lancashire, had few opportunities to encounter the new ideas and thus remained predominantly Catholic. Conversely, ports and areas where cloth was manufactured or traded often became Protestant centres, for the new beliefs were often imported by sailors and foreign visitors, and the mobility of clothworkers facilitated an easy exchange of ideas. Political factors also influenced the religious configuration of a region. Those places where committed Protestant clergy or gentry possessed land and patronage frequently became important evangelizing centres; Archbishop Cranmer, for example, used his patronage rights to introduce Protestant preachers into Suffolk and Kent during the reigns of Henry VIII and Edward VI. In the same way, the influence of a conservative landlord could also be considerable; the anti-heretical Gage family were able to keep the downland area of East Sussex Catholic despite the spread of Protestantism further to the east. Finally, it seems that relatively prosperous regions may have been more readily attracted to Protestantism than those that were more economically backward, perhaps because their inhabitants had the education to read Protestant works and the independence of outlook which helped them to make the break with traditional beliefs.

After 1553, committed and outspoken Protestants reacted to Mary's counter-Reformation in several different ways. Fearing reprisals from the new government, those most closely implicated in the Duke of Northumberland's unsuccessful coup fled abroad as soon as they could. The duke's chief supporters in Cambridge, Edwin Sandys, Thomas Lever, and Sir John Cheke, escaped to Strasbourg, and a number of others who were not in immediate danger also chose to leave the country. Twenty-six Cambridge men, many of whom had reached high office under Edward, went into self-imposed exile before the beginning of the Marian persecutions in February 1555; thereafter, the drift accelerated and altogether nearly 800 men, women, and children departed for the continent. They left partly through fear and partly to keep their Protestant beliefs alive and pure, uncompromised by the need to conform to popery. A number of other Protestants, however, some of whom had been former associates of Northumberland, chose to remain in England throughout Mary's reign. William Cecil and Matthew Parker, for example, both outwardly conformed and retired from public life, while after a spell in prison Northumberland's three surviving sons even fought for Mary and her Spanish allies in the war against France in 1557.

Some of the Edwardian Protestants who were unable to escape abroad refused to recant or conform and kept their faith alive by meeting secretly for worship in underground congregations. Although the precise number who attended these conventicles is unknown, John Foxe claimed that some meetings attracted as many as 200 participants, and described specific gatherings at which forty people were present. Some of these congregations were presided over by an ordained Protestant minister who used the Edwardian Prayer Book, but others were sectarian in character and were led by laymen who introduced their own individual forms of worship. Those who were caught at such meetings often suffered a heretic's death. The first Protestant martyr was John Rogers, a Cambridge MA, who refused to recant even at the moving sight of his wife and eleven children gathered round the fire; 290 other martyrs followed him, the majority coming from London, the south-east, and East Anglia. A large proportion of them were young people in their late teens or twenties; more than 50 were women, and 105 of the 151 whose occupation was recorded were artisans, traders, and labourers from the lower orders. They cannot, however, be taken as an accurate social anatomy of Protestantism, for in the main their ranks were filled by those Protestants who lacked the wealth and social connections to avoid arrest and punishment. The Marian martyrs were probably only the ringleaders of the active Protestant cells, but there is no way of knowing the number or size of the conventicles they led or attended. Much to the alarm of the authorities, spectators attending the burnings seem to have pitied and admired the victims. In January 1556, the privy council ordered the Mayor and Sheriff of London to stop 'apprentices or other servants to be abroad' at the time of the burnings, and commanded that anyone found 'comforting, aiding or praising the offenders' should be arrested. Yet, despite the unpopularity of the persecutions, the government was able to rely upon the co-operation both of conservative Justices of the Peace to round up Protestants, and of jurors to inform against them. Nor was there any serious incident of violence in support of the victims; indeed, the only rebellion of Mary's reign, that led by Wyatt, erupted well before the policy of persecution had been initiated.

Despite the burnings, Mary failed in her mission to extirpate heresy. Sizeable underground Protestant communities survived the persecution, and at Elizabeth's accession significant numbers of closet

Protestants emerged from the shadows to worship openly once more. Along with those Protestants who now returned home from exile, these men and women looked to Elizabeth to bring in a new, thoroughly reformed religious order. However, for reasons of personal preference and political expediency, Elizabeth decided to proceed cautiously and to retain many ceremonial practices deemed popish by the most committed Protestants. As a consequence, the Elizabethan religious settlement disappointed many ardent Protestants; while some chose to uphold it hoping for changes at a later stage, others found it unacceptable and agitated unsparingly for its reform. Both contemporaries and historians have dubbed this latter group of Protestants 'Puritans'. In the past some historians misrepresented Puritanism as a radical Protestant opposition to mainstream Anglicanism. More recently, Peter Lake[3] has shown that the Puritans and their so-called 'Anglican' opponents had much of importance in common, in particular the same Calvinist theology and anti-papalism. The Puritans, therefore, are better characterized in Lake's words as 'those Protestants whose enthusiasm and zeal in the cause of true religion marked them off from their more lukewarm and profane contemporaries'.

The first major conflict between these Puritans and the authorities erupted in 1564, when two recently returned Marian exiles at Oxford University, Thomas Sampson and Lawrence Humphrey, were summoned to appear before Archbishop Parker for failing to comply with the queen's order that all clergy should wear the correct clerical dress: the white surplice for all liturgical occasions and the long clerical gown and square cap for outdoor attire. This move was followed by a more general drive, not only to secure uniformity of dress but also to suppress 'what diversities there are in our clergy' in all matters of 'ceremonies and rites'. This governmental attempt to secure conformity, misnamed the vestiarian controversy, dragged on for several years. Puritans who refused to conform appealed to Protestant leaders abroad for support, and both sides published books and pamphlets to arouse public opinion at home. Sampson was deprived at Oxford, the master of a Cambridge college was disciplined, and nearly forty London ministers were suspended. The debate ended in an uneasy victory for the queen. Conformity of dress was enforced and all but a handful of the London ministers returned to their pulpits, but the victory was incomplete, for in practice diversity of ceremonials persisted. Godly ministers continued to use bread rather than the prescribed wafers for communion, and they still refused to incorporate into their services practices which they regarded as superstitious, such as the signing of the cross on the infant's head during baptism. They also continued to shorten the liturgy to allow more time for sermons. Furthermore, Elizabeth's partial victory was achieved at a very high cost, for many Puritans now turned against the bishops for upholding 'popery' within the church, and out of their anger and frustration the radical force of English Presbyterianism was born.

Elizabethan Presbyterians demanded a wholesale reform of the church, and in particular of its governmental structure. They sought to replace the existing episcopal hierarchy with a four-part parochial ministry elected by individual congregations: a pastor to preach the Word, a doctor to teach true doctrine, lay elders to regulate discipline, and deacons to collect and distribute alms. Congregations would remain the basic unit of ecclesiastical government, but they would be linked together in a network of representative assemblies – local classes and provincial and national synods. These revolutionary ideas, which appeared to advocate the incorporation of elements of democracy into the running of the church, ran counter to the existing authoritarian structures of ecclesiastical government, and not surprisingly alarmed and appalled most of those who held high office in the church and state. They first came to public attention in 1570, when they were championed by the Cambridge theologian, Thomas Cartwright, in a series of lectures at the university on the Acts of the Apostles. For this display of radicalism, Cartwright was deprived of his professorship and forbidden to preach in the university. Two years later, a detailed Presbyterian programme was outlined by John Field and Thomas Wilcox in *An Admonition to the Parliament*, a tract that, although ostensibly addressed to the MPs then meeting at Westminster, in reality represented an appeal to a wider public opinion. The authors were incarcerated in Newgate gaol for their offence, but Cartwright took up their cause and further publicized the Presbyterian position by entering into a lengthy public debate on the issues with John Whitgift, master of Trinity College, Cambridge.

During the 1580s, Presbyterianism developed into a well organized, though never unified or broadly based movement. Presbyterians petitioned parliament, introduced parliamentary Bills to change the government of the church, and established an embryonic synodical organization in some parts of the country. Their energetic radicalism was a reaction to their disillusionment with the established church, which in their view had failed both to purge itself of popery and to provide preachers to spread the Word. Indeed, far from dedicating himself to bringing about the reforms they desired, the new Archbishop of Canterbury, John Whitgift, seemed bent on repressing all signs of nonconformity. For a while, the Presbyterians enjoyed the support of moderate Puritans who shared their alarm that Whitgift's policies threatened to deprive the church of all godly preachers and leave it vulnerable to the attacks of Catholics. At this stage, hostility to Whitgift was expressed not only in parliament but also in the privy council, where prominent royal advisers, such as Lord Burghley, the Earl of Leicester, and Sir Francis Walsingham, protested against the use of the prerogative Court of High Commission to punish Puritans, many of whom were their own clients. However, this moderate support was soon lost, both because Whitgift showed himself capable of compromise, and because during 1588 and 1589 the radical wing of the Presbyterians produced and disseminated widely a number of 'Marprelate Tracts', such as *The Protestation of Martin Marprelate*. The appearance of these works, which attacked the bishops with virulent, satirical rhetoric, provided Whitgift with the excuse to break up the Presbyterian movement. Their secret presses were raided and silenced, and Presbyterian leaders were prosecuted before the Courts of High Commission and Star Chamber. By 1592, English Presbyterianism had been driven underground, and it was not to re-emerge as an effective religious force until the middle of the seventeenth century.

The Presbyterians were not, however, the most radical of the Elizabethan Protestants, for there also existed small groups of men and women, labelled separatists, who went so far as to question the need for any established state church at all. These separatists must not be confused with the radical Puritans who 'gadded' to sermons outside their own parishes and often met in their own households for Bible reading; although the boundaries are often blurred, the latter were not strictly speaking separatists, for they accepted the state church and attended parish services, while supplementing them with voluntary religious activities for their personal edification. The separatists, by contrast, established their own autonomous congregations and totally dissociated themselves from the Elizabethan church with its ungodliness and 'open abominations of anti-christ'. Their separated or 'gathered' churches, which were often presided over by laymen, had first appeared in England during the period of the Marian persecutions, and a few congregations, mainly in London but also in several provincial centres, had continued to meet secretly after Elizabeth's accession. One group, known as the Family of Love, or Familists, which had been brought together by the founder of the movement in the Netherlands, Henry Niclaes, apparently listened to scriptural expositions late at night in isolated houses in East Anglia, and upheld their own rituals and beliefs, far removed from mainstream Protestantism. Further separatist congregations were established in London and East Anglia during the 1580s under the leadership of Robert Browne, John Greenwood, and Henry Barrow. The authorities subsequently became so alarmed by their activities that they executed Greenwood and Barrow for sedition in 1593. This left the gathered congregations in disarray, and shortly afterwards many of the London separatists chose to escape further persecution by emigrating to Holland; others went into hiding, not to reappear publicly until James I's reign.

These radical Protestants were not, of course, the only ones to dissent from the established church in the sixteenth century. Many Roman Catholics too protested against and refused to conform to the religious changes imposed by the Tudor monarchs. Under Henry VIII, 308 people were executed under the Treason Law of 1534, sixty-three for simply speaking against the royal supremacy. Countless others suffered more minor punishments, mainly the pillory, for seditious behaviour that fell short of treason. The most serious Catholic resistance took the form of full-scale rebellions – the Pilgrimage of Grace of 1536–7, the Western Rebellion of 1549, and the Northern Rebellion of 1569. None of these risings was exclusively religious in origin, but all three included religion among the grievances of the rebels and were accompanied by actions demonstrating hostility to recent religious changes, and two of the three were led by priests. The Pilgrims reopened monasteries, the Western rebels marched under religious banners, while the Northern rebels celebrated the mass at Durham and Ripon. All failed, however, principally because the monarchy could count on the loyalty and military support of its leading subjects, Catholic as well as Protestant.

Elizabeth's Catholic subjects did not face quite the same tribulations as Protestants had under her sister, for they were not burnt or forced to recant. Elizabeth's main concern was to enforce obedience to the law, not to change people's beliefs. Her subjects, she argued, could believe whatever they wished, provided that they attended the religious services prescribed by the state and declined to practise their own religion, even in secret. The official penalties for non-compliance included hefty fines for non-attendance at church or for hearing mass. The more prominent Catholic families also had to reconcile themselves to losing their positions of power and prestige. After 1563, professing Catholics were barred from the House of Commons, and Protestants gradually replaced Catholics as justices of the peace. Initially, most Elizabethan Catholics decided to conform outwardly, to attend their parish church, and await better times, for it seemed likely that Elizabeth would either marry a Catholic prince or else die without issue, thereby leaving the throne to the Catholic queen of Scotland, Mary Stuart. At this stage, there were no martyrs to set an example of resistance and no strong papal leadership to rally the Catholic cause. Yet, while they ostensibly conformed, many of these 'church-papists' remained attached to Catholic objects of piety such as rosaries and missals. Nor had all the elements of the old religion to which they remained loyal entirely disappeared from the parish churches; some parishes continued to use their altars, vestments, and chalices, and those Catholic clergy who still held benefices often conducted secret masses and attempted to incorporate traditional Catholic practices into the new services. As a consequence, for a time there seemed little need for Catholics to separate from the established church, and many indeed drifted into conformity or conversion.

Recusancy began on a small scale in the late 1560s in many areas of the country; it was evident, for example, in Lichfield and Peterborough, and in parts of Herefordshire, Lancashire, and Worcestershire. Its appearance was partly a response to governmental success in imposing Protestant conformity on the Marian clergy, and partly as a result of the mission of the papal envoy, Lawrence Vaux, who had forbidden English Catholics to attend their parish churches. It was only, however, after the arrival of missionary priests in England in the early 1570s that church-papists were given sustained encouragement to absent themselves from church. Thereafter, the numbers of recusants grew rapidly. A national survey taken in 1577 identified 1,500 recusants, but this was a serious underestimate, which listed only the gentry and a number of other conspicuous malcontents. By the beginning of James I's reign, there were probably as many as 40,000 committed Catholic recusants in England, or about 1.5 per cent of the population. They were no longer, however, evenly spread over the country, but were concentrated in the northern counties; thus while a census of Yorkshire recusants contained 3,500 names, only 266 adults were recorded as recusants in Sussex, a county which had been a Catholic stronghold in the 1560s. Most recusants were members of aristocratic or gentry families and were thus able to afford the cost of supporting a priest as a private chaplain. Very often, the head of a Catholic household continued to attend church services in order to protect his estates from the heavy fines imposed by the government; his wife, meanwhile, became a recusant, took responsibility for educating the children in Catholic doctrine, and organized the household regime around the cycle of Catholic feasts and holy days. The country seats of these Catholic gentry families provided a network of 'safe houses' for the priests who secretly travelled around the country ministering to the spiritual needs of the faithful.

This 'manor house Catholicism' could not have survived without priests to administer the sacraments. During the first fifteen years of Elizabeth's reign, the Marian priests had played their part in keeping the faith alive, but from 1573 onwards the task was taken up by missionaries from abroad. Initially they were trained at the seminary at Douai in the Spanish Netherlands, established in 1568 by the former Oxford don, William Allen. During the 1580s, they were joined by a small group of Jesuits led by Edmund Campion and Robert Parsons. Despite the extreme danger of the enterprise and the torture and execution of some 130 priests, there was no shortage of missionaries, and at the time of Elizabeth's death about 400 secular priests and a dozen Jesuits were active in England. Yet, for a number of reasons their missionary effort was less effective than it might have been. As the missionaries tended to work in the south and east of the country rather than in the north where recusancy was strongest, the Catholic heartlands often lacked priests to say masses, hear confessions, perform marriages, and baptize children. Furthermore, the arrival of the missionaries had in some ways made life more difficult for the recusant community, since their presence had alarmed the authorities and made them more vigilant in proceeding against lay Catholics. New penal laws were passed in parliament and more than sixty lay Catholics were executed for treason after 1581. Only the most committed or best protected could withstand this kind of persecution. Finally, the missionary effort was hampered by disagreements over tactics and objectives. In general, the Jesuits wanted England to return to the papal fold, favoured mass conversions, and supported the Spanish invasion attempt of 1588. The lay leadership and most of the secular priests, on the other hand, remained loyal to the English crown and reconciled to a future in which Catholicism would continue only as a minority religion. This difference of outlook led to a serious rift in the priestly ranks in the 1590s.

The role of the seminary priests and the Jesuits in the survival of Catholicism under Elizabeth has been a subject of controversy in recent years. While John Bossy[4] has argued that the missionary effort of the 1570s should receive the credit for constructing 'a viable

Catholic community' out of the debris of the destroyed English
Catholic church, Christopher Haigh[5] has conversely maintained that
the Catholic community was largely the product of survivalism from
the Marian period, and should thus not be seen as 'a new post-
Reformation creation of missionaries from the Continent'. Haigh
is undoubtedly right to draw attention to the work of the Marian
priests in keeping Catholic practices alive in the 1560s, and also to
demonstrate that recusancy pre-dated the arrival of the priests from
Douai, but he overstates his case and belittles the missionary effort
of the 1570s and 1580s. It is highly unlikely that church-papistry
or recusancy could have survived into the late Elizabethan period
without the efforts of the seminary priests, except perhaps in the most
conservative and remote of parishes. All the evidence suggests that
Catholicism remained strong where it had the support of the gentry
who could maintain seminary priests, rather than in those areas which
had retained a strong commitment to traditional religion before and
during the Reformation but which had no gentry households to sus-
tain the faith during the difficult Elizabethan years. Haigh may also
exaggerate the role of the Marian clergy in the long-term survival of
Catholicism. There is indeed a strong counter-argument which suggests that those Marian priests who clung on to Catholic observances
in the 1560s may ultimately have assisted the establishment of Protestantism, since their continued presence in the established church
and their retention of traditional practices may have made it easier
for conservatives to conform during the early years of Elizabeth's
reign, and helped them to make the transition from Catholicism to
Protestantism in slow and relatively painless stages.

By the end of Elizabeth's reign, a great many church-papists had
been absorbed into the Church of England, and the Protestant critics
of the Elizabethan Settlement had been largely silenced. Elizabeth
and her own distinct brand of conservative Protestantism had apparently triumphed. In the parishes, however, the reality was somewhat
different. While it is true that only a tiny number of separatists and
a slightly larger group of recusants had entirely refused to conform,
the state church continued to exhibit a very broad spectrum of
divergent religious practice. Relations between the different factions
were often tense, and incidents of verbal abuse and even violence
appear regularly in the records of the ecclesiastical courts. Given this
religious diversity, it is a testament to the strength and sound policies
of the monarchy that, unlike France and the Netherlands, England
experienced no massacres or wars of religion in the later sixteenth
century.

On the accession of James I in 1603, the Puritan or godly element within the English church initially had high hopes that the new monarch, who possessed an impeccable Calvinist background, might be prepared to support the liturgical and ceremonial reforms which they had been pressing on Elizabeth for over forty years. Within weeks of the start of the new reign, James was presented with a petition signed by a large number of godly clergy, and much to the annoyance of his bishops, he responded by calling a conference to consider their demands. This theological debate between the king, the bishops, and the representatives of the Puritans took place at Hampton Court Palace at the beginning of 1604. At one time, historians believed that this conference had ended abruptly in failure after one of the representatives of the Puritans was unwise enough to arouse James's anger by advocating Presbyterianism. In the early 1960s, however, the work of Mark Curtis[6] demonstrated that the conference itself was quite productive, but that its recommendations were subsequently stymied by a number of leading bishops. According to Curtis, James I took a full part in the debates at Hampton Court and adopted a stance independent of his bishops. While he baulked at any suggestions that might have reduced the powers of the bishops, he was also fully aware of the need to conciliate Puritan opinion by reforming crucial areas of the church. Immediately after the ending of the conference, the Puritans appeared reasonably pleased with what they had achieved, and James for his part was not dissatisfied. Over the next few months, however, several of the bishops, in particular Whitgift and Bancroft, set about nullifying the effects of the conference, with the result that few of its reform proposals were ever put into practical effect. In Curtis's view, therefore, the ultimate failure of the Hampton Court Conference should be blamed not on James or the leaders of the Puritan cause, but rather on the English bishops, who were quite incapable of believing that any good could come from a dialogue with their radical opponents. While not disagreeing with the general tenor of Curtis's findings, Patrick Collinson[7] has subsequently stressed James's determination not to allow anyone at Hampton Court to question his overall control over the church, and has argued that the king should bear at least some of the responsibility for the actions of his bishops.

Following the lost opportunity of the Hampton Court Conference and the subsequent appointment of the conservative Richard Bancroft to replace Whitgift as Archbishop of Canterbury, the early years of James's reign witnessed the implementation by the ecclesiastical authorities of a hard line against those clergy and laity who were looking for further reform of the English church. As a result, large numbers of godly ministers surrendered their livings rather than conform to the conservative establishment. On Bancroft's death, however, his successor at Canterbury, George Abbot, adopted a much more lenient approach towards moderate Puritans who sought to purify the church but were prepared to accept episcopacy, and who wished to reform rather than destroy the ecclesiastical establishment. By turning a blind eye to those who failed to conform fully to every canonical regulation, Abbot and his colleague at York, Toby Matthew, once more enabled many Puritans to remain within the state church.

From 1611 to 1625, James's church, like Elizabeth's, was kept broad enough to contain all but the most extreme of radicals, and as a direct result nonconformity remained a relatively insignificant force. English Presbyterianism continued to reel from the attacks launched upon it at the end of the sixteenth century, and while separatism was able to re-establish itself in several parts of the country, it made little headway in terms of conversions. As we saw above, a number of the gathered churches established in England in the second half of the sixteenth century had escaped persecution by emigrating to the more tolerant United Provinces, where they could preach and worship in peace. There, many of their members had absorbed some of the more radical ideas of the continental anabaptists, who were notorious for their rejection of infant baptism. In 1612, a group of these radicalized émigrés returned from Amsterdam to found the first permanent separatist church in England at Spitalfields near London, and shortly afterwards further congregations were founded in Coventry, Lincoln, Tiverton, and Salisbury. While the leaders and theorists of this movement were generally individuals from a landed background who had attended one of the universities, their gathered churches appear to have been peopled largely by small, independent craftsmen and their families. Rejecting all formalism and ceremonialism, these men and women practised a simplified form of worship, within which *ex tempore* prayer and free discussion of scripture predominated. Highly suspicious of a professional ministry, they generally allowed the laity to play an important part in church services and organization.

In the period before 1625, this separatist movement grew only very slowly, acquiring no more than 150 members throughout the whole country. However, with the accession of Charles I and the subsequent rise to power within the church of the Laudians, the religious climate was to turn full circle yet again. Convinced that even moderate Puritans were a dangerous fifth column within the church, Laud and his fellow bishops initiated a period of severe persecution of any who upheld even the most limited of reformist aspirations or godly lifestyles. Their drive towards uniformity and attacks on what had previously been considered mainstream practices and beliefs, seriously divided the church, alienated many of the moderate episcopalian Puritans who up until 1625 had been prepared to remain within the church, and ultimately drove them into an alliance with the small, radical minorities of Presbyterians and separatists. The Puritan, John Davenport, for example, who had conformed during the early 1620s despite his dislike of popish ceremonies, found that once the Arminians had 'stolne in and taken possession of the house' his position became untenable, and in 1633 he withdrew to Amsterdam.

Largely as a reaction to Laudian ecclesastical policies, then, separatism proliferated during the 1630s. By 1640, there appear to have been some ten separatist congregations in London, as well as meetings for worship in a growing number of provincial centres, particularly in Kent and East Anglia. Among the most important of these separatists were the Baptists, who had adopted the practice of adult baptism by total immersion. By the eve of the civil war, the movement had split into two factions over the question of predestination; while the Particular Baptists upheld the Calvinist belief in the rigid division of the world into the saved and the damned, the General Baptists rejected this idea in favour of the concept that 'Christ died for all men'. All Baptists severed their links with the national church through the rite of re-baptism. Some other radicals, however, attempted to combine worship in gathered churches with continued attendance at their parish churches, a form of 'semi-separatism', which had been advocated by the early seventeenth-century reformer, Henry Jacob. By 1640, two such early Independent, or congregationalist, churches were meeting in London, one led by Henry Jessey, the other by Praise-God Barebone.

At the other end of the denominational spectrum, the small but growing number of Catholic recusants in England also remained firm in their opposition to the established religious system. Early seventeenth-century Catholic recusancy retained its appeal at a popular level only in the north of England and Wales – 'the dark corners of the land' which had been least exposed to Protestant evangelizing. Elsewhere, it survived as a manor house religion, maintaining a covert existence in the country seats of recusant gentlemen. A steady stream of missionary priests continued to risk mutilation and death by secretly entering England from the continent to bring succour to their co-religionists. Largely as a result of their work, the number of Catholics in England grew steadily during the first forty years of the seventeenth century, reaching a peak of around 60,000 in 1640. Although this represented a very small proportion of the total population of the country, most English Protestants none the less believed that the recusant community represented a serious threat to the very existence of the English state, and Catholics continued to be regarded with a mixture of extreme disgust and pathological fear and suspicion. Protestant fears of popery were nurtured by the propaganda that followed incidents such as the 1605 Gunpowder Plot – the atypical last occasion on which English Catholicism was involved in political terrorism – and the uprising of the Catholic Irish of Ulster in 1641. The fact that in reality the great majority of English Catholic recusants remained loyal to the crown and politically quiescent did nothing to lessen these Protestant anxieties, and anti-Catholicism was to remain an extremely potent force throughout the seventeenth century.

Between 1640 and 1660, the religious situation in England was totally transformed by the civil war and the subsequent political dominance of the Long Parliament and the New Model Army. These developments had an especially dramatic impact on the position of nonconformists, for many of those who had faced harassment and persecution in the pre-1640 period now found themselves part of the new ecclesiastical status quo. By the end of the civil war in 1646, both episcopacy and the Book of Common Prayer had been abolished, and a new Presbyterian national church had been created. Following the military coup of December 1648 and January 1649, many Independents and Baptists were also incorporated into a loosely structured and flexible Interregnum state church, and during the 1650s it was ironically the Anglicans who were numbered among the dissenters.

Soon after assembling at Westminster in November 1640, the MPs of the Long Parliament made clear their sympathetic attitude towards nonconformity by freeing from prison a number of religious radicals who had fallen foul of the Laudian authorities during the 1630s; two of these, William Prynne and Henry Burton, returned to London shortly afterwards as popular heroes. Over the next few years, the legislation enacted by the Long Parliament MPs transformed the status of English Presbyterianism from the oppressed ideology of a small minority to the orthodox, even conservative theory underpinning the established church. Following a long period of lassitude during the early decades of the century, Presbyterianism had begun to win new converts during the 1630s from among those opposed to Arminianism, and after 1640 it experienced a rapid rise to prominence within the House of Commons. This parliamentary success came about partly through the efforts of preachers such as Edmund Calamy and Stephen Marshall, and partly through the literary propaganda produced by leading Presbyterian writers. Ultimately, however, it was secured by the Long Parliament's dependence on the military assistance of the Scots, the price for which was a promise to impose a strict, Scottish-style Presbyterian church on England once the war had been won. By the middle of the civil war, Presbyterians like Denzil Holles had gained effective control of parliamentary business, and at the beginning of 1645, the MPs authorized a Directory of Public Worship, which outlined the liturgy and governmental structure of a new Presbyterian state church. Following the end of the civil war, this Presbyterian majority at Westminster attempted to enforce Sunday attendance at parish churches and to ban all unlicensed preachers, and in 1648 they passed a Blasphemy Act, imposing prison sentences on any convicted of questioning the legality of the compulsory church establishment, denying predestination, or advocating anabaptism.

Despite the hostility of this new Presbyterian establishment, the war years also saw some considerable expansion in the numbers of Baptist and Independent gathered churches, both in the capital and elsewhere. It is important to remember, however, that although some contemporaries believed they were witnessing a rapid and dangerous explosion of sectarianism which might ultimately destroy the state church, in reality the total membership of all these churches never amounted to more than about 7 per cent of the population. With the breakdown of effective press censorship during the war, some conservative commentators embarked on a full-scale literary debate with the radicals on the merits of separatism. Among the radicals' leading critics were the Presbyterian ministers, Daniel Featley and Thomas Edwards. While Featley castigated the re-baptizers in his tract *The Dippers Dipped*, Edwards began his assault on the sects in 1641 with the publication of *Reasons Against the Independent Government of Particular Congregations*, and intensified his campaign in 1646 by bringing out the three-part work *Gangraena*, in which he catalogued in detail several hundred 'errors of the sectaries'. For these writers, toleration of the gathered congregations constituted a grave threat both to the conservative moral code and the established social order of the English state. They claimed that as a result of the activities of the sects, England was beginning to resemble the religiously plural city of Amsterdam, and might even degenerate into another Munster, the scene of anabaptist excesses in the 1530s. One of the earliest of the radicals to answer such criticisms in print was the prominent sectary, Katherine Chidley, whose *Justification of the Independant Churches of Christ* was published in 1641. However, the fact that women were now involving themselves in theological debate merely confirmed the worst fears of Edwards and his fellow conservatives.

Although it remained dominated by Presbyterians, the Long Parliament contained a number of Independent MPs, including Oliver Cromwell, who were anxious to defend the rights of the separatists. The task of defending religious toleration and the gathered churches was also vigorously taken up by the leaders of the radical Leveller party. Furthermore, by 1647 a new and potentially extremely powerful ally of the radicals had emerged in the shape of the New Model Army. This force, which had been raised by parliament during 1645 and had played a major role in the subsequent defeat of Charles I, included within its ranks large numbers of Independents and Baptists, whose radical fervour was sustained by listening to the fiery sermons of chaplains such as John Saltmarsh, William Erbury, and Hugh Peter. Alarmed and frustrated by the Presbyterian domination of the House of Commons and by the unwillingness of the MPs to listen to their grievances, the soldiers exerted increasing pressure on parliament during 1647 and 1648, and in December 1648 they finally purged the House of all the leading Presbyterians and MPs unsympathetic to their political and religious outlook. Over the next few weeks, the army leaders proceeded to put on trial and execute the head of the English church, Charles I, and to declare England a republic. This New Model Army *putsch* sounded the death knell for the already unpopular Presbyterian church establishment. During the 1650s, Oliver Cromwell and his army colleagues presided over the widest and most liberal English ecclesiastical establishment to be seen in early modern England, within which Presbyterians, Independents, and Particular Baptists all worshipped side by side.

However, despite this considerable stretching of the boundaries of conformity, some groups, both conservative and radical, remained beyond even this very extensive religious pale. With regard to the conservatives, official toleration continued to be denied to both Roman Catholics and episcopalian Anglicans, or 'prelatists' as they were known. Neither of these groups, however, was subjected to a sustained campaign of harassment at the hands of the new rulers of England. English Catholics who had taken up arms for Charles I during the 1640s generally received very short shrift from the

Interregnum regimes, but many others found, sometimes to their great surprise, that for most of the time they were able to exercise their religion unmolested. Similarly, although in theory those who attended services conducted according to the Anglican Book of Common Prayer ran the risk of arrest and imprisonment, many Anglicans, like the diarist John Evelyn, continued to worship according to the old rite, or a close approximation to it, without suffering serious consequences.

In addition to these conservatives, membership of the broad Interregnum church was also rejected by an assortment of new radical sects – Fifth Monarchists, Seekers, Muggletonians, Ranters, and Quakers. Frequently, the disruptive activities of these groups stretched the tolerance and patience of Oliver Cromwell and his fellow politicians to breaking point. Seekers, Fifth Monarchists, and Muggletonians all shared a common millenarian stance and believed the second coming of Christ was imminent. The Muggletonians saw their two leaders, Ludowick Muggleton and John Reeve, as messengers sent from God to bring about conversions as a prelude to the second coming. Seekers were particularly numerous in the north of England. Their movement, which may have developed out of sixteenth-century Familism, was a loose, amorphous alliance of individuals who had rejected all existing forms of ecclesiastical organization and were waiting for God to send his prophets to construct the true church. While Seekers opposed any attempts to hasten the coming of the Lord or his envoys, the Fifth Monarchists in contrast advocated a policy of active and even violent intervention in politics with the aim of removing all obstacles standing in the way of Christ's return. During the early 1650s, Fifth Monarchism gained some real influence within the English army, and in 1653 it was the Fifth Monarchist officer, Thomas Harrison, who helped to persuade Oliver Cromwell to call together the members of Barebone's Parliament. A small caucus of Fifth Monarchists was chosen to sit in this assembly; it subsequently came to dominate proceedings and pressed ahead with a radical programme of economic and social reform. Within six months, conservative opinion had become alarmed and Barebone's Parliament was wound up, but Fifth Monarchism remained an active revolutionary force, and it was only finally broken up in the early 1660s following an unsuccessful armed insurrection in London.

The Ranters, who emerged in the late 1640s, were a radical antinomian group who believed that as they had been predestined to salvation, they had been freed from any obligation to adhere to the traditional Christian moral code. Some of them denied the concept of sin and questioned the independent existence of God by advocating a muddled form of pantheism within which the divine was to be found within man and the natural world. They outraged their more conservative contemporaries by allegedly indulging in excessive eating, drinking, swearing, smoking, and casual sexual intercourse. When threatened with serious punishment by the authorities, most Ranters quickly recanted their opinions, and the movement died away within a few years. Nevertheless, it appears to have caused some considerable short-term alarm, and to have confirmed the worst fears of conservatives about the dangers of toleration. The historian J. C. Davis[8] has recently argued that the importance of the Ranter movement has been greatly exaggerated, originally by a number of hostile contemporary observers, but more recently by a group of sympathetic left-wing historians, including A. L. Morton[9] and Christopher Hill.[10] Davis believes that some conservative contemporaries of the Ranters deliberately played up stories of their outrages in order to provoke a moral panic and shore up attachment to traditional morality. He has also suggested that those struggling to gain control of other sectarian groups may have used accusations of Ranterism as a means of discrediting their opponents. Even more controversially, he has accused a number of modern historians with left-wing affiliations of conspiring to promote these seventeenth-century radicals as early hippies. Davis's conclusion that the Ranters never really existed has been disputed by a number of historians, including Gerald Aylmer,[11] and is clearly an overreaction to the historiographical distortions he has exposed. None the less, his work has demonstrated that the Ranters were a tiny group whose contemporary impact was extremely limited.

Quakerism, or the Society of Friends, which emerged in the north-west of England in the early 1650s, was one of the most remarkable and dynamic movements in English religious history. Its rapid initial dissemination and subsequent survival owed much to the enormous energy, great personal magnetism, and untiring evangelizing of one of its founders, George Fox. Fox began his preaching ministry in the Midlands in the late 1640s, but it was in the early 1650s that he began to win over large numbers of converts among the Baptists and Seekers of the Lake District. In the summer of 1654, Fox and around seventy other Quaker missionaries returned south to bring their message to the rest of the country. Later, other Friends, like the redoubtable Mary Fisher, would journey as far afield as Rome, Malta, Turkey, Jerusalem, and North America to spread the Quaker message. In England, Quaker evangelizing was remarkably successful, and by the end of the 1650s there were in the region of 30,000 Quakers in the country, many of whom were women. Fox and his followers advocated a radical form of Christianity, free of the literalism which had become a feature of the more established sects of his day. He rejected the doctrine of predestination, claimed that all could achieve salvation, and argued that the 'Inner Light', which each Christian carried within him or her and which could never be entirely extinguished, was more important than scripture as a source of religious truth. Liturgically, Fox and his fellow Quakers rejected a professional ministry and all ritualism, and worshipped in services with no set format, during which men and women spoke as and when the spirit moved them. Quakers were reluctant to perform the customary signs of social deference; they refused to remove their hats when in the presence of superiors and addressed them using the colloquial term 'thou' as opposed to the more respectful 'you'. These practices, together with their frequent interruption of services in parish churches and refusal to swear oaths or pay tithes, made the Quakers appear a serious threat to public order, and despite Cromwell's personal tolerance towards them, many ended up in prison. In 1656, the prominent Quaker James Nayler seriously undermined the wide measure of religious toleration that Cromwell presided over by re-enacting at Bristol Christ's entry into Jerusalem, an escapade which resulted both in severe punishment for Nayler himself and in a virulent conservative backlash against the activities of the extreme radicals.

Two of the leading present-day authorities on early Quakerism, Christopher Hill[12] and Barry Reay,[13] have argued that the Quaker movement of the 1650s was significantly different from that which emerged after the Restoration. They claim that the Quakers only withdrew from political activity and adopted their now famous stance of uncompromising pacifism and quietism as a direct result of the return of the Stuarts, and that in contrast during the 1650s Quakerism was an active and subversive revolutionary political force bent on overthrowing what it saw as a socially unjust as well as ungodly state. While Hill and Reay are right to stress the volatility of sectarian politics and the turbulence of the religious scene during the Interregnum, they probably overstate the discontinuity. Furthermore, writing from a position of late twentieth-century unbelief, they seem reluctant to acknowledge the predominantly New Testament origins of the social radicalism of Quakerism, a movement which both before and after 1660 embodied what was essentially a liberation theology.

Following the restoration of the monarchy in 1660, the freedom which many religious denominations had enjoyed during the 1650s came to an abrupt and violent end. The re-establishment of a narrow and intolerant state church and the reimposition of severe penalties on those who refused to conform, finally put an end to godly aspirations that the English church might be reformed from within. The 1662 Act of Uniformity and the other legislative measures of the Clarendon Code – the Corporation Act, the Five Mile Act, and the Conventicles Acts – expelled from the established church even the more conservative Presbyterians, subjected the whole of the nonconformist community to almost thirty years of sustained persecution, and cemented the division in English religious life between church and chapel which has remained down to the present day. Forbidden by the Conventicles Acts from holding gatherings of more than five people, some congregations divided and worshipped in groups of four. Others met at secret locations or in the middle of the night, their ministers officiating from behind curtains or on horseback in order to hide their identities and facilitate escape. The Quakers on the other hand eschewed all such compromises and continued to meet openly and to suffer passively the inevitable assaults, arrests, and imprisonments which resulted.

The intensity of the persecution of nonconformists under the Clarendon Code varied from year to year, and in some places its severity was mitigated by a local reluctance to implement it with its full rigour. None the less, during the course of Charles II's reign thousands of dissenters were arrested and imprisoned and many of them languished for months or years in overcrowded and disease-ridden gaols, such as Newgate in London. It has been estimated that over 15,000 Quakers suffered fines, exile, imprisonment, or deportation during these years. Very few dissenters, however, appear to have succumbed to this pressure and rejoined the Anglican church; indeed the years of persecution may have seen a small increase in the numbers refusing to conform. That this persecution served merely to strengthen the resolve of the dissenters and convince them of the surety of ultimate victory is illustrated by the appearance during these years of some of the greatest works of nonconformist spiritual literature. Books such as William Penn's *No Cross, No Crown* and John Bunyan's *The Pilgrim's Progress* and *Grace Abounding to the Chief of Sinners* all stressed that the road to salvation was a narrow and difficult one, marked by a great number of attractive and beguiling temptations.

It is very difficult to estimate with any degree of accuracy the extent of dissent during Charles II's reign. A religious census commissioned in 1676 by the king's chief minister, Thomas Danby, revealed that out of an adult population of some two-and-a-half million, the country contained about 108,000 nonconformist Protestants and about 13,000 Catholic recusants. According to this source, therefore, Protestant nonconformists made up no more than about 3 per cent of the adult population, and Catholics less than 1 per cent. However, as Danby's main purpose in collecting the figures was to dissuade the king from policies aimed at placating the dissenters, the census probably seriously underestimates the numbers of those absenting themselves from their parish churches. Nor was it able to identify those who conformed occasionally by turning up at those churches from time to time. It has been suggested that somewhere between 15 and 20 per cent of the population of London may have been dissenters during Charles II's reign, although the figure for the country as a whole would have been appreciably lower than this.

As a result of Charles's personal sympathy towards the Roman religion, Catholicism made great strides at court during the period following the Restoration. A sizeable minority of the English aristocracy also retained an attachment to popery, and unlike in the pre-1640 period many of these Catholic peers remained in close contact with the Catholic gentry within their local spheres of influence. For their part, these recusant gentry more and more looked to them and to the king to break down the implacable opposition of the Protestant county establishments. None the less, despite this relatively favourable climate in high places, the numbers of these Catholic gentry families were in decline, for heavy recusancy fines, estate mismanagement, and the failure of male lines had all taken their toll. Those families that stayed loyal to the papacy continued to be hated and feared by the vast majority of the Protestant political nation and their representatives in parliament. The ease with which anti-Catholic feeling could be exploited was shown in 1678 during the Popish Plot. Following dubious revelations of a Catholic plot to assassinate the king, anti-Catholic hysteria spread rapidly and resulted in physical attacks on Catholics and several executions based on the flimsiest of evidence. Anti-Catholicism also figured prominently in the propaganda of the First Whigs, who between 1679 and 1681 strongly lobbied Charles II to exclude from the succession his Catholic brother, James, Duke of York. As a means of survival in this hostile climate, many recusant families retreated into the rigours of an austere and introspective household piety, thereby distancing themselves further from their suspicious Protestant neighbours.

When James II succeeded to the throne in 1685 as the first Catholic king of England for a century and a half, both Roman Catholics and Protestant dissenters experienced a rapid improvement in their circumstances. In May 1686, James extended a general pardon to dissenters, as a result of which 1,200 Quakers were subsequently released from gaol. The following year he issued a Declaration of Indulgence, suspending all the penal laws against those refusing to conform to Anglicanism. The position of the Protestant dissenters was further improved when the Anglican hierarchy, alarmed at the seriousness of the threat from James's Catholic policies, began to court them as allies in the struggle against popery.

In 1688, James's energetic promotion of Roman Catholicism led to his deposition. He was replaced by another non-Anglican monarch, the Calvinist William III, and the following year saw the passing of the Toleration Act, which for the first time in English history gave trinitarian Protestant dissenters the right to worship openly in their own meeting-houses. Though important, this measure was a very limited one. It had originally been conceived of as a limited concession for the very small group of nonconformists who refused to worship within the wider, more comprehensive church which William wished to preside over. When this comprehensive church foundered on the opposition of the Anglican bishops, the 1689 Toleration Act was left applying to a much larger group than those who had drawn it up had envisaged. Nonconformist worship remained subject to a number of petty and annoying restrictions, and a whole range of civil disabilities prevented dissenters from attending the universities or holding military or civil office. During the period 1689 to 1714, the dissenting community was to suffer continued harassment at the hands of Tories and High Anglicans, who considered them a serious threat to the survival of the established church. With the accession of the Hanoverian dynasty in 1714, however, the gains of 1689 were confirmed and the survival of Protestant dissent was finally assured. During the eighteenth and nineteenth centuries, the dissenting community was to prove one of the most dynamic elements, not only in the spheres of religion and spirituality, but also in the political and industrial development of modern Britain.

NOTES

1 J. J. Scarisbrick, *The Reformation and the English People* (Oxford, 1984).
2 A. G. Dickens, 'The early expansion of Protestantism in England 1520–1558', *Archiv für Reformationsgeschichte* 78 (1987); Christopher Haigh (ed.), *The Reformation Revised* (London, 1987)

3 Peter Lake, *Anglicans and Puritans? Presbyterian and English conformist thought from Whitgift to Hooker* (London, 1988).
4 John Bossy, *The English Catholic Community 1570–1850* (London, 1975).
5 Christopher Haigh, 'The continuity of Catholicism in the English Reformation', *Past and Present* 93 (1981).
6 M. H. Curtis, 'The Hampton Court Conference and its aftermath', *History* 46 (1961).
7 Patrick Collinson, 'The Jacobean religious settlement: the Hampton Court Conference', in Howard Tomlinson (ed.), *Before the English Civil War* (London, 1983).
8 J. C. Davis, *Fear, Myth and History: The Ranters and the historians* (Cambridge, 1986).
9 A. L. Morton, *The World of the Ranters: Radical religion in the English Revolution* (London, 1970).
10 Christopher Hill, *The World Turned Upside Down: Radical ideas in the English Revolution* (London, 1972).
11 Gerald Aylmer, 'Did the Ranters exist?', *Past and Present* 117 (1987).
12 Hill, *The World Turned Upside Down.*
13 Barry Reay, *The Quakers and the English Revolution* (Oxford, 1985).

SUGGESTIONS FOR FURTHER READING

The standard work on the later Lollards is J. A. F. Thomson, *The Later Lollards, 1414–1520* (Oxford, 1965), but some new research can be found in A. Hope, 'Lollardy: The stone the builders rejected?', in P. Lake and M. Dowling (eds), *Protestantism and the National Church in Sixteenth-century England* (London, 1987); and D. Plumb, 'The social and economic spread of rural Lollardy: a reappraisal', in W. J. Sheils and D. Wood (eds), *Voluntary Religion*, Studies in Church History 23 (Oxford, 1986). The importance of Lollardy to the Reformation has been discussed in a number of works. The classic statement was made by A. G. Dickens in 'Heresy and the origins of English Protestantism', which is reprinted in A. G. Dickens, *Reformation Studies* (London, 1982). Also important are M. Aston, 'Lollardy and the Reformation: survival or revival?', *History* 49 (1964); and J. F. Davis, *Heresy and Reformation in the South-east of England, 1520–1559* (London, 1983).

The early impact of Lutheranism is examined in W. Clebsch, *England's Earliest Protestants* (New Haven, CT, 1964); H. Porter, *Reformation and Reaction in Tudor Cambridge* (Cambridge, 1958); R. M. Fisher, 'Reform, repression and unrest at the Inns of Court, 1518–1558', *Historical Journal* 20 (1977); and Susan Brigden, 'Youth and the English Reformation', *Past and Present* 95 (1982). The response of English humanists and others to Luther is the subject of R. Rex, 'The English campaign against Luther in the 1520s', *Transactions of the Royal Historical Society*, 5th series, vol. 39 (1989); and is also discussed in M. Dowling, *Humanism in the Age of Henry VIII* (London, 1986).

The current debate about the progress of the English Reformation is summarized in R. O'Day, *The Debate on the English Reformation* (London, 1986). The arguments are presented by their respective protagonists in J.

J. Scarisbrick, *The Reformation and the English People* (Oxford, 1984); C. Haigh (ed.), *The Reformation Revised* (London, 1987); and A. G. Dickens, 'The early expansion of Protestantism in England 1520–1558', *Archiv für Reformationsgeschichte* 78 (1987). Local studies which provide evidence about the advance of Protestantism include Susan Brigden, *London and the Reformation* (Oxford, 1990); M. Bowker, *The Henrician Reformation in the Diocese of Lincoln under John Longland 1521–1547* (Cambridge, 1981); P. Clark, *English Provincial Society from the Reformation to the Revolution: Religion, politics and society in Kent 1500–1640* (Sussex, 1977); C. Haigh, *Reformation and Resistance in Tudor Lancashire* (Cambridge, 1975); D. MacCulloch, *Suffolk and the Tudors* (Oxford, 1986); J. Oxley, *The Reformation in Essex to the Death of Queen Mary* (Manchester, 1968); D. M. Palliser, *The Reformation in York, 1534–1553*, Borthwick Paper no. 40 (York, 1971); M. C. Cross, 'The development of Protestantism in Leeds and Hull 1520–1640: the evidence from wills', *Northern History* 18 (1982); R. A. Houlbrooke, 'The persecution of heresy and Protestantism in the diocese of Norwich under Henry VIII', *Norfolk Archaeology* 35 (1973); G. J. Mayhew, 'The progress of the Reformation in east Sussex 1530–1559: the evidence from wills', *Southern History* 5 (1983); K. G. Powell, 'The beginnings of Protestantism in Gloucestershire', *Transactions of the Bristol and Gloucester Archaeological Society* 90 (1971); and J. Ward, 'The Reformation in Colchester', *Essex Archaeology and History* 15 (1983). The problems in interpreting wills are discussed in M. Spufford, *Contrasting Communities* (Cambridge, 1974); and M. L. Zell, 'The use of religious preambles as a measure of religious beliefs in the sixteenth century', *Bulletin of the Institute of Historical Research* 50 (1977).

The Marian Protestants can be approached through D. Loades, *The Oxford Martyrs* (London, 1970); N. M. Sutherland, 'The Marian exiles and the establishment of the Elizabethan regime', *Archiv für Reformationsgeschichte* 78 (1987); and J. Martin, 'The Protestant underground in Mary's reign', *Journal of Ecclesiastical History* 35 (1984).

The best surveys of English Catholicism under Elizabeth and the Stuarts are J. C. H. Aveling, *The Handle and the Axe: The Catholic recusants in England from Reformation to emancipation* (London, 1976); and A. Dures, *English Catholicism 1558–1642* (London, 1983). The controversy between Bossy and Haigh can be followed in John Bossy, *The English Catholic Community 1570–1850* (London, 1975); and many articles by Christopher Haigh, including 'The continuity of Catholicism in the English Reformation', *Past and Present* 93 (1981). Patrick McGrath makes some additional points in 'Elizabethan Catholicism: a reconsideration', *Journal of Ecclesiastical History* 35 (1984).

An excellent short introduction to Puritanism is Patrick Collinson, *English Puritanism*, Historical Association Pamphlet (London, 1983). More detailed studies of Elizabethan and early Stuart Puritanism include Patrick Collinson, *The Elizabethan Puritan Movement* (London, 1967); Peter Lake, *Moderate Puritans and the Elizabethan Church* (Cambridge, 1982); William Lamont, *Godly Rule: Politics and religion 1603–1660* (London, 1969); W. J. Sheils, *The Puritans in the Diocese of Peterborough 1558–1610* (Northampton, 1979); R. Marchant, *The Puritans and the Church Courts in the Diocese of York 1560–1642* (London, 1960); and R. Richardson, *Puritanism in*

North-west England (Manchester, 1972). For James I's relations with the Puritans, see M. H. Curtis, 'The Hampton Court Conference and its aftermath', *History* 46 (1961); and Patrick Collinson, 'The Jacobean religious settlement: The Hampton Court Conference', in Howard Tomlinson (ed.), *Before the English Civil War* (London, 1983).

A comparison of the outlook and beliefs of Presbyterians and conformist Protestants is made in the interesting but difficult book by Peter Lake, *Anglicans and Puritans? Presbyterian and English Conformist Thought from Whitgift to Hooker* (London, 1988). Also useful on the Presbyterians in the seventeenth century is C. G. Bolam, *The English Presbyterians: From Elizabethan Puritanism to modern Unitarianism* (London, 1968). Separatism is usefully surveyed in R. J. Acheson, *Radical Puritans in England 1550–1660* (London, 1990); B. R. White, *The English Separatist Tradition* (Oxford, 1971); and Paul Christianson, *Reformers and Babylon: English apocalyptic visions from the Reformation to the eve of the civil war* (Toronto, 1978).

On the civil war and Interregnum sects, see J. F. Macgregor and B. Reay, *Radical Religion in the English Revolution* (Oxford, 1984); Christopher Hill, *The World Turned Upside Down: Radical ideas in the English Revolution* (London, 1972); and Murray Tolmie, *The Triumph of the Saints* (Cambridge, 1977). Particular sects are discussed in G. F. Nuttall, *Visible Saints: The congregational way 1640–1660* (Oxford, 1957); W. C. Braithwaite, *The Beginnings of Quakerism* (Cambridge, 1955); Barry Reay, *The Quakers and the English Revolution* (Oxford, 1985); B. Capp, *The Fifth Monarchy Men* (London, 1972); A. L. Morton, *The World of the Ranters: Radical religion in the English Revolution* (London, 1970); J. F. Macgregor, 'Ranterism and the development of early Quakerism', *Journal of Religious History* 9 (1976–7); B. R. White, 'The organization of the Particular Baptists, 1644–1660', *Journal of Ecclesiastical History* 17 (1966); G. Yule, *The Independents in the English Civil War* (Cambridge, 1958); H. J. Maclachan, *Socinianism in Seventeenth-century England* (Oxford, 1951); and Christopher Hill, William Lamont, and Barry Reay, *The World of the Muggletonians* (London, 1983). For the recent controversy over the Ranters, see J. C. Davis, *Fear, Myth and History: The Ranters and the historians* (Cambridge, 1986); and Gerald Aylmer, 'Did the Ranters exist?', *Past and Present* 117 (1987). An interesting study of the local impact of the religious radicals is M. C. Cross, 'Achieving the millennium: The church in York during the Commonwealth', *Studies in Church History* 4 (Leiden, 1967).

On the post-Restoration dissenters, see Michael Watts, *The Dissenters*. Vol. I: *From the Reformation to the French Revolution* (Oxford, 1978); R. B. Knox (ed.), *Reformation, Continuity and Dissent* (London, 1977); Christopher Hill, *A Turbulent, Seditious and Factious People: John Bunyan and his church* (Oxford, 1988); F. Bate, *The Declaration of Indulgence of 1672* (Farnborough, 1968); C. E. Whiting, *Studies in English Puritanism 1660–1688* (London, 1931); and D. R. Lacey, *Dissent and Parliamentary Politics in England 1661–1689* (New Jersey, 1969).

7 The bishops

Historians have long been aware that the English bishops of the pre-Reformation era were primarily lawyers, royal servants, and neo-feudal lords, rather than spiritual and pastoral leaders. What has only become clear more recently, however, is that despite the many inherent contradictions between their worldly and spiritual roles, many of them managed to perform all their various functions with striking efficiency and relatively little corruption. Thomas Wolsey, who held several sees in plurality and brazenly promoted his son to a dozen or so ecclesiastical offices, was the exception rather than the rule; far from embodying the abuses of the pre-Reformation church, he was unique in his flouting of canon law. Most of the fifteenth- and early sixteenth-century bishops, including Wolsey, were well educated and suitably trained. Over 90 per cent were graduates, usually of law, and thus well equipped to deal with both the judicial business of their dioceses and the demands of royal and governmental service. Many indeed proved very able diocesan administrators, personally supervising their church courts, imposing discipline on their clergy, and prosecuting heretics. When absent from their sees, usually on royal business, they appointed conscientious deputies, with the result that few sees showed signs of neglect, even when, as in the case of Bishop Richard Fox of Winchester who was Lord Privy Seal for thirty years, their absences were frequent and prolonged.

Furthermore, not satisfied with merely carrying out routine diocesan business efficiently, a number of bishops were also responsible for initiating significant reform. Some, like Bishop Robert Sherburne of Chichester, overhauled the judicial machinery of their dioceses; others, such as William Waynflete of Winchester and John Fisher of Rochester, dissolved decaying monasteries and nunneries, using their resources to fund new schools and colleges. Nor were these last two isolated examples, for many bishops proved substantial patrons of learning; during the late fifteenth and early sixteenth centuries, at least twelve founded educational establishments, and twenty provided endowments and scholarships at the two universities. While many of these new foundations were traditional in outlook and curriculum, some reflected the impact of the New Learning, indicating that a number of the bishops had come under the influence of the continental educational reform movement known as humanism. John Fisher, for example, was sympathetic towards the ideas of the humanist scholar, Erasmus, and as chancellor of the university of Cambridge he encouraged the study of the three biblical languages (Hebrew, Greek, and Latin). Even Thomas Wolsey can be regarded as a reforming bishop. Not only did he use his legatine power to curb abuses of sanctuary and benefit of clergy, but he also dissolved some thirty decaying monastic houses, employing their assets to endow new colleges at Ipswich and Oxford. Furthermore, in drawing up the statutes for Cardinal College at Oxford, he prescribed the study of classical texts as well as the traditional scholastic method for defending the true faith.

Henry VIII's attack on the church and papacy came, therefore, as a cruel blow to a group of bishops who were conservative in religion and had been loyal servants and supporters of the newly established Tudor dynasty. None the less, episcopal opposition to Henry's policies was for the most part both half-hearted and ineffectual. At critical points, the upper house of convocation failed to ward off the royal attack on the church; moreover, despite their substantial presence in the House of Lords, the bishops were also unable to block the legislation which brought about the break with Rome and established the royal supremacy. There were no deprivations for disobedience, and only one bishop, John Fisher, actively resisted the king, suffering imprisonment and subsequent execution after calling upon the Emperor Charles V to invade England and depose Henry. To some extent this absence of episcopal resistance can be explained by what was for Henry a series of timely episcopal vacancies in the early 1530s. During the crucial five years between 1532 and 1536, the deaths of the Archbishop of Canterbury, William Warham, and six other bishops allowed Henry to promote to the episcopal bench a group of clerics who favoured the annulment and supremacy, including Thomas Cranmer, who became the new archbishop, and the royal chaplain, Thomas Goodrich, who was elevated to Ely.

Many of the other bishops, however, continued to harbour grave private doubts about the king's ecclesiastical policies. While some of these were probably too frightened to make a stand, and others were awed by habits of obedience, most simply failed to realize the significance of what was happening and were lulled into acquiescence by the apparent conservatism of the Henrician Reformation. In practice, Henry appeared to be doing or saying nothing that was very new. From the beginning of his reign he had strongly promoted his claims to power over the church, and in asserting the royal supremacy, he justified it with plausible arguments based on precedent, which would have made a great deal of sense to bishops with a training in civil law. As a consequence, a man like Bishop Stephen Gardiner of Winchester was able to reassure himself that the king had the right to legislate on matters of faith simply by referring to the *Codex Justinianus*, a basic undergraduate text which he had encountered while studying at Cambridge. Furthermore, in the period following the Act of Supremacy, Henry intervened little in ecclesiastical business and left episcopal jurisdiction intact. This also did much to placate the more conservatively minded bishops and to guarantee their continued co-operation. Bishop John Longland of Lincoln, for example, initially found the supremacy difficult to accept, and declared in a sermon that he could only acknowledge the king as supreme head as long as he refrained from intruding onto the jurisdiction of the church. Subsequently, Longland's authority was indeed threatened for some months by Henry's vicegerent in spirituals, Thomas Cromwell, but when in 1538 his jurisdiction was fully restored, he felt able to remain loyal to the crown.

Nor did Henry launch any wholesale attack on the wealth of the bishops. Although royal income was boosted from time to time by informal and piecemeal expropriation of episcopal lands, there was no general or co-ordinated assault on episcopal property to mirror the attack on the monasteries, and on occasions the king was responsible for restraining the more rapacious instincts of his influential lay subjects. Part of the reason for Henry's self-control was his recognition that the bishops needed a substantial income if they were to fulfil their traditional role as administrators and dispensers of charity. Indeed, in an attempt to improve the effectiveness of episcopal administration, the king created six new dioceses between 1539 and 1542, endowing them, albeit insufficiently, with the revenues from confiscated monastic land. This again did much to reassure the episcopal doubters, and encouraged them to view the king not as the wolf at the door, but rather as the protector of the church against the threats from anti-clerical common lawyers and other vested interest groups that wished to destroy its immunities, privileges, and wealth.

Finally, the bishops were generally more concerned about the threat of doctrinal and liturgical change than about the annulment and break with Rome. A small number, including Cranmer, Hugh Latimer of Worcester, and for a time Nicholas Shaxton of Salisbury, were attracted to the beliefs of the Protestants, but most remained staunchly Catholic. Some, like Cuthbert Tunstall of Durham and Gardiner of Winchester, worked to overthrow the reformist factions at court, led by Cromwell in the 1530s and Cranmer in the 1540s. Others, such as Longland of Lincoln and John Stokesley of London, tried to prevent the spread of heretical ideas in their dioceses. Although never certain of the future direction of Henrician policy, these bishops continued to regard the king as a bastion against heresy, and were thus able to remain his loyal and active servants as long as the Catholic doctrine and liturgy of the church was left intact.

The reign of Edward VI, however, was to test the loyalty of the conservative bishops much more severely, for Protestant beliefs became the official doctrine of the state church, and episcopal authority was seriously challenged by the governments of both Lord Protector Somerset and the Duke of Northumberland. New commissions issued to the bishops in 1547 referred to them as 'delegates', and declared that they held their authority only during the prince's good pleasure. In addition, the abolition of the procedure of *congé d'élire*, whereby new episcopal incumbents were officially appointed by cathedral chapters, ended the semblance of independent elections; at a stroke the bishops were transformed from ordinaries with their own independent jurisdictional powers into little more than crown civil servants. At the same time, their political influence was also substantially reduced; no longer did they serve as presidents of the regional councils or as temporary ambassadors abroad, and Cranmer was their sole remaining representative on the privy council. These changes reflected the Edwardian government's Erastian principles and the Protestant image of the bishop as a pastor rather than a politician. The status of the bishops was further eroded by the expropriation of substantial amounts of episcopal land during the general plunder of ecclesiastical assets in the early 1550s.

The group of committed Protestant bishops on the Edwardian bench numbered no more than ten; it included Archbishop Cranmer and a number of new appointments, such as Miles Coverdale, John Hooper, Nicholas Ridley, John Scory, and John Ponet. Most of the remaining bishops were Henrician Catholics – supporters of the royal supremacy but believers in purgatory and transubstantiation.

Only five, however – Edmund Bonner of London, George Day of Chichester, Gardiner of Winchester, Nicholas Heath of Worcester, and Tunstall of Durham – were prepared to disobey the government and suffer deprivation for their conservatism or refusal to conform to the new Protestant order. The majority found the habit of obedience difficult to break, and continued to conform outwardly to a religious establishment to which they were privately opposed; Bishop Thomas Thirlby, for example, retained his position and upheld the Edwardian regulations, while at the same time consistently voting against any religious innovations and labouring quietly to prevent the dissemination of Protestantism in his diocese of Norwich.

With the accession of Mary in 1553, the radical bishops were soon deprived of their sees and replaced by the original occupants who had been ousted and imprisoned under Edward. These restored bishops had originally accepted the royal supremacy, but their subsequent opposition to the religious changes of Edward's reign had led them to change their minds and to seek a return to papal rule as the only sure protection for doctrinal orthodoxy. Bishop Stephen Gardiner, for example, who had earlier argued in favour of the supremacy in his *De Vera Obedientia*, had by 1553 abandoned this intellectual stance and was ready to see England restored to the papal fold. During the course of Mary's short reign, no fewer than twelve bishops died in office. They were replaced by clerics who had conspicuously demonstrated their loyalty to Roman Catholicism during the previous two reigns: men like Richard Pate who had sacrificed a diplomatic career to join Cardinal Pole in Rome in 1541, and who was now rewarded with the see of Worcester. As a consequence, by the later stages of Mary's reign the episcopal bench was united in its religious outlook, a circumstance which was unique during the period from 1536 to 1570, and one which was of great advantage to the government. The strength of the episcopal commitment to the Marian order can be clearly seen on the accession of Elizabeth, when the bishops not only put up a strong fight against the 1559 Bills of Supremacy and Uniformity, but also (with the lone and relatively insignificant exception of Bishop Anthony Kitchen of Llandaff) refused to conform to the new Protestant Settlement.

The Marian bishops were less united, however, in their attitude to the government's policy of heresy trials and burnings. The persecutions, which were initiated by Cardinal Pole, were enthusiastically supported by Bishop Cuthbert Scott, whose vigorous attempts to eradicate heresy in Cambridge culminated in the exhumation and burning of the remains of the prominent continental reformer,

Martin Bucer, who had taught at the university during the previous reign. Few others, however, shared this fanaticism; Tunstall of Durham and Nicholas Heath of York were certainly averse to persecution, while even Bonner, who was responsible for the Smithfield burnings in London, was less enthusiastic than his royal mistress. Four Edwardians bishops – Cranmer, Hooper, Ridley, and Robert Ferrar of St David's – themselves perished at the stake, as did the Henrician bishop, Hugh Latimer, who had resigned from the see of Worcester at the time of the Act of Six Articles in 1539, but who had been a regular preacher at court during Edward's reign. These men soon came to be regarded as Protestant martyrs, and their deaths did much to add dignity to a cause whose image had suffered as a result of the squalid looting of ecclesiastical wealth in the early 1550s.

The Marian counter-Reformation also involved the restoration of episcopal independence and political influence. Five of the Marian bishops were royal councillors, while Thirlby and Thomas Goldwell of St Asaph were employed as ambassadors. The financial position of the bishops was improved by parliament's decision that they should receive the first fruits and tenths which had been coming to the crown since the 1530s. They were not, however, restored to all their pre-Reformation wealth and property; Henry VIII had already sold a great deal of ecclesiastical land to the laity in order to finance the wars of the 1540s, and Mary made no attempt to make a general restitution of the estates alienated during the reigns of her father and brother.

This brief return to something approaching their pre-Reformation status ended for the bishops with Mary's death, for her successor Elizabeth was determined to follow her father's policy of subordinating her prelates to firm royal control and treating ecclesiastical property as her own personal resource. Her first parliament not only returned annates and tenths to the crown, but also paved the way for the more systematic plunder of episcopal lands by passing an Act of Exchange, which stipulated that while a see was vacant the crown could exchange spiritual revenues appropriated since the Reformation for episcopal lands of an equivalent value. Exploiting this legislation, Elizabeth forced the bishops to grant her long leases of episcopal land, many of which she passed on to courtiers and councillors; despite vehement episcopal protests, some fifty-seven long leases were extracted from the bishops in the period 1574 to 1603. Elizabeth also kept episcopal sees vacant for unjustifiably long periods, either pocketing their revenues herself or allowing them to fall into the hands of royal favourites. The Earl of Sussex, for example, enjoyed an income from the vacant see of York when acting as lord president of the Council of the North, while the Earl of Oxford was given a pension out of the revenues of Ely – a diocese which was left without a bishop for nineteen years. At the same time, however, the queen shared her father's attachment to the traditional governmental structure of the church and to the customary role of the episcopate. Hence, she continued to observe *congé d'élire* and dispensed with the Edwardian commission to the bishops. For the same reason, she would later have no truck with the Presbyterian ideas which surfaced in the 1570s, and she resisted any proposals for a wholesale reform of diocesan administration which aimed at transforming the bishops into pastors with a purely spiritual function.

As a direct consequence of Elizabeth's conservative instincts, the Reformation affected the long-term position of the English episcopate far less than that of the higher clergy elsewhere in Protestant Europe. It did, none the less, have a number of important repercussions, both for its economic position and for its administrative function. During the first half of the sixteenth century, the English and Welsh bishops lost a total of 150 manors through lay expropriations, with the result that their earlier concentrations of landed power, particularly in the south-east, largely disappeared, causing a significant weakening of their traditional authority in the localities. There was also an overall drop in the rental income from episcopal lands, from an estimated £26,000 per annum in 1535 to £17,200 in 1603. The adverse effect of such a reduction was offset by a corresponding rise in the value of spiritualities, the result of the crown policy of granting rectories, tithes, and tenths to bishops in exchange for land. During the same period, annual revenue from this source grew from £3,450 to £9,800, an increase which in most English dioceses largely compensated for the loss of estate revenue. During the last decades of Elizabeth's reign, a few dioceses, such as London, Hereford, and Bath and Wells, also raised their rental income by introducing more efficient estate management. Nevertheless, in perhaps as many as a quarter of the English dioceses, bishops were experiencing severe financial difficulties during the later sixteenth century, and finding it increasingly difficult to maintain themselves in the style expected by their contemporaries. Some were sufficiently desperate to resort to highly irregular expedients, such as the misappropriation of royal taxes, in order to survive financially.

At the same time as the incomes of the post-Reformation bishops were becoming more precarious, most of them had to shoulder the additional financial burden of supporting wives and children. As most prelates had no private incomes or salaries with which to provide for their families, they were frequently obliged to 'nourish and maintain their children, not according to their calling, which is properly their own, but according to their estate of maintenance which should be for the church and the poor'. Scandalous stories of episcopal nepotism abounded, and while some were unfounded, abuses certainly did occur. Bishops gave leases to members of their immediate families on favourable terms, used their patronage to advance their sons, and paid substantial dowries on their daughters' marriages. The scale of such corruption should not be exaggerated; only one bishop's son in Elizabeth's reign became a bishop in his own right. None the less, in this respect at least, the Reformation extended the scope for ecclesiastical abuse and encouraged a round of new complaints about the higher clergy and their often large families.

Certainly, none of the Elizabethan bishops, married or single, could afford the grand lifestyle of their medieval predecessors. Lay plunder had robbed them of their episcopal palaces, sixty-seven of which were granted or leased away during Elizabeth's reign, often following acrimonious disputes with the laymen who coveted them. Furthermore, the rise in food prices which resulted from the inflation of the sixteenth century had increased the costs involved in maintaining an open house; as a consequence, the households of the Elizabethan bishops were smaller than those of their late medieval counterparts, their hospitality more restrained, and their funerals generally less lavish. They tended, therefore, to live and die in the style of a modest nobleman or gentleman, rather than that of a great lord or prince.

The function of the late sixteenth-century episcopate was also changed as a result of the Reformation. Although the bishops continued to act as royal servants, they no longer held the highest state offices or represented the queen on missions abroad, and only Archbishop John Whitgift sat on the privy council. They now fulfilled less important administrative tasks, serving as justices of the peace and members of regional councils, and keeping the government informed about events in the provinces. At the same time, a greater emphasis was placed upon their pastoral role as preachers and propagators of the gospel, and they were required to be theologians and biblical scholars rather than administrators and lawyers. Many of Elizabeth's bishops were specifically chosen for their pastoral credentials and took this side of their work very seriously. Nearly all were resident in their dioceses, preaching and carrying out regular visitations. Most also took a keen interest in ensuring the appointment of learned ministers to their parishes, personally examining ordinands in an attempt to raise clerical standards. Some also founded or endowed schools and colleges.

As a result, however, of this shift of focus towards their spiritual duties, a number of bishops began to encounter increased problems in coping with their legal and bureaucratic responsibilities; Bishop Thomas Bentham, in particular, experienced considerable difficulties in administering his diocese of Coventry and Lichfield. By the later decades of the sixteenth century, few bishops were able to supervise their ecclesiastical courts personally, and some neglected to appoint satisfactory subordinates to stand in for them. In short, the much needed wholesale reform of diocesan administration was quite beyond the limited administrative capacities of Elizabeth's bishops, who could aspire no further than the implementation of the 1559 settlement, and the maintenance of financial solvency.

The first generation of Elizabethan bishops was drawn in the main from the ranks of those committed Protestants who had chosen to go into exile during Mary's reign. Men like Edmund Grindal of London, Edwin Sandys of Worcester, Richard Cox of Ely, John Parkhurst of Norwich, and Robert Horne of Winchester returned from the radical Protestant centres of Germany and Switzerland determined to create a truly Reformed church in England. Elizabeth, for her part, had more conservative objectives. She appointed these zealous Protestants to the episcopal bench because she needed their help in imposing the 1559 settlement on her more reluctant and hostile subjects. As her first Archbishop of Canterbury, however, she chose Matthew Parker, a scholar whose moderate opinions coincided much more closely with her own views. Parker had been her mother's former chaplain and had remained in England during Mary's reign without conforming to her short counter-Reformation. Devoted to the new queen, he was much more to Elizabeth's personal taste than the uncompromising Marian exiles. Hardly surprisingly, tensions soon arose between the 'godly' bishops and their more conservative monarch. The first crisis of conscience for the Marian exiles occurred in 1564, when the queen insisted upon conformity to the prescribed clerical dress and the ceremonials of the Prayer Book. While the bishops disapproved of 'popish' ceremonials and attire and hoped that they would in time be dispensed with, they did not consider them important enough to warrant mass resignations from benefices or disobedience to the law. Their attitude was summed up by Grindal, who commented that to 'desert our churches for a few ceremonies' would threaten the unity of the church and the progress of the gospel. Ignoring therefore their private opinions, the bishops co-operated with their supreme governor in enforcing conformity during the mid- and late 1560s, thereby alienating many of their former friends among the hardline Protestants.

Following his appointment as Archbishop of Canterbury in 1575, Edmund Grindal was to find it far more difficult to appease his conscience while at the same time obeying his queen. Despite his earlier readiness to deprive dissident clergy when Bishop of London, he was not lacking in Protestant zeal, and in particular was dedicated to the ideal of achieving an educated preaching ministry. Consequently, when in 1576 he was ordered by Elizabeth to suppress prophesyings, which he considered to be an essential instrument in the training of preachers and spreading of the gospel, he refused to obey. For his temerity and implicit challenge to the royal supremacy, he was sequestered from his see and, but for the support of his fellow bishops and a number of privy councillors, he would have been deprived. He died in office in 1583, having been archbishop in name only during the previous six years. Although Grindal was the only bishop to make a public stand against the attack upon prophesyings, a number of his colleagues undoubtedly supported his position; of those bishops whose opinions are known, eight were favourable to the practice and only four hostile.

In the aftermath of Grindal's fall, Elizabeth's episcopal appointments reflected her concern for discipline and obedience rather than reform and zeal. At Norwich, for example, Parkhurst was succeeded by Edmund Freke; while the former had been reluctant to discipline Protestant activists, Freke in stark contrast was prepared to ally himself with religious conservatives and even Catholics in his efforts to impose uniformity within his diocese. The appointment of Whitgift as Grindal's successor at Canterbury was part of the same trend, and ushered in a new era of harmony between Elizabeth and her bishops, as crown and episcopate came to share the common purpose of eradicating political Puritanism and grass-roots Presbyterianism.

During the 1570s, the need to respond to the threat from Presbyterianism forced Elizabeth's bishops to devise arguments to justify their very existence. Whitgift was the first to take up the challenge, but he made only very modest claims in defence of episcopacy. To counter Thomas Cartwright's assertion that there was no scriptural authority for the episcopal order, Whitgift responded that, as no specific form of church government had been prescibed by scripture, the matter was *adiaphora* and could thus be determined by the supreme governor. At the outset, this Erastian approach was shared by a number of other bishops, and it was only in the late 1580s that some, like John Bridges of Oxford and Richard Bancroft of London, began to assert the divine right of episcopacy. Bridges declared in a sermon that the bishops 'had superiority over the inferior clergy, otherwise than by and from her Majesty's authority, namely by divine right'. Initially, Bancroft was somewhat more restrained than his colleague, claiming only that episcopacy had existed as a superior order within the church since the time of the apostles; in 1593, however, in his *Survey of the Pretended Holy Discipline*, he stated unequivocally that the episcopal order had been instituted by God.

In 1604, shortly after the start of James I's reign, Bancroft succeeded Whitgift as Archbishop of Canterbury. As he fully shared in his predecessor's conservative and disciplinarian approach, his appointment did much to alienate the godly, whom the new king had so recently been trying to accommodate at the Hampton Court Conference. Bancroft's insistence on conformity and opposition to Puritanism led to the ejection of large numbers of parish clergy during the early years of James's reign. On his death in 1610, however, he was succeeded by George Abbot, a churchman much more in the mould of Grindal, who during the next ten years did much to restore peace to the English church. A committed evangelical Calvinist, Abbot believed passionately in the doctrine of predestination and possessed a profound fear and loathing of popery. To counter what he considered to be the pressing danger from Roman Catholicism, he placed great importance on the need for an effective preaching ministry, and was extremely reluctant to persecute godly minsters, whom he considered to be among the best preachers in the church, simply because they failed to adopt all the ceremonial injunctions laid down by his predecessor. He thus adopted a tolerant approach towards the many moderate episcopalian Puritans, while at the same time remaining vehement in his condemnation of Presbyterians.

In order further to advance the cause of the godly, Abbot played a very active role in the faction fighting at James's court, and was one of those responsible for introducing the king to George Villiers, the future Duke of Buckingham, in an attempt to reduce the influence of the pro-Catholic Howard faction. During the early years of his primacy, Abbot found himself in broad agreement with the king on religious issues, such as the threat from Catholicism and the need to convert the Irish to Protestantism. Following the outbreak of the Thirty Years' War in 1618, however, his outspoken advocacy of a militant Protestant foreign policy led to a breach with James; his influence was already in decline by the early 1620s, and after his accidental killing of a gamekeeper in 1621 he was forced into virtual retirement for the remaining twelve years of his life.

The overall calibre of the remainder of the Jacobean bishops has been the subject of some debate among historians. Hugh Trevor-Roper[1] has regarded them as little more than 'lay courtiers holding clerical sinecures', labelling them 'indifferent', 'negligent', and 'secular'. Other historians, however, have subsequently done much to restore their reputation, by emphasizing the undoubted abilities and dedication of many of those appointed or promoted by James. The Jacobean episcopal bench certainly contained some men of great learning and evangelical commitment, a fact that is clearly illustrated by the example of Toby Matthew of Durham. Although undoubtedly a scheming and ambitious cleric, Matthew also preached over 2,000 sermons between 1580 and 1620, and on his death he left a huge private library of over 3,000 books. While John Williams of Lincoln was famous among his contemporaries for his well-stocked wine cellar and lavish entertainment of the gentry, according to his biography *Scrinia Reserata*, he was also an accomplished preacher, tireless scholar, and attentive administrator. Establishing harmonious relations with lay neighbours was a legitimate and important part of the episcopal function, and one that was taken seriously by other Jacobean bishops as well as Williams. John Jegon, Bishop of Norwich from 1603 to 1618, co-operated closely with local Puritan gentry in the establishing of preaching ministries, and as a consequence won the respect of these potential opponents; on one occasion he was assured by the Suffolk Puritan, Nicholas Bownde, 'how ready we are, and shall be to yield obedience to all Your Lordship's godly proceedings'.

For many godly English men and women, bishops like Abbot, Williams, and Jegon were exemplars of the pure apostolic government which had existed within the early church. Their approach to their episcopal duties was popular with the laity, and as a result at the close of James I's reign anti-episcopalianism attracted the support of only a tiny radical minority in England. During the fifteen years that followed the accession of Charles I in 1625, however, popular attitudes towards the bishops were to change dramatically for the worse, the predominant cause for the deterioration being the elevation to the episcopal bench of a number of conservative Arminian clerics, such as Richard Montagu, Matthew Wren, Richard Neile, and William Laud. The beginnings of this shift in opinion can be seen in the

angry reaction to the appointment of the Arminian controversialist
Richard Montagu as Bishop of Chichester in the late 1620s; John
Pym, who was to lead the attack on Charles's government in the
early 1640s, remarked in parliament that Montagu's promotion had
dishonoured an otherwise honourable order, and John Eliot, who
was later to die in prison as a result of his opposition to Charles's
fiscal policies, similarly declared: 'I reverence the order, I honour
not the man.' A decade later, the Arminian bishops had become
some of the most feared and hated men in England, and, as a direct
result of their activities, far fewer laymen continued to 'reverence'
the episcopal order.

A recognizable Arminian party had grown up within the English
church during James's reign, and even before 1625 it had secured
several positions on the episcopal bench; Richard Neile, the effective
leader of the Arminians until 1625, was appointed to Durham in 1617,
Lancelot Andrewes to Winchester in 1618, and George Montaigne to
London in 1621. William Laud was made Dean of Gloucester in 1616,
and appointed Bishop of St David's in 1621. During the later years of
James's reign, the group's activities were co-ordinated at meetings
held at Neile's London residence, Durham House. Nevertheless, at
this stage they had only a limited influence within the church, and it
was only after the accession of Charles I in 1625 that they grew rapidly
in strength through the support and patronage of the new monarch.
William Laud was appointed Bishop of Bath and Wells in 1626, and
of London in 1628; in 1633 he succeeded Abbot as Archbishop of
Canterbury. Thereafter, virtually all episcopal vacancies were filled
by Laudians and only a small group of bishops, such as Williams of
Lincoln and Archbishop James Ussher of Armagh who was in overall
control of the Irish Protestant church, attempted to resist the new
primate's dominance.

During the remainder of the 1630s, Laud and his fellow Arminian
prelates alienated moderate episcopalian Calvinist opinion on a mas-
sive scale by their redefinition of the doctrinal boundaries of the
church and consequent proscription of predestination; by their harsh
punishment in the ecclesiastical courts of all who opposed them, irre-
spective of their social background; and above all by their imposition
of liturgical ceremonies and decorational features regarded by many
as the trappings of popery. Undoubtedly, their actions gave rise to
intense anxiety and engendered deep resentments within an influential section of the English political nation. John Morrill[2] has argued
recently that it is 'almost impossible to overestimate the damage
caused by the Laudians'. Another inevitable consequence was a

change in attitudes towards the episcopal office itself, for as the 1630s progressed, Laud's opponents were forced to consider drastic remedies, and as Nicholas Tyacke[3] has pointed out, 'presbyterianism emerged as the cure for the Arminian disease'.

During May 1640, William Laud's palace at Lambeth was attacked on several occasions by large crowds of Londoners, and in the months that followed the meeting of the Long Parliament in November, petitions calling for the 'root and branch' abolition of episcopacy flooded into the House of Commons from all parts of the country. One, which the House received in early December, claimed that episcopal government had been found 'by woeful experience to be a main cause and occasion of many foul evils pressures and grievances of a very high nature unto His Majesty's subjects in their own consciences, liberties and estates'. Laud was arrested on the orders of Parliament and imprisoned in the Tower of London, where he languished until his public trial and execution in 1645. During the spring of 1641, negotiations took place at Westminster with the aim of avoiding the radical 'root and branch' solution by creating a new form of pastoral episcopacy modelled on that of the early church. The supporters of the proposal included parliamentary leaders like John Pym and bishops such as Williams and Ussher, as well as a number of Puritan lower clergy; they envisaged an episcopal bench with far less wealth and political influence, which would never again be able to repeat the Laudian tyranny. The plan foundered, however, at an early stage when the House of Lords rejected the attempts of the Commons to exclude the bishops from their seats in the Upper House. In a similar attempt to dilute the strength of the hostility directed at episcopacy, Charles I created eleven new bishops between 1641 and 1643, most of whom were committed Calvinists in the tradition of Abbot rather than Laud. However, with the Presbyterians growing increasingly dominant at Westminster during the civil war, the bishops' days were numbered. Following its military victory in the summer of 1646, parliament delivered the *coup de grâce* to the beleaguered system; in October 1646 it officially abolished episcopacy, replacing it with a Presbyterian classis system recommended by the Westminster Assembly of Divines.

Normal episcopal administration had, however, broken down long before this, for on the outbreak of the war in 1642 most of the bishops had abandoned their palaces and official duties, and concentrated their attentions upon protecting their own property. Matthew Wren, Bishop of Ely, who was almost as hated as Laud, was held as a prisoner in the Tower of London. The remainder kept a very low profile throughout the Interregnum period, and no doubt shared the view of Brian Duppa, Bishop of Salisbury, who remarked at the time that he survived 'the same way as the tortoise doth, by not going out of my shell'. Bishop Henry King of Chichester devoted himself to his poetry, and William Juxon of London to his hunting hounds; the others remained in what one historian has called 'impenetrable obscurity'. As a group, they failed to give any lead to their parish clergy on issues such as their continued use of the Prayer Book, or their attitude to the new ecclesiastical establishment. However, if as a group they neglected to make any clear public stand in favour of the old pre-war church, several of them, notably Bishop Robert Skinner of Oxford, did carry on with the important work of ordination, and as a result helped to assure the continued attachment of large numbers of the parish clergy to the traditions of the Elizabethan church. By the late 1650s, the dwindling number of bishops was causing some anxiety at the exiled Royalist court, where it was feared that the apostolic succession of the Anglican bishops, which had descended from Thomas Cranmer, might be broken. In an attempt to prevent this, during the months that preceded the Restoration the surviving bishops received express instructions from the king to proceed with the consecration of replacements to the vacant sees.

Following the return of the monarchy, the restoration of episcopacy was one of the chief priorities of the new government. During the second half of 1660, sixteen new bishops were nominated and three surviving bishops were translated to new sees. Charles II, who appears to have taken a very active part in the choice of the new prelates, appointed a group of churchmen who exhibited a wide spectrum of Anglican opinion. Still at this stage hoping to restore a comprehensive church which could accommodate within its confines those who held Presbyterian as well as Anglican views, the king passed over most of the more obvious conservative candidates and those who had been closely associated with Laud. Indeed, he went so far as to offer bishoprics to several prominent Presbyterians, including Richard Baxter and Edmund Calamy, and he left Coventry and Lichfield vacant until 1661 in the hope that Baxter might be persuaded to accept it. In the event, however, only one Presbyterian accepted the king's offer, Edward Reynolds agreeing to become Bishop of Norwich.

As a group, the occupants of the restored episcopal bench were characterized principally by the diversity of their religious outlooks, a heterogeneity which reflected Charles II's Erastian outlook and his determination not to become the prisoner of any one ecclesiastical faction. Most of the new bishops – men like William Lucy, Nicholas Monck, Hugh Lloyd, William Nicholson, and Gilbert Ironside – were relatively obscure clerics who had supported the Royalist cause during the 1640s, but had distanced themselves both from the Arminians in the 1630s and the Interregnum church in the 1650s. As they set about the business of reinstating the apparatus of episcopal government by refounding deans and chapters and ecclesiastical courts, and conducting extensive visitations of their parish clergy, they adopted varying approaches towards the problems they encountered. While some of them, like Robert Sanderson of Lincoln and Brian Walton of Chester, attempted to force the use of the Book of Common Prayer, others, such as Ironside at Bristol and Humphrey Henchman at Salisbury, adopted a more tolerant approach towards their clergy. Edward Reynolds at Norwich and John Gauden at Exeter even involved the Presbyterians of their dioceses in the ordination of new clergy.

For his first Archbishop of Canterbury, Charles II chose William Juxon. Juxon had been closely associated with Laud, but he was now old and in very poor health, and thus quite unable to take any active role in the restoration of the church. On his death in 1663, he was succeeded at Canterbury by the Bishop of London, Gilbert Sheldon. In the months immediately following the Restoration, Sheldon had supported the king's attempts to achieve a comprehensive church settlement. However, during the debates at Westminster on the Bill of Uniformity, he had become aware of the strong commitment of the MPs in the Cavalier Parliament and the provincial gentry they represented to the old church. He had therefore decided to adopt a more aggressive and uncompromising line, and had lent his full support to the legislation of the Clarendon Code. As an able administrator and shrewd political operator, Sheldon was a churchman particularly well equipped to organize the restoration of the national church, and his increasingly uncompromising line towards nonconformity and promotion of measures such as the ending of separate clerical taxation did much to cement the emerging alliance between the restored church and English landed society.

Sheldon also realized that the church's power was ultimately dependent on its economic well-being, and shortly after his elevation he commissioned an extensive survey of episcopal revenues. This revealed that the economic position of the restored bishops was markedly superior to that of their sixteenth-century predecessors. The surveyors found that the total value of the English bishoprics was in the region of £50,000 per annum, representing an increase of about 25 per cent over the previous seventy-five years, and since the survey was designed to show that the bishops were not excessively wealthy, it may have underestimated the scale of the improvement in their economic fortunes. Certainly, the late seventeenth-century bishops both complained about their poverty and fell into serious debt far less frequently than their Elizabethan counterparts. While some dioceses, like Hereford and Exeter, still possessed fairly modest resources, other bishops were now in a very comfortable financial position; during the 1680s Canterbury was yielding something in the region of £6,000 per annum, Winchester £5,000, and Ely over £3,000. In such dioceses, efficient estate management had more than compensated for the adverse effect of alienations and inflation.

The close alliance between crown, church, and gentry, which Sheldon had started to forge in the 1660s, was further developed after 1677 by his successor, William Sancroft. Sancroft was another keen disciplinarian who worked hard to improve the quality of the lower clergy, and who was anxious to take every opportunity to extend the influence of a resurgent Anglicanism over English society. A devoted follower of the Stuarts, Sancroft regarded the monarchy with an almost mystical devotion. In the late 1670s, he gave his full backing to Charles II's opposition to parliamentary demands for the exclusion from the succession of the Catholic heir to the throne, James, Duke of York. Following the failure of this Exclusion campaign, he accepted James's assurances that he would not, as a Catholic monarch, pose any threat to the established Anglican church, and during the last years of Charles's reign he helped to build up a strong Yorkist faction at court.

Having staked so much on James's avowed willingness to work with the Anglican hierarchy, Sancroft was to find the religious developments of James's short reign a cruel disappointment. By 1687, he had come to the conclusion that the king's policy of catholicization did represent a major threat to his church, and in the summer of 1688 he became involved in a bitter, public confrontation with the crown. In May 1688, James ordered that the Declaration of Indulgence suspending the penal laws against dissenters and Catholic recusants should be read from the pulpits of all the Anglican churches in the country. When Sancroft and six of his episcopal colleagues protested by presenting a petition to James, the king declared their action 'a standard of rebellion' and charged the seven bishops with seditious libel. They were held for some weeks in the Tower of London and put on trial in June 1688, only to be acquitted by the jury amid scenes of great rejoicing. The incident was a humiliating defeat for the king, and an ominous sign of the strength of the country's attachment to Anglicanism and its opposition to James's Catholic reforms. It also marked a dramatic change-around in the popularity of the bishops since the fall of Laud half a century earlier.

Despite the increasing alarm with which the bishops had regarded James's policies and the tacit acknowledgement by some of them of the necessity of his removal, the expulsion of the king in 1688 and his replacement with his daughter Mary and son-in-law William was to cause severe embarrassment to a church hierarchy which had been for many years firmly committed to the ideas of the divine right of kings and the unlawfulness of resistance. When Sancroft and five other bishops refused to compromise their consciences by swearing an oath of allegiance to the new monarchs, they were ejected as 'non-jurors'. As several other bishops had travelled into exile in France with James II, and a number of sees had fallen vacant through the deaths of their incumbents, William was called upon to nominate no fewer than sixteen new bishops between 1688 and 1691. In the main, he chose clerics whom he believed would help to bolster up his new regime and cool down the religious passions engendered by his predecessor. In 1691, Sancroft was replaced as Archbishop of Canterbury by the moderate and conciliatory John Tillotson, who possessed a far less elevated view of the role of the Anglican church and who favoured major concessions to nonconformity. The Anglican bishops of the late seventeenth century had served their Stuart masters with great dedication and loyalty, but their undoubted devotion had gone largely unrewarded.

NOTES

1 Hugh Trevor-Roper, 'James I and his bishops', *History Today* 9 (1955).
2 John Morrill, 'The religious context of the English civil war', *Transactions of the Royal Historical Society*, 5th series, vol. 34 (1984).
3 Nicholas Tyacke, 'Puritanism, Arminianism and counter-revolution', in Conrad Russell (ed.), *The Origins of the English Civil War* (London, 1973).

SUGGESTIONS FOR FURTHER READING

The bishops of the late medieval period, along with various other aspects of the fifteenth-century church are discussed by Christopher Harper-Bill in *The Pre-Reformation Church in England* (London, 1989). The best study of the sixteenth-century episcopate is Felicity Heal, *Of Prelates and Princes: A study of the economic and social position of the Tudor episcopate* (Cambridge, 1980). The political role of the bishops and their reactions to the events of the Reformation are well examined in L. B. Smith, *Tudor Prelates and Politics* (London, 1953). For the Tudor episcopacy's relations with the crown and its formulation of divine right theories, together with useful documents, M. C. Cross, *The Royal Supremacy in the Elizabethan Church* (London, 1969) is helpful. There are several important articles on different aspects of the Elizabethan episcopate; Ralph Houlbrooke, 'The Protestant episcopate 1547–1603: the pastoral contribution', in Felicity Heal and Rosemary O'Day (eds), *Church and Society in England: Henry VIII to James I* (London, 1977); P. Collinson, 'Episcopacy and Reform in England in the later sixteenth century', in G. J. Cumming (ed.), *Studies in Church History* 3 (Leiden, 1966); R. B. Manning, 'The crisis of episcopal authority during the reign of Elizabeth I', *Journal of British Studies* 11 (1971); and Joel Berlatsky, 'The Elizabethan episcopate: patterns of life and expenditure', in Rosemary O'Day and Felicity Heal (eds), *Princes and Paupers in the English Church 1500–1800* (New Jersey, 1981). There are many studies of individual Tudor bishops. Among the most interesting and important are Peter Gwyn, *The King's Cardinal: The rise and fall of Thomas Wolsey* (London, 1990); Brendan Bradshaw and Eamon Duffy (eds), *Humanism, Reform and Reformation: The career of Bishop John Fisher* (Cambridge, 1989); M. Bowker, *The Henrician Reformation: The diocese of Lincoln under Bishop John Longland, 1521–1547* (Cambridge, 1981); Glyn Redworth, *In Defence of the Church Catholic: The life of Stephen Gardiner* (Oxford, 1990); R. Pogson, 'God's law and man's: Stephen Gardiner and the problem of loyalty', in C. Cross, D. Loades, and J. J. Scarisbrick (eds), *Law and Government under the Tudors* (Cambridge, 1988); G. Alexander, 'Bonner and the Marian persecutions', *History* 60 (1975); P. N. Brooks, 'The principle and practice of primitive Protestantism in Tudor England', in P. N. Brooks (ed.), *Reformation Principles and Practice: Essays in honour of A. G. Dickens* (London, 1980); and P. Collinson, *Archbishop Grindal 1519–1583: the struggle for a reformed church* (London, 1979).

The Jacobean bishops can best be approached through Kenneth Fincham, *Prelate as Pastor: The episcopate of James I* (Oxford, 1990); J. Rogan, 'King James' bishops', *University of Durham Journal* 48 (1956); D. E. Kennedy, 'The Jacobean episcopate', *Historical Journal* 5 (1962); H. R. Trevor-Roper, 'James I and his bishops', *History Today* 9 (1955); Kenneth Fincham, 'Prelacy and politics: Archbishop Abbot's defence of Protestant orthodoxy', *Historical Research* 61 (1988); P. Collinson, *The Religion of Protestants* (Oxford, 1982); and S. B. Babbage, *Puritanism and Richard Bancroft* (London, 1962).

Charles I's Arminian bishops are dealt with as a group by Nicholas Tyacke in *Anti-Calvinists: The rise of English Arminianism c. 1590–1640* (Oxford, 1987); and also in 'Puritanism, Arminianism and counter-revolution', in Conrad Russell (ed.), *The Origins of the English Civil War* (London, 1973). On William Laud, see H. R. Trevor-Roper, *Archbishop Laud* (London, 1962); and Charles Carlton, *Archbishop William Laud* (London, 1987). For the damage caused by the Arminian bishops, see John Morrill, 'The religious context of the English civil war', *Transactions of the Royal Historical Society*, 5th series, vol. 34 (1984).

For the bishops during the period of the civil war and Interregnum and at the Restoration, see M. C. Cross, 'The church in England, 1646–1660', in G. E. Aylmer (ed.), *The Interregnum: The quest for settlement 1646–1660* (London, 1972); Peter King, 'The episcopate during the civil wars', *English Historical Review* 83 (1968); John Morrill, 'The church in England, 1642–9', in John Morrill (ed.), *Reactions to the English Civil War 1642–9* (London, 1982); Robert S. Bosher, *The Making of the Restoration Settlement, 1649–1662* (London, 1951); I. M. Green, *The Re-establishment of the Church of England* (Oxford, 1978); and Ronald Hutton, *The Restoration: A political and religious history of England and Wales 1658–1667* (Oxford, 1985). For the conflict between the seven bishops and James II, see R. Thomas, 'The seven bishops and their petition, 18 May, 1688', *Journal of Ecclesiastical History* 12 (1961). There is no study of the seventeenth-century episcopate comparable to that of Heal for the sixteenth century.

8   The parish clergy

The parish clergy of the late fifteenth and early sixteenth centuries have generally received a bad press, being condemned by
both contemporary moralists and many later historians as ignorant,
unchaste, and too often absent from their benefices. In recent years,
however, research into ecclesiastical records has revealed that the
accusations against them have been grossly exaggerated, and that the
great majority of them were fulfilling their duties adequately. While
only a few of the late medieval parish clergy could be considered
biblical scholars, most were literate and well able to absorb the
handbooks and preaching aids specifically written to help them
write their sermons and instruct parishioners in the rudiments of
the faith. Again, although many priests undoubtedly found their
vows of clerical celibacy difficult to keep, only a small percentage
were denounced by their churchwardens for sexual misconduct. As
a result of the episcopal visitations within the diocese of Lincoln
during the period 1515 to 1527, only 10 per cent of the clergy were
accused of immorality, while a visitation of the archdeaconry of
Winchester conducted during 1527 and 1528 threw up a mere eleven
cases of misconduct from 230 parishes; furthermore, in both areas
a significant number of those accused were subsequently cleared.
Absenteeism among the lower clergy was certainly a feature of the
late medieval church, with between a quarter and a third of all English
parishes having a non-resident incumbent. The great majority of
these parishes were not, however, neglected for they were served
by chaplains and curates; the number of ordinations in England had
soared during the later decades of the fifteenth century, and there was
thus a large pool of unbeneficed priests ready to take up a cure for a
meagre stipend. Within very few parishes, therefore, were liturgical
and pastoral duties not performed by either a beneficed cleric or a
curate; only 4 per cent of the clergy were accused of such neglect in

the diocese of Lincoln, and a number of these were old and infirm rather than lazy or irresponsible.

The relatively small number of complaints against parish priests has encouraged some historians to question the existence of anti-clericalism in England on the eve of the Reformation. Christopher Haigh[1] has argued that the absence of widespread criticism of clerical misconduct indicates one of two things: either that the clergy were not breaking their vows and neglecting their cures, or that, if they were, most of their parishioners did not care. In either case, the laity cannot be considered anti-clerical. This is a persuasive argument, which is given further weight by the fact that outside London relatively few parish priests appear to have found themselves in dispute with their parishioners over clerical dues and fees; in the diocese of Norwich there were only ten tithe suits in 1524, and in the diocese of Canterbury only four in 1531. Even in the city of London there were only between ten and twenty-five tithe suits a year in the early sixteenth century.

On the other hand, historians should not be too quick to dismiss the possibility of the existence of anti-clericalism. While there is little evidence of a popular hostility to the idea of the priesthood on the eve of the Reformation, there are many stories of 'rubs and rows' between individual priests and their parishioners, and it is possible that the extent of lay discontent with the clergy was greater than Haigh admits. Extant visitation records may not tell the whole story; not only are they incomplete, but also some parishioners could have been inhibited from testifying against their priest by communal loyalty, distrust of the ecclesiastical machinery, fear of being accused of heresy, or simply the preference for a quiet life. While tithe and mortuary disputes may not have been prolific, the evidence from London demonstrates that they could poison a whole community against a priest who was thought to be demanding dues to which he was not entitled. The popularity of chantries and lay fraternities on the eve of the Reformation may be a sign of a healthy religion, but it may also indicate that some members of the laity were not receiving sufficient spiritual comfort from their parish priests and had been obliged to seek it elsewhere. In the absence of some equivalent of the modern opinion poll, historians can only guess at the extent of lay dissatisfaction with the parish clergy in the early sixteenth century, and are left to speculate about its significance for the impending religious crisis.

Although Protestantism won over a small number of parish priests during the period of the early Reformation, the vast majority of the English lower clergy remained fundamentally conservative in religious outlook until well into Elizabeth's reign. Only a minority, for example, took advantage of the ending of clerical celibacy in 1549 by marrying during the remaining years of Edward's reign; in Lancashire as many as 95 per cent of parish priests remained single, while even in the south-east, where Protestant influences were strongest, only between a quarter and a third married. Yet, despite this widespread clerical attachment to the old religious order, most clerics adopted the approach made famous by the vicar of Bray in Berkshire and outwardly conformed without protest to the rapid succession of major religious changes. The reigns of Henry VIII and Edward VI witnessed no mass resignations from livings, and few within the ranks of the lower clergy became martyrs to the papal or Catholic cause. Similarly, on the accession of Mary in 1553, the vast majority of the parish clergy readopted their allegiance to Rome, including some 2,000 priests who had married in the early 1550s but who now quickly repudiated their wives. When Mary was in turn succeeded by Elizabeth in 1558, only about 300 of the lower clergy were deprived for refusing to take the oath of supremacy, no more than 70 or 80 chose to go into exile, and only just over 100 were imprisoned.

To a large extent, the acquiescence of the parish clergy in the Reformation changes was a product of the fear of government reprisals against those who offered resistance. Some of the clergy had played a prominent role in the Lincolnshire and Yorkshire rebellions of 1536, spreading the rumours which sparked off the risings, ringing their church bells to raise the country, and distributing money to those prepared to follow the rebel leaders. The failure of these uprisings, however, and the particularly severe punishment meted out to those clerics implicated in them, acted as a deterrent against further acts of defiance. Although sixty-three of the laymen who were convicted as rebels after the Lincolnshire rebellion were spared by an act of royal clemency, every priest without exception was executed, including the rector of Sotby, who had been prevented from playing any meaningful part in the rising by his great age and blindness.

If most of the parish clergy preferred to remain quietly in their posts, many of them none the less worked discreetly within their parishes to undermine the Protestant religious innovations introduced by the governments of Edward and Elizabeth. In December 1549, a proclamation complained that many priests were failing to use the new English Prayer Book, and ordered that the old service books be destroyed. Under Elizabeth, the Marian clergy retained many Catholic practices in their parish worship and continued to preside at communion services which were kept as much like the mass as possible. Visitation records reveal that altars, images, rosaries, and holy water persisted well into the 1570s. In addition, numbers of clergy were indicted before the ecclesiastical courts during the 1560s and 1570s for trying to 'counterfeit the mass' when conducting the Protestant communion service, by facing eastwards, using wafers rather than bread, and continuing to elevate the chalice.

The primary reason for the failure of Elizabeth's government to purge the ranks of the lower clergy of these residual Catholic elements was that in 1558 there was an insufficient number of Protestant ministers to put in their place. The early years of Elizabeth's reign experienced an acute shortage of clerical manpower; this had been partly caused by the influenza epidemic of 1556, but was also a legacy of the long-term slump in ordinations which had begun with the religious upheavals of the 1530s. In 1561, some 10 per cent of all livings in the country were vacant, and but for the co-operation of the Marian priests who continued to serve their cures, Elizabeth would have found it impossible to implement her religious settlement. Even so, for the first few years of the reign, many bishops were obliged to accept unqualified candidates as deacons, while both the Archbishop of Canterbury and the Bishop of London had to resort to mass and almost indiscriminate ordinations to meet the manpower crisis.

If the Elizabethan church was to win over a predominantly Catholic laity to Protestantism, the creation of an educated and well-trained parish clergy was absolutely essential. The role of a Protestant minister was not that of a priest, whose office alone gave him the power to mediate between man and God, but rather that of a preacher and pastor who was expected both to edify his parishioners through his sermons and to teach them 'to live well and christianly' through his discipline and good example. The bishops, however, were not in a position to impose higher standards for ordinands until the recruitment crisis was over and better qualified candidates came forward. It was some twenty years before this began to happen, and it was only in the last quarter of the sixteenth century that there was a steady and general improvement in the quality of ordinands.

By this stage, a large proportion of new recruits had attended a grammar school and university, where they had been given a sound grasp of Protestant theology, and many were also graduates in divinity; within the small diocese of Ely, for example, which benefited from its close proximity to Cambridge University, 73 per cent of the new recruits to the ministry during the 1570s were university trained. The entry of such men into the ranks of the parochial clergy led to a gradual raising of clerical standards, but as they could only be appointed to livings on the death or resignation of the previous incumbent, infiltration was slow and progress towards the goal of an all-graduate clergy varied greatly from diocese to diocese. In 1576, for example, the archdeaconry of Leicester still contained nineteen ministers who had been ordained in the 1530s and 1540s, all but three of whom were found to be 'indifferentlie learned', 'meanlie learned', or simply 'ignoraunt' in their knowledge of Latin and the scriptures. Another area of slow progress was the diocese of Coventry and Lichfield where only 24 per cent of the clergy were graduates on Elizabeth's death. At the other end of the scale came the diocese of London, where by the end of Elizabeth's reign three-quarters of the incumbent clergy and half the curates were graduates.

Potential ministers were encouraged to go to university by the new ordination requirements of 1575, which laid down that prospective deacons – the first rung on the career ladder – had to be at least twenty-three years old. The progress towards a university-trained ministry was also assisted by the generosity of the queen, individual bishops, and the godly laity. Elizabeth effectively created a number of university scholarships for intending clerics by setting aside the income from all crown prebends valued at less than £20 per annum for theology students. Bishops such as Matthew Parker, Edmund Grindal, Edwin Sandys, and John Whitgift also gave sums of money to promote the education of future clerics at the grammar schools and universities. Of most value, however, were the endowments of Emmanuel and Sidney Sussex Colleges at Cambridge by two Puritans, Sir Walter Mildmay and Frances, Countess of Sussex, respectively, for these colleges were created for the sole and express purpose of 'rendering as many persons as possible fit for the sacred ministry of the word and sacraments'.

The existing pool of largely unlearned clergy was also affected by the drive to raise educational standards. Throughout Elizabeth's reign, non-graduate clerics were offered a number of opportunities for 'in-service training', aimed at equipping them to cope better with the new, more onerous pastoral demands which had been placed upon them. In 1559, the government ordered that archdeacons should supervise instruction in biblical studies for all clergymen without an MA degree, and in major dioceses such as London, Durham, York, Chester, Lincoln, and Winchester regular checks on their progress were made during quarterly and half-yearly synods. Prophesyings – conferences of clergy at which a text from scripture was debated in front of senior churchmen – were also used as a means of educating unlearned ministers. By the mid-1570s, these were a regular occurrence not only in large towns like Norwich and Northampton, but also in many smaller urban centres. According to Patrick Collinson,[2] those bishops who took part in prophesyings considered them 'the most convenient and efficient means of sending the clergy to school', and when in 1576 Elizabeth decided to ban them they were deeply unhappy. Following their suppression, new methods of educating the clergy were investigated; in 1587, for example, convocation drew up orders for the appointment of 'certain grave and learned preachers' who would be responsible for giving individual instruction to small groups of their unlearned colleagues. There is, however, little evidence to suggest that any of these initiatives proved particularly successful, for as Collinson[3] has commented, much of the manpower brought into the church in the 'lean years' of the mid-Tudor period proved educationally 'irredeemable'.

The best hope for an improvement in the standard of the clergy continued to lie with the universities. There could, however, be no guarantee that new graduate entrants to the ministry would possess either the necessary vocation or the qualities appropriate for a pastor. Those who examined ordinands normally directed most of their attention towards a candidate's educational attainments, and only rarely investigated vocational commitment. As a result, a number of clearly unsuitable graduates became ministers. In 1585, Robert Jones, the graduate curate of Brightling in Sussex, was 'vehemently suspected for loose life' and accused of being 'a gamester, a quarreller, a fighter'. Some time later the graduate William Holland, minister of the nearby parish of Etchingham, was reported to have been 'so drunk that his soles were cut or pulled from his shoes'.

Nor should it be automatically assumed that even the more committed young graduates were necessarily well equipped to perform the varied and taxing duties of the parochial ministry, for their university education had probably provided little or no specific training in preaching or pastoral work. Certainly, the seminary role was strongly reflected in the teaching at some of the newer university colleges, like Emmanuel and Sidney Sussex at Cambridge, as well as at a number of older endowments which had retained a strong clerical tradition, such as St John's, Christ's, and Gonville and Caius, Cambridge. Elsewhere, however, undergraduates followed a broad, humanist curriculum of little direct relevance to the realities of parochial work. In this context, it is significant that despite the high percentage of graduate clergy within the diocese of Ely, as late as 1584 only 40 per cent of them were considered suitable to be licensed as preachers. Moreover, as a direct result of their educated backgrounds, some Elizabethan clergy may have found it increasingly difficult to relate to the majority of their more ignorant parishioners. Overzealous clergymen could also sometimes provoke bitter divisions within their parishes; when, for example, Henry Pye, a young minister, attempted to suppress an unlicensed ale-house in his parish of Peasmarsh in Sussex in 1584, he caused a storm which resulted in a legal case in the Court of Queen's Bench.

The rise in the clergy's social and educational standing during the second half of the sixteenth century was not always matched by a corresponding improvement in their economic position. Superficially all appeared well, for the traditional sources of clerical revenue – tithes, dues, and offerings – survived the Reformation and continued to be paid to the Elizabethan clergy. Furthermore, it has been calculated that the average value of livings increased fourfold over the period from 1535 to 1603, enough to compensate for the effects of the sustained inflation of those years. Such overall estimates, however, conceal extreme inequalities in the value of individual livings, and hide the disastrous impact of inflation, taxation, and lay plunder on the incomes of some of the poorest clergy. Rectors who were fortunate enough to enjoy an extensive glebe or uncommuted 'great tithes' of grain and hay were generally relatively secure, and some actually benefited from inflation. On the other hand, incumbents who received a fixed stipend, or officiated in parishes where the tithes had been commuted or where the glebe was small, struggled to keep pace with rising prices. The country's 3,800 vicars were particularly hard hit by inflation and many had great difficulty in making ends meet. The economic position of the post-Reformation clergy was rendered still more difficult by its changing lifestyle, duties, and expectations. Graduate clergymen who had invested considerable time and money in acquiring an education wished to live as gentlemen, and many of them also now had to support and make provision for large families.

In some parishes even the most efficient exploitation of the glebe and the most rigorous exaction of clerical dues failed to produce an adequate income for the incumbent, with the result that many clergy were forced to resort to pluralism. Pluralism and its corollary non-residence were far from abolished at the Reformation. On the contrary, due to the desperate shortage of clergy at the start of Elizabeth's reign, they were more prevalent during the early 1560s than at any other time throughout the Reformation period. In Archbishop Parker's diocese of Canterbury, for example, 17 per cent of the beneficed incumbents were pluralists in 1559, 44 per cent in 1561, 32 per cent in 1569, and 18 per cent in 1575. While some instances of pluralism can be attributed to the temporary crisis in manpower and the poverty of livings, many others were the result of the survival of the patronage system. Whether the laymen who acquired large numbers of monastic advowsons during the 1530s and 1540s were more or less simoniacal in the exercise of their patronage than their clerical predecessors is open to question, but there are certainly many examples of lay patrons using advowsons to reward their servants or advance their kinsmen; in 1562 the Marquis of Winchester numbered among his retinue three non-resident clergymen, who between them held four livings; and throughout Elizabeth's reign the Earl of Derby employed as his chaplain the non-resident incumbent of the parish of Eccleston in Lancashire.

It would be a mistake to conclude that every instance of pluralism and non-residence resulted in the neglect of cures. As we have seen, in both the pre- and post-Reformation periods, curates were normally employed to stand in for incumbents and many ran their parishes conscientiously. In addition, where two parishes were small and lay close to each other, both could be adequately served by one man; in the archdeaconry of Norwich in 1561, for example, nearly one third of the pluralists held adjacent parishes. It is, none the less, undeniable that some parishes which were too large and impoverished to attract a replacement cleric continued to suffer as a consequence of non-residence. Some of the most glaring incidents of neglect of cures occurred in Lancashire, a county with a particularly large number of extensive, poorly endowed parishes. Elimination of this problem could only have been achieved through the complete overhaul of the parochial structure of the church and the revision of the patronage system – reforms which were unthinkable in the conservative climate of Elizabethan England.

The improvement in the standard and conduct of the parish clergy, which had begun in the last quarter of the sixteenth century, continued during the first two decades of the seventeenth century, and by the 1620s the gradual process of educating and professionalizing the English parish clergy was virtually complete. While many individual ministers still fell short of the Protestant ideal and the most remote parts of the country remained poorly served, most contemporaries were by now agreed that there had been a marked general improvement in standards. In 1621, one MP declared in the House of Commons: 'I speak it confidently, there were never better ministers since this kingdom stood'; and three years later Joseph Hall, who was later appointed Bishop of Exeter, described the parish clergy as *stupor mundi* – 'the wonder of the world'. Candidates for the ministry now poured out of the two universities in considerable numbers, and as a result almost all new clergymen were graduates. In view of their plentiful supply, ordinands were subjected to rigorous examinations, and some bishops took advantage of the new 'buyers' market' to reject large numbers of applicants.

Those who were successful now found themselves members of a profession with a more clearly defined career stucture. The wide and often unbridgeable gap between beneficed and unbeneficed clergy, which had existed down to the Reformation, had disappeared, and it had become normal practice for an ordinand to serve as a curate before proceeding naturally to the acquisition of a benefice. The clergy's growing sense of professional identity was fostered by increased contact with ministers from neighbouring parishes. One of the main vehicles for this was the combination lecture – the equivalent of the modern research seminar – at which the clergy took it in turns to preach to their colleagues. Furthermore, clergymen began to show a marked tendency to marry into other clerical families, and thus to develop their own clerical dynasties. During the first half of the seventeenth century, for example, a third of the daughters of the Kentish clergy married clergymen, and in the 1630s the sons of clergy accounted for 15 per cent of all students at Oxford University. However, if the clergy were increasingly coming to see themselves as a profession, they remained a profession within which the rewards for service were still very unequally distributed. By the early seventeenth century, some of the more fortunate rectors had become extremely prosperous and begun to acquire the lifestyle and affectations of the landed gentry; at the same time, however, thousands of poorer vicars were still engaged in a constant struggle to make ends meet.

While these changes created a body of parochial clergy who were generally more capable, self-confident, and efficient, they also set ministers further apart from the majority of their parishioners. From the late sixteenth century onwards, the graduate parish clergyman was clearly marked off from his flock by his different interests, language, and lifestyle, and his new, more elevated status was reflected in the use of the new honorific title of 'Master'. Even though some clergymen in rural parishes – such as Ralph Josselin, the minister of Earls Colne in Essex – continued to involve themselves in the secular life of their communities as farmers and schoolmasters, they none the less had to put aside an increasing proportion of their week for private study and the preparation of sermons. How these developments affected relations between the clergy and the laity is an important but complicated question. Some historians have recently argued that the new, educated preaching ministry created by the Reformation was far more unpopular than its late medieval counterpart. Christopher Haigh,[4] for example, has provocatively asserted that: '"Anticlericalism", in short, was not a cause of the Reformation; it was a result'; and Rosemary O'Day[5] has similarly suggested that the roots of the rampant anti-clericalism which surfaced in some areas during the 1640s and 1650s should be sought in these pre-civil war tensions. There is certainly no shortage of evidence of disputes between ministers and their parishioners in the ecclesiastical court records of the late sixteenth and early seventeenth centuries. Most commonly these involved attacks on the clergy's right to interpret scripture, to discipline parishioners, and to collect tithes. Complaints were also frequently made about the growing pretensions and arrogance of some clergymen. None the less, it is important to remember that those clergy who did quarrel with their parishioners remained a relatively small minority, and that many hundreds of clergymen managed to remain on amicable terms with their parishioners. While some of the laity doubtless resented the loss of the earlier, more equal relationship with the local clergyman, others may well have been happy to show a greater respect and deference to this new pillar of the local community.

Following the Laudian takeover of the church in the late 1620s, both the new conservative episcopate and its godly opponents realized the importance of maximizing their support within the ranks of the parish clergy. Although Laud and his fellow Arminian bishops were extremely eager to appoint like-minded clerics to parochial benefices, they failed to achieve their objective of an Arminian parish clergy, and during the 1630s their ceremonial innovations were widely resisted by the parochial clergy. The failure of the Arminians to reshape the lower clergy in their own image was partly attributable to the relative infrequency with which parochial vacancies arose, but more importantly to the patronage system. For when livings did fall vacant, the rights of presentment were often in the hands of lay patrons, many of whom had no sympathy with Laud and his supporters. In order to restrict the influence of the bishops, some of Laud's most committed Puritan opponents deliberately set out to acquire additional rights of presentment. In 1625, a number of godly clerics, merchants, and lawyers founded the Feoffees for Impropriations, a body created with the express purpose of purchasing impropriated livings and appointing to them Puritan preachers and ministers.

During the late 1620s, the godly laity of London contributed more than £6,000 to further the work of the Feoffees and by the early 1630s they had acquired patronage rights in eighteen counties. In 1633, their activities were outlawed by the Laudian authorities, but individual Calvinist gentlemen continued to appoint godly ministers to livings in their gift throughout the 1630s. Further opposition to the reforms of the Laudian bishops was provided by parish lecturers. These unbeneficed clergy, who were often of a Puritan disposition, were appointed to provide the laity of London and other major urban centres with regular weekly preaching; a number of them exercised considerable influence and became the focus for opposition to the conservative ecclesiastical regime.

If the membership of the beneficed clergy remained relatively unaffected by the dramatic changes in the leadership of the church during the 1630s, this was certainly not the case once the political crisis which Laud had done so much to provoke erupted in the early 1640s. As a result of the political and religious turmoil of the 1640s and 1650s, somewhat under 3,000, or 28 per cent, of the 8,600 parish clergy in England suffered either the loss of their living or some other form of serious harassment. Many were summarily ejected or put under great pressure to resign from their livings; others were imprisoned or forced to pay substantial composition fines for giving support to the Royalist cause. Initially, the parliamentarian attack upon what were labelled 'delinquent', 'scandalous', and 'malignant' clergy was both sporadic and uncoordinated, and the intensity of local persecution varied greatly across the country. After receiving a flood of petitions calling for reform of the ministry during the early months of its sitting, in December 1642 the Long Parliament established a Committee for Plundered Ministers, and entrusted to it the task of removing Royalist clergy from livings and replacing them with parliamentarian ministers who had suffered from Royalist depredations. This committee set to work in 1643, but shortly afterwards in an attempt to speed up the process, parliament authorized local county committees to carry out ejections too. Thereafter, the fate of individual Royalist and Anglican clergymen was largely determined by the nature of local politics.

Ejections occurred most frequently in those parts of the country where the purging of the ministry was considered a high priority by members of the local parliamentarian elite. In such areas the authorities acted swiftly and uncompromisingly. Following the granting of a commission for the removal of suspect ministers to the Earl of Manchester in early 1644, the following summer and autumn witnessed a spate of ejections in East Anglia. Similar commissions were subsequently issued to Sir Thomas Fairfax in Yorkshire and Sir William Brereton in Cheshire, and numerous ejections again ensued. In some other counties the latter stages of the civil war saw the emergence of a new breed of more radical parliamentarians, such as John Pyne in Somerset and Thomas Cooke in Essex, and these men too were responsible for directing concerted local campaigns against clergy whose commitment to their cause was in doubt. Elsewhere, however, local committees appear to have been more reluctant to act, with the result that substantial numbers of moderate clergymen who, although not fervent supporters of parliament, had refrained from any active involvement in the Royalist cause, were left unmolested. Furthermore, many ministers seem to have been protected from harassment by influential lay patrons. Consequently, there were large regional variations in the scale of ejections. The highest level occurred in London, where 36 per cent of the clergy lost their posts, and the rate was also above average in Kent, East Anglia, the east Midlands, the north-west, and the far south-west. Conversely, a lower than average number of ejections occurred in the west Midlands, the Severn Valley, and the southern Pennine region.

As almost certainly a substantial majority of the lower clergy sympathized with the king during the civil war, it is not surprising that charges of Royalism were extremely common. Clergy persecuted under this heading, however, included not only those whose attachment to the king's cause was obvious and uncompromising, but also in some areas those who had attempted to remain neutral or whose merely lukewarm commitment to parliament and its godly cause was considered inadequate to the task of promoting the establishment of Calvinist Zions in their parishes. Another group of ministers were attacked for their conspicuous support for William Laud. Of these, only a relatively small number were singled out for their attachment to Arminian doctrines, such as salvation through works; a far greater number were arraigned for continuing to conduct ceremonies such as marriage and the churching of women in a 'popish' manner, or for insisting that their parishioners bow their heads at the name of Jesus and receive communion kneeling at the altar rails. Yet another group of clergymen who fell foul of the parliamentary authorities were those considered to be incapable of adequately performing their pastoral duties, and a few were also charged with immoral behaviour – most frequently excessive drinking and gaming. Pluralists were another obvious target for those who wished to improve the quality of pastoral care in the localities; the need for action to deal with this problem was highlighted by the members of the Westminster Assembly in the mid-1640s, and non-residence continued to cause concern to the authorities throughout the Interregnum.

It was rare for a minister to be denounced to the authorities by a majority of his parishioners; far more frequently charges were brought by small caucuses of the more godly, and often more wealthy parishioners with particularly high pastoral expectations. The views of these 'well-affected' minorities were frequently at odds with those of their less zealous lay neighbours, and ejection cases frequently reveal the existence of serious divisions within those parishes where ministers came under attack. In such cases, the clergyman often found himself caught in the crossfire between the hostile factions. One issue that frequently led to conflict was the observance of the sabbath, and ministers were regularly accused of upholding the *Book of Sports* and condoning their parishioners' indulgence in activities such as archery and football on Sundays. After 1645, the clergy's attitude towards the newly promulgated Directory of Public Worship also caused tensions and disputes.

While the overall effect of these ejections upon the quality and popularity of the English lower clergy in the 1640s and 1650s was almost certainly deleterious, care must be taken to avoid exaggerating the damage. Of the nearly 3,000 ministers who suffered harassment of one kind or another during this period, over 1,000 managed to remain within the ranks of the beneficed clergy; 400 of those ejected were later appointed to a different parish, around 200 pluralists were able to retain one of their parishes, and another 270 clerics managed to cling on to their parishes despite the active hostility of the authorities. It should not, therefore, be assumed that the old pre-war church was eradicated at the grass-roots level. Indeed, John Morrill[6] has recently pointed out that as late as 1649 between two-thirds and three-fifths of English livings remained in the hands of the clergymen who had held them in 1642. These men had in the main been ordained during the primacy of Laud's predecessor, George Abbot, and they shared the firm attachment of the laity to the doctrines and liturgy of the traditional, pre-Laudian English church.

During the 1650s, new candidates for the ministry were examined by a committee of thirty-eight 'triers' which met regularly at London, while incumbent clergy who were suspected of inadequacy or immorality were called before local committees of 'ejectors'. None the less, as a result both of the tolerant religious outlook of successive Interregnum regimes and the temporary shortage of ordinands occasioned by the disruptions in the universities, many moderate Anglican clergy continued to occupy parochial livings throughout the Interregnum, and they were left relatively free to organize services as they saw fit. Many of the new recruits to the ministry also remained essentially conservative in outlook, and considerable numbers were ordained by the pre-war bishops, especially Robert Skinner of Oxford, who provided this service for considerable numbers of new Oxford graduates. It has recently been suggested that only one in four of the incumbent parish clergy of the 1650s exhibited clear Independent or Presbyterian allegiances. Ironically, another focus of support for those sympathetic to Anglicanism was provided by some of the lectureships attached to the London parishes, which had so recently been the favourite vehicles of the Puritans. The conservatism of the Interregnum clergy is further illustrated by the great popularity of the book *The Country Parson*, which was published in 1652. Written during the early 1630s by the Arminian cleric and poet, George Herbert, the work outlined a deeply conservative conception of the role and responsibilities of the rural clergyman. Despite, therefore, the pressure exerted upon them by the religious radicals who governed Interregnum England, a large majority of the parochial clergy retained a more traditional religious approach, and most were happy to see the return of the monarchy and Anglican church in 1660.

In the weeks immediately following the Restoration, many English parishes witnessed confrontations between their present ministers and previous incumbents who had been ejected during the course of the preceding twenty years. Charles II promptly referred this problem to the MPs of the Convention Parliament, and in September 1660 they passed an Act for the Settling of Ministers. This legislation restored the 700 or so surviving sequestered ministers to their original positions, but otherwise confirmed the 1660 holders in their posts, with the result that large numbers of the Interregnum clergy managed to retain their livings. The new king clearly wished to preside over the restoration of a broadly based church, and when vacancies occurred during the following months in livings to which the crown presented, he used the opportunity to add to the ranks of the parochial clergy some 600 individuals with widely differing theological and liturgical views. In the immediate aftermath of the Restoration, therefore, it appeared that the authorities wished to accommodate a wide range of opinion within the church, and would not enquire too deeply into the practices and attitudes of individual ministers.

These early signs, however, proved misleading, for during 1661 and 1662 a conservative backlash headed by the restored bishops and the MPs of the Cavalier Parliament began to gather steam. Despite his own liberal inclinations, in 1662 Charles was obliged to bow to episcopal and parliamentary pressure and give his assent to an Act of Uniformity which imposed a narrow doctrinal and liturgical test upon the whole body of the clergy. As a result of the passing of this measure, over 900 parish ministers were expelled or resigned; London lost one third of its beneficed clergy, and in' some counties, such as Leicestershire and Cheshire, three-quarters of parishes changed hands. Thirty years later, following the expulsion of James II and his replacement by William and Mary, another 400 clergymen were ejected as non-jurors for refusing to swear an oath of loyalty to the new joint monarchs. On both occasions, included among those who lost their positions were some of the most able and committed of the parish clergy. Their departure and the failure of the bishops to find adequate replacements certainly caused a temporary weakening of the church at the parochial level. In time, however, new ministers of comparable stature did come forward, and the quality of the lower clergy was not permanently damaged by these rounds of expulsions.

In terms of status and quality, therefore, the parochial clergy recovered relatively quickly from the disruptions of the mid-seventeenth century. However, because the restored ecclesiastical establishment failed to grasp the nettle of the great inequalities in the value of livings, the economic difficulties of the many poorer clergymen persisted down to 1700 and beyond. At the end of the seventeenth century, just over half of the livings in England and Wales were still worth less than £50, and roughly one-third less than £35. Dioceses that contained particularly large numbers of poor parishes included Norwich, Bath and Wells, York, Chester, Hereford, Carlisle, St David's, Llandaff, and Bangor. Significant progress towards the elimination of this widespread clerical poverty only began with the launching of Queen Anne's Bounty in 1704. Under this scheme, the crown and wealthy members of the laity and clergy contributed to a central fund out of which grants were made to needy clerics. During the course of the eighteenth century, £2.5 million was raised and over 6,000 individual grants dispersed. The clear success of the Bounty is shown by the reduction in the number of livings worth less than £50 from 5,600 in 1700 to only 1,000 in 1800.

Perhaps the most significant development with regard to the lower clergy in the second half of the seventeenth century was the forging of an extremely close alliance between the Anglican minister and his aristocratic and gentry neighbours. Landed society and the established church had both been taught a hard lesson during the 1640s and 1650s, and as a consequence had come to realize that their fortunes were interdependent and that in the future they would stand or fall together. They now saw that it was in their mutual interest to join together to oppose the forces which had created the mid-century crisis. As the lower clergy co-operated more and more closely with the gentry, they came to exercise increasing power within local society, and as an inevitable corollary became still further divorced from the needs and aspirations of the majority of their poorer parishioners. As one contemporary observed, the local clergyman was becoming 'the patriarch of his parish, its ruler, its doctor, its lawyer, its magistrate, as well as its teacher'. This new partnership between parson and squire was already well established by 1700, and it was to remain one of the quintessential features of English provincial life for the next two centuries.

NOTES

1 Christopher Haigh, 'Anticlericalism and the English Reformation', *History* 68 (1983).
2 Patrick Collinson, *The Religion of Protestants* (Oxford, 1982).
3 ibid.
4 Haigh, 'Anticlericalism and the English Reformation'.
5 Rosemary O'Day, *The English Clergy: The emergence and consolidation of a profession 1558–1642* (Leicester, 1979).
6 John Morrill, 'The church in England 1642–9', in John Morrill (ed.), *Reactions to the English Civil War 1642–9* (London, 1982).

SUGGESTIONS FOR FURTHER READING

A good survey of the clergy on the eve of the Reformation is P. Heath, *The English Parish Clergy on the Eve of the Reformation* (London, 1969), although, being written in pre-revisionist times, it tends to emphasize the failings of priests rather than their strengths. An indispensable local study is M. Bowker, *The Secular Clergy in the Diocese of Lincoln 1495–1520* (Cambridge, 1968). For the clergy's relations with the laity, see Susan Brigden, 'Tithe controversy in Reformation London', *Journal of Ecclesiastical History* 32 (1981); Ralph Houlbrooke, *Church Courts and the People during the English Reformation 1520–1570* (Oxford, 1979); and R. Wunderli, *London Church Courts and Society on the Eve of the Reformation* (Cambridge, Mass., 1981). Christopher Haigh's views on anticlericalism appear in 'Anticlericalism and the English Reformation', *History* 68 (1983).

Margaret Bowker has written two articles which throw light on the behaviour of the parish clergy during the Henrician Reformation: 'Lincolnshire

1536: heresy, schism or religious discontent?', in D. Baker (ed.), *Schism, Heresy and Religious Protest*, Studies in Church History, vol. 9 (Cambridge, 1972); and 'The Henrician Reformation and the parish clergy', *Bulletin of the Institute of Historical Research* 50 (1977).

Examples of the conservative practices of the parish clergy in Elizabeth's reign can be found in C. Haigh, 'The Church of England, the Catholics and the people', in C. Haigh (ed.), *The Reign of Elizabeth I* (London, 1984); and T. J. McCann, 'The clergy and the Elizabethan settlement in the diocese of Chichester', in M. J. Kitch (ed.), *Studies in Sussex Church History* (Brighton, 1981).

Local studies of the clergy during the Reformation period include J. I. Daeley, 'Pluralism in the diocese of Canterbury during the administration of Matthew Parker 1559–1575', *Journal of Ecclesiastical History* 18 (1967); J. F. Fuggles, 'The parish clergy in the archdeaconry of Leicester 1520–1540', *Transactions of the Leicestershire Archaeological and Historical Society* 46 (1970–1); F. Heal, 'The parish clergy and the Reformation in the diocese of Ely', *Proceedings of the Cambridge Antiquarian Society* 66 (1977); J. Goring, 'The reformation of the ministry in Elizabethan Sussex', *Journal of Ecclesiastical History* 34 (1983); and M. Zell, 'The personnel of the clergy in Kent in the Reformation period', *English Historical Review* 89 (1974).

The change in the status of the clergy in the late sixteenth and early seventeenth centuries is the subject of R. O'Day, *The English Clergy: The emergence and consolidation of a profession 1558–1642* (Leicester, 1979); and R. O'Day, 'The anatomy of a profession: the clergy of the Church of England', in W. Prest (ed.), *The Professions in Early Modern England* (London, 1987). O'Day discusses clerical education in 'The reformation of the ministry, 1558–1642', in R. O'Day and F. Heal (eds), *Continuity and Change: Personnel and administration of the church in England 1500–1642* (Leicester, 1976); and also in *Education and Society, 1500–1800: The social foundations of education in early modern Britain* (London, 1982). For the financial position of the parish clergy, see R. O'Day and F. Heal (eds), *Princes and Paupers in the English Church 1500–1800* (Leicester, 1981). Patrick Collinson considers the quality of the post-Reformation lower clergy in *The Religion of Protestants* (Oxford, 1982).

The effect of the rise of the Laudians on the parish clergy is dealt with by Nicholas Tyacke in *Anti-Calvinists: The rise of English Arminianism* c. *1590–1640* (Oxford, 1987). For the Feoffees for Impropriations, see Isabel M. Calder, *The Activities of the Puritan Faction in the Church of England, 1625–1633* (London, 1957). The problems of the parish clergy during the civil war are discussed in Clive Holmes (ed.), *The Suffolk Committees for Scandalous Ministers 1644–1646*, Suffolk Records Society Publications, vol. 13 (1970); I. M. Green, 'The persecution of "scandalous" and "malignant" parish clergy during the English civil war', *English Historical Review* 94 (1979); J. Morrill, 'The church in England 1642–9', in J. Morrill (ed.), *Reactions to the English Civil War 1642–9* (London, 1982); and J. Sharpe, 'Scandalous and malignant priests in Essex: the impact of grassroots Puritanism', in C. Jones, M. Newitt, and S. Roberts (eds), *Politics and People in Revolutionary England* (Oxford, 1986).

For the Restoration clergy, see R. S. Bosher, *The Making of the Restoration Settlement 1649–1662* (London, 1951); I. M. Green, *The Re-Establishment of the Church of England* (Oxford, 1978); and R. A. Beddard, 'The Restoration church', in J. R. Jones (ed.), *The Restored Monarchy* (London, 1979). For a lively and detailed picture of the everyday life of a seventeenth-century parish clergyman, see Alan Macfarlane (ed.), *The Diary of Ralph Josselin 1616–1683* (London, 1976).

9 The religious orders and society

On the eve of the Reformation there were nearly 900 religious communities in England and Wales, containing between them some 12,000 men and women who had taken monastic vows. In many houses the numbers had been growing steadily, if not spectacularly, during the late fifteenth century. The new recruits tended, however, to come from yeoman families who saw a monastic career as a means of social advancement for sons, rather than, as earlier in the medieval period, from those within the ranks of the gentry and aristocracy who had been attracted to the monastic ideal either for its own sake, or as a means for younger sons to preserve an elevated social status. By the early sixteenth century the monasteries had to a great extent departed from their original purpose and function. In many of the larger houses, the monks were neglecting their liturgical duties for the secular tasks of estate management, while in the smaller houses they were often prevented from carrying out their spiritual obligations by inadequate resources. Almost everywhere, strict observance to the monastic rule had been relaxed, with the result that few late fifteenth- and early sixteenth-century monks lived the life of austerity and self-denial laid down by their founders. Only relatively few orders – the Observant Franciscans and the new foundations of the Carthusians, and the Bridgettines at Syon – retained their religious fervour and internal discipline.

At the same time as monasticism was losing its role as a model of the purest form of Christianity, it was also failing to make any significant contribution to contemporary religious and social life. The spiritual needs of the laity were now largely met by the secular clergy: chaplains in pious landed households, curates, incumbents, and chantry priests in parishes. Although the monasteries were still recognized as centres of scholarship, they no longer produced intellectual giants with an international reputation, and the schools they provided for children faced competition from those run by the secular clergy and laity. Only in the fields of charity and hospitality were the monks still fulfilling a useful purpose, yet even here it is questionable whether they were meeting the real needs of their contemporaries. During the early sixteenth century, *ad hoc* provision for the poor in the form of doles and individual pensions was coming under attack from members of the laity, who argued for the introduction of a more organized system of relief which would discourage begging and benefit only the deserving poor. As a direct result of this general decline in standards and service, although there was little open hostility to English monasticism on the eve of the Reformation, there was also little real commitment to it; while a great many wills from the early sixteenth century left endowments to the secular clergy and their parochial churches, only a minority of testators gave bequests to the regular clergy.

Some significant reform of the English monasteries had taken place during the half-century preceding Henry VIII's dissolutions; in particular, a number of decaying religious communities had been dissolved by bishops prior to 1530. These earlier dissolutions, however, differed from those of Henry VIII in several fundamental respects. Whereas the pre-Reformation dissolutions were usually initiated by a bishop and were carried out with the permission of the founder or patron as well as that of the king and pope, the later dissolutions were solely the work of the king in parliament and any objections from patrons were simply swept aside. More importantly, the pre-Reformation dissolutions had normally involved a redistribution of ecclesiastical assets within the church – a transfer of endowments from a decaying monastery to a collegiate church or academic college – with the result that the church suffered no overall loss of resources. When Bishop Fisher of Rochester dissolved the decaying nunneries of Bromhall in Berkshire and Higham in Kent, he allocated the proceeds to St John's College, Cambridge; similarly, Cardinal Thomas Wolsey's closure of twenty-nine monasteries between 1524 and 1529 had financed the building of Cardinal College, Oxford, and a school at Ipswich. In contrast, although some of the revenue from the Henrician dissolutions was used for ecclesiastical and educational purposes, most ended up in the royal coffers. The clearest distinction of all, however, was that while the earlier dissolutions were selective and aimed at bringing about reform, the governmental initiatives of the 1530s represented a frontal assault on the whole idea of monasticism and were to lead to its rapid extinction.

Henry's dissolutions were carried out under the direction of Thomas

Cromwell, vicar-general of the new English church. Cromwell was undoubtedly hostile towards the regular clergy and shared in the humanist desire for monastic reform, but his main purpose in promoting the dissolutions of 1536 was less the reform of the church than the strengthening of the monarchy. Although the preamble to the 1536 Act stated that the smaller houses were being suppressed to encourage the development of a more streamlined and better disciplined monasticism, this was mere propaganda, for there was no attempt to impose stricter order upon the surviving houses and very little reform ensued. Cromwell's true intentions are to be found not in the Act's preamble but rather in an anonymous document dating from the autumn of 1534 which was discovered among his private papers; this recommended that the church be disendowed 'for an increase and augmentation of the king's most royal estate and for the defence of the realm'. Similarly, Henry VIII, who was much influenced by theories of imperial kingship, had as early as 1533 expressed his intention to 'reunite to the Crown the goods which churchmen held of it, which his predecessors could not alienate to his prejudice'. Although he was subsequently to reject proposals for a wholesale disendowment of the church, both he and Thomas Cromwell were clearly attracted to the idea of a limited confiscation of ecclesiastical property to augment the crown's income and power.

That the government set its sights on monastic wealth, rather than episcopal or chantry lands, was partly due to Cromwell's personal hostility to the religious orders and partly because of the precedent of the earlier dissolutions. Furthermore, the monasteries' foreign links increased their vulnerability to royal attack, for the allegiance owed by the English priories to parent houses on the continent was seen as both incompatible with the royal supremacy and a potential threat to the security of the realm. This was especially so once the Franciscan Observants, the London Carthusians, and the Bridgettines at Syon had demonstrated their opposition to the break with Rome by refusing to subscribe to the oath of supremacy.

The campaign against the lesser monasteries began in 1535 with the compilation of a survey of ecclesiastical property for taxation purposes. This survey, the *Valor Ecclesiasticus*, provided the government with detailed information about the number and location of the religious houses, and the value of their revenues. A few months after its completion, Cromwell used his powers as vicar-general to appoint commissioners to carry out a visitation of the monasteries, and his six visitors began their investigations in September 1535, armed with a questionnaire containing eighty-six articles of inquiry and twenty-five articles of injunction. These men carried out their task in record time, and their report, the *Comperta*, was brought before parliament within six months. Even so, the Dissolution Bill had by then already been drafted, and the contents of the report did little more than provide further justification for a government which had already decided to dissolve the smaller houses. The overriding importance of the financial incentive behind the 1536 Act can be clearly seen in the purely monetary distinction – a net annual income of £200 per annum – which separated the smaller houses to be dissolved from the larger ones which were allowed to remain. The king's pecuniary purpose is also revealed by his decision to reprieve about seventy houses on the payment of a fee. However, the fact that, in addition to allowing these exemptions, the government also permitted a number of monastic refoundations, suggests that at this stage Henry and Cromwell did not envisage the complete eradication of monasticism, but rather intended to siphon off a considerable amount of ecclesiastical wealth while leaving the church with a limited number of monastic endowments.

The enactment of the 1536 Bill was followed by an eighteen-month hiatus during which no further measures were taken against the 202 larger houses which remained. In December 1537, however, the great priory at Lewes in Sussex was induced to surrender its property to the king, and over the next two years the remaining houses followed suit by offering themselves for dissolution and transferring their lands to the king. A few heads of houses refused to comply, most notably the abbots of Colchester, Reading, and Glastonbury, who were executed for treason, and a number of abbesses, who were treated more leniently. The last house to go was Waltham Abbey in Essex which capitulated in March 1540. The second Act of Dissolution passed in 1539 merely, therefore, confirmed the surrender of most of the larger houses and authorized the king to seize the assets of any of the remainder which 'heretofore shall happen to be dissolved'. Once again, it was Henry's financial needs that had provided the primary impetus for the confiscations, since the threatened invasion of England by the Emperor Charles V and the French king, Francis I, on behalf of the pope, had necessitated heavy governmental expenditure on fortifications and defence.

The dissolutions have long been lamented, particularly by scholars and connoisseurs of the arts. The architectural loss of fine medieval buildings was immense, for a third of the houses disappeared without trace and another third were left in ruins. Many important examples of medieval craftsmanship were destroyed as a result of the seizure and melting down of monastic plate, of which there are virtually no surviving examples. Although Henry and his agent, John Leland, made concerted efforts to rescue the manuscript collections of the monasteries for the royal archives, all the manuscripts of many smaller houses and substantial parts of the collections of the larger houses were also destroyed, lost, or dispersed. To those today with a keen appreciation of the importance of the nation's heritage, the Henrician dissolutions appear a deplorable act of state vandalism, and a similar view was clearly held by some contemporaries; when explaining to the authorities why he had taken up arms in defence of the monasteries, Robert Aske, one of the leaders of the Pilgrimage of Grace, declared: 'the abbeys was one of the beauties of the realm, to all men and strangers passing through the same.'

In other respects the loss of the monasteries was generally less catastrophic in effect, although for some contemporaries their closure did prove particularly traumatic. Most directly affected, of course, were those who lived and worked in the dissolved houses. While many of the abbots and priors received generous pensions and soon obtained substantial alternative livings, the majority of the displaced monks found themselves without homes and employment, and despite the slump in ordinations after 1535, less than half of them were subsequently absorbed into the ranks of the secular clergy. The average pension awarded to an ex-religious was £5 10s a year – barely a subsistence wage – and many received even less. Worst affected were the nuns and friars. Eighty-eight per cent of the nuns in the diocese of Lincoln received less than £5 a year, and 60 per cent less than £2, clearly an insufficient amount to live on. The friars were numbered among the 1,000 or so ex-religious who were left totally unpensioned. In personal terms, therefore, there were undoubtedly many cases of great hardship. None the less, the overall social impact of the appearance of this new group of poor was negligible. As somewhere between a third and a half of the English population were already living on or below the poverty line during the early sixteenth century, the addition of the unpensioned ex-religious to their number made relatively little difference. Nor did the plight of the lay poor markedly deteriorate as a result of the disappearance of monastic charity, for private philanthropy, communal urban initiatives, and state legislation all helped to fill the void. Many individuals continued to leave bequests to the poor in their wills, and from Edward VI's reign onwards contributions towards doles for the poor were regularly collected in parish churches. In addition, towns such as Ipswich and London constructed almshouses and hospitals for the needy, and provided free or heavily subsidized grain rations in times of dearth.

Similarly, any adverse effect that the dissolutions had on education was very limited. The loss of monastic schools was not a major setback to educational provision, since other schools had existed alongside them in the pre-Reformation period, and royal grammar schools took over the functions of monastic cathedral schools at Canterbury, Carlisle, Ely, Norwich, Rochester, and Worcester. Indeed, to some extent education, and in particular the two universities, benefited from the seizure of monastic wealth. The revenues from ex-monastic property were used to endow Christ Church, Oxford, with £2,200 per annum, and Trinity College, Cambridge, with £1,640 per annum; they also helped to fund new Regius professorships at Oxford and Cambridge and to maintain students and readers in divinity at both universities.

Although the deleterious effects of the loss of the monasteries on charity and education should not, therefore, be exaggerated, it none the less remains true that the dissolutions represented a lost opportunity for reform of the church. Despite promising to do so, Henry entirely failed to redirect the 'redundant' monastic resources to other areas in the church; only sixteen monastic buildings continued to be used for ecclesiastical purposes, two being refounded as shortlived collegiate churches and the other fourteen as secular cathedrals. Of these fourteen, only six became the seats of newly created dioceses (Bristol, Chester, Gloucester, Oxford, Peterborough, and Westminster), and the income diverted to them was barely adequate for their bishops to fulfil their tasks of imposing conformity and encouraging reform. The diocese of Chester, for example, was assessed for tax purposes as having an income of only £420 1s 8d per annum and, as Christopher Haigh[1] has commented, its bishop 'remained solvent only by abdicating from the real government of the diocese'. As a consequence, the English church continued to contain both a great many over-large dioceses and a small number of underendowed ones. In the same way, all proposals to employ monastic wealth for educational and social purposes, such as the endowment of preachers, schools, hospitals, and humanist studies, were rejected in the face of the pressing financial needs of the crown.

Altogether the dissolutions brought to the crown lands valued at some £132,000 per annum, but the possibilities presented by this huge windfall were largely wasted. Had he retained his new lands and managed them wisely, Henry might have laid the economic foundations which would have allowed his successors to build an absolutist monarchy in England. In the event, however, the opportunity was missed, for large amounts of land soon passed from the king to the laity. Although relatively little property was simply given away to favoured courtiers, Henry's decision to go to war after 1540 forced him to sell many estates and thus to dissipate much of his new-found wealth. By 1547, some two-thirds of the land had been alienated, with the crown raising about £80,000 from the sales. By 1558, the proportion had increased to three-quarters, and Cromwell's dream of making the crown financially independent had failed to materialize. Even with this huge increase in cash reserves, the financial needs of the crown were not satisfied. During the 1540s, Henry started to nibble away at the assets of some other ecclesiastical institutions, including the secular colleges, the religious guilds, and the chantries, and under his successor, Edward, their resources too were totally swallowed up by the crown.

Although the dissolutions and the subsequent royal sales of ex-monastic lands did lead to some redistribution of landed wealth, they did not, as some historians once thought, either revolutionize the pattern of landownership among the laity or create a new class of property owners. Regional studies have found that the monastic lands were generally purchased by families who already owned property in the locality, and that when lands were bought by outsiders, in most cases the purchasers were already established within the ranks of the gentry in other parts of the country. In Devon, for example, less than 10 per cent of the available land was purchased by outsiders, and there, as in Cornwall, Norfolk, Yorkshire, and most other parts of the country, the general result of the dissolutions was the enlargement of pre-existing, moderate gentry estates. As a consequence, the sales of monastic land had the overall effect of reinforcing the social structure by strengthening the position of the existing landed classes.

Along with their lands, the new owners of monastic property also acquired the tithes which had previously been paid to the monks, and often a number of advowsons (the right to present clergymen to parochial livings), which had formerly been under the control of the monasteries. In the diocese of Canterbury, for example, the laity's share of presentations jumped from 16 per cent in 1534 to 38 per cent in the period 1540 to 1553. Only in London did the church itself benefit from the redistribution of advowsons. The fact that a number of monasteries had been selling rights of presentation to laymen in the period leading up to the dissolutions may have led some contemporaries to conclude that the effects of the transfer of patronage during the middle decades of the sixteenth century would not be particularly momentous. In reality, however, lay impropriation of both tithes and advowsons did significantly reduce the authority of the higher clergy at the parochial level, and greatly extend the influence of the laity over the late sixteenth- and early seventeenth-century church.

Considering the marked shifts in wealth, power, and patronage, which resulted from the dissolutions, their long-term political impact was surprisingly limited. The redistribution of lands in favour of the laity, and particularly the gentry, has in the past been viewed by some historians as a social change of the most fundamental importance, and even as the underlying cause of the English civil war of the 1640s. Few, however, would now attribute such significance to any 'rise of the gentry', for the increase in the numbers of gentry did not amount to the rise of a new social class and was certainly not accompanied by a corresponding growth in the power and political assertiveness of the House of Commons. The removal of the twenty-nine abbots from the House of Lords did end the majority of the spiritual lords in the Upper House, but the resulting ascendancy of the laity had little practical impact upon parliamentary business or relations with the crown. The regulars had had a poor attendance record before the dissolutions and their presence was thus not greatly missed. The clerical majority in the Lords had not stopped Henry gaining parliamentary sanction for the break with Rome; nor did the removal of the abbots prevent the Lords from putting up fierce resistance to Elizabeth's religious settlement in 1559.

Although the great majority of the English laity had in no way suffered from the loss of the monasteries and some members of the landed classes had positively benefited, there is no evidence of any popular enthusiasm for the dissolutions. Closure does not appear to have been accompanied by any mass looting of the monastic buildings or mob violence against their former inmates. On the contrary, most recorded episodes of violence were directed against the commissioners who arrived to shut down the religious houses. In Exeter, one commissioner broke a rib after leaping from a tower to escape a group of women armed with shovels, pikes, and stones; at Hexham, two commissioners were confronted by 'many persons assembled with bills, halberds, and other defenceable weapons, ready standing in the street, like men ready to defend a town of war'. In addition, many of the rebels who took up arms during the Pilgrimage of Grace wished 'to have the monasteries [which have been] suppressed to be restored unto theyr howses, land and goodes'. Not all opponents of the dissolutions resorted to such violence. Some individuals petitioned men at court to use their influence in an attempt to save their local monastic houses; the Earl of Shrewsbury, for example, begged one of the king's gentleman-ushers to intervene on behalf of 'the poor house of Wormsley . . . which is of my foundation', where most of his ancestors lay buried. Yet, some of these same laymen who pleaded in 1536 for the preservation of specific houses, subsequently participated eagerly enough in their plunder. Once it became clear that there was to be a general division of monastic spoils, men like Shrewsbury joined in petitioning the king for a grant of property. Nor was it only the lands themselves which were up for grabs, for the stonework, stained glass, and lead from the medieval buildings were often incorporated into the new secular residences constructed by the lay heirs of the monks.

Unsurprisingly, those who had acquired monastic property during the later years of Henry's reign were extremely unwilling to return it to the church after the accession of his Catholic daughter, Mary. As a result of their blanket refusal to contemplate the surrender of these lands, Mary and Cardinal Pole were forced to negotiate a reconciliation with the pope, which allowed for the continued alienation of the ecclesiastical property. The eventual agreement did not, however, leave the laity with an absolute legal title to the lands, but merely allowed them possession by right of a papal dispensation which might be revoked in the future. Mary herself refounded several monastic houses, but her endowments were not generous; her subjects meanwhile entirely failed to follow her lead. By the summer of 1557, only six houses had been re-established, four for men and two for women, and there was no rush of recruits to take up residence within their walls, the total number of religious not rising beyond 100. Nor was there any attempt to introduce into England any of the new religious orders which were doing so much to revitalize Catholic religious life on the continent; on the contrary, Cardinal Pole specifically rejected an offer of help from the founder of the Jesuits, Ignatius Loyola.

With Mary's death, the attempt to revive English monasticism was stillborn. None the less, for a number of English men and women, Catholic and Protestant alike, the monastic ideal was to continue to exercise a strong hold on the imagination for many years after the dissolutions. Its appeal for the English Catholic community remained especially strong. From the 1590s onwards a steady stream of recusants and converts entered monasteries on the continent, some of them rising to prominent positions; Walter Montagu, for example, brother of the parliamentary general, Edward Montagu, Earl of Manchester, was abbot of the monastery at Pontoise in France during the 1640s. Others preferred to found or enter English houses on the continent. During the early seventeenth century the number of English monastic communities in Europe grew rapidly, from fewer than ten in 1600 to almost 100 in the 1660s. The English recusant community also continued to harbour ambitions of taking back the pre-Reformation sites of the dissolved English monasteries. For this reason, throughout the seventeenth century the English Benedictines continued to grant senior monks honorific titles such as Abbot of Westminster, Abbot of St Alban's, Prior of Durham, and Cathedral Prior of Norwich. The Franciscans actually acquired the sites of some medieval friaries, as well as old Catholic shrines such as Osmotherley in Yorkshire and the Holy Well in Wales. During the late 1680s, the succession of a Catholic king, James II, once again led to fresh hopes of a re-establishment of English monasticism. The English religious orders returned home to acquire premises, start up schools, and practise their missions openly, and rumours soon spread that the Jesuits were planning to annex St Alban's and a number of other medieval monastic sites. In the event, Catholic hopes of a restoration of the monasteries were once again to be disappointed, for before any significant moves could be put in motion, James was expelled in 1688.

The monastic ideal also had a deep appeal for some seventeenth-century English Protestants, particularly those who adhered to Arminianism. In the 1620s, the Arminian Nicholas Ferrar, a member of a wealthy London merchant family and a friend of the poet George Herbert, abandoned his commercial activities and founded a lay monastic community for his family at Little Gidding near Huntingdon. After acquiring the manor house at Little Gidding in 1624, Ferrar and his mother quickly set about repairing the ruined parish church, and in 1626 Nicholas was ordained a deacon by William Laud. Soon afterwards, Ferrar's brother and sister and their families joined him at Little Gidding, thereby increasing the size of the community to about thirty. Over the next twenty years, the Ferrars led a life of discipline and austerity; they said prayers every hour of the day, chanted matins and evensong in the church, recited the whole of the psalter through the night, and observed regular fasts and vigils. Family members also visited the sick of the local community and catechized the village children. In addition to these devotional and pastoral activities, the community engaged in bookbinding and manuscript illumination. The members of the community clearly gained great spiritual satisfaction from their monastic regime. Ferrar explained to one visitor to Little Gidding that they had previously 'found diverse perplexities, distractions and almost utter ruin in their callings', and that 'if others knew what comfort God had ministered to them since their sequestration, they might take the like course'.

While many English Calvinists were, of course, profoundly suspicious of this 'protestant nunnery', most of those who experienced the community at first hand were impressed by its order and tranquillity. Bishop John Williams of Lincoln, who visited Little Gidding in 1633, could find nothing to object to, and another visitor remarked: 'I find them full of humanity and humility.' Charles I was a particularly keen admirer of the Little Gidding community, which he visited on several occasions; during a hurried visit in 1642, he is reputed to have remarked: 'I did not think to have seen a thing in this kind that so well pleaseth me. God's blessings upon the founders of it.' After Nicholas Ferrar's death in 1637, the community continued under the direction of his brother John and son Nicholas, but in 1647 following the parliamentary victory in the civil war, it was broken up, and the church and manor house were ransacked by parliamentary soldiers. Although Ferrar had at no time attempted to found an order or engage in any missionary work, the story of his community at Little Gidding illustrates the enduring attachment of some in post-Reformation England to the idea of monastic withdrawal from the world.

During the later seventeenth century, further evidence of a continuing interest in the English monastic past can be seen in the academic researches of several of the period's most prominent scholars. During the 1640s and 1650s, a group of antiquarians, including William Dugdale, Henry Spelman, and Roger Dodsworth, brought together a mass of original documentation relating to the Benedictine, Cluniac, Cisterian, and Carthusian monasteries of medieval England. These were subsequently published as the *Monasticon Anglicorum*, the first part of which appeared in 1655. In 1691, the young clergyman Henry Wharton published a large-scale study of the pre-Reformation church under the title *Anglia Sacra*, devoting the first volume to the study of the 'cathedral churches possessed at one time by monks'. Several years later, in 1695, Thomas Tanner published *Notitia Monastica*, which as the subtitle explained, consisted of a 'short history of the foundation and chief revolutions of all our religious houses'. This academic interest in the history of English monasticism did not, however, meet with universal approval. Some saw the publication of the *Monasticon* as an attempt to popularize Catholicism, and Wharton later became involved in a fierce controversy with Bishop Gilbert Burnet, who was led to declare at one point: 'the barbarous style, the mixture of so much fable, the great want of judgement that runs thro' the writings of the Monks, have so disgusted me at their works that I confess I could never bring myself to read them with pleasure.' Unfortunately for medieval scholarship, eighteenth-century opinion tended to share Burnet's outlook. The Age of Reason was to turn its enlightened back on the monasteries and universally to despise them as the institutions most closely associated with the obscurantism, superstition, and ritual of popery.

NOTE

1 Christopher Haigh, 'Finance and administration in a new diocese: Chester 1541–1641', in Rosemary O'Day and Felicity Heal (eds), *Continuity and Change: the personnel and administration of the church in England 1500–1642* (Leicester, 1976).

SUGGESTIONS FOR FURTHER READING

The fullest account of the dissolutions of the monasteries is M. D. Knowles, *The Religious Orders in England*. Vol. III: *The Tudor Age* (Cambridge, 1959). Some useful documents, along with a valuable introduction which concentrates on the legal aspects of the dissolutions, are contained in J. Youings, *The Dissolution of the Monasteries* (London, 1971).

Henry VIII's intentions are further explored in E. Hallam, 'Henry VIII's monastic refoundations of 1536–7', *Bulletin of the Institute of Historical Research* 51 (1978). C. Kitching, 'The disposal of monastic and chantry lands', in F. Heal and R. O'Day (eds), *Church and Society in England: Henry VIII to James I* (London, 1977) provides a useful summary of research into the new lay property owners. Regional examples of the effects on ecclesiastical patronage can be found in M. Zell, 'The personnel of the clergy in Kent in the Reformation period', *English Historical Review* 89 (1974); and M. Bowker, *The Henrician Reformation in the Diocese of Lincoln under John Longland, 1521–1547* (Cambridge, 1981). For the financial problems of the new dioceses, see C. Haigh, 'Finance and administration in a new diocese: Chester, 1541–1641', in R. O'Day and F. Heal (eds), *Continuity and Change: The personnel and administration of the church in England 1500–1642* (Leicester, 1976).

Popular reactions to the dissolutions are discusssed in J. J. Scarisbrick, *The Reformation and the English People* (Oxford, 1984); and C. Haigh, *The Last Days of the Lancashire Monasteries and the Pilgrimage of Grace* (Manchester, 1969). For Mary's attempted restoration, see D. M. Loades, *The Reign of Mary Tudor* (London, 1979).

For the importance of monasticism to the Catholic community in the seventeenth century, see J. C. H. Aveling, *The Handle and the Axe* (London, 1976). The Little Gidding experiment is the subject of G. P. Peckard, *The Life of Nicholas Ferrar* (London, 1852). Seventeenth-century antiquarian interest in monasticism is discussed in D. Douglas, *English Scholars 1660–1730* (London, 1951).

10   The church and social control

The Christian church had assumed the role of regulator of the moral behaviour of the English laity centuries before the Reformation, and by the early sixteenth century it was exercising this social influence chiefly through three formal mechanisms: the sacrament of penance (confession), the ecclesiastical courts, and the sermons and homilies delivered by the clergy. All combined a private and public function. Although not yet carried out in secret, the confession of sins, which was required at least once a year during the Easter period, was essentially a private matter, concerned with the individual sinner's spiritual well-being and requiring a personal examination of conscience as a condition of absolution. At the same time, however, the sacrament had the public function of reconciling well-known sinners to the parish community, and its crucial importance in the imposition and maintenance of communal ethics is now widely acknowledged by historians. While the church courts dealt with individual cases of immorality, they also enforced a practical and social code of Christian conduct and endeavoured to resolve disputes within communities. Among their penalties was public penance, a ritual of personal repentance and public reconciliation of the sinner with his local community, which was designed both to deter others from sin and give satisfaction to the congregation that the wrong-doing of one of its members had been punished. Similarly, the sermons and homilies that the clergy delivered from their pulpits addressed both private and public concerns.

As a procedure that has left no written records, the study of auricular confession poses particular problems for historians, but since it was condemned by all but the most conservative of English Protestants, it had anyway ceased to play any significant part in the lives of the laity by the middle of the sixteenth century. Conversely, the church courts survived the Reformation and the pulpit flourished within the new Protestant environment. As most of the courts kept meticulous and detailed records, and as a great many sixteenth- and seventeenth-century sermons have survived in published form, there are fewer obstacles to the investigation of their social impact.

Although it had not been entirely without disciplinary influence in the pre-Reformation period, the role of the sermon as a regulator of social conduct was to be considerably enhanced by the emergence of an English Protestant church which laid great stress on the importance of preaching. Some of the new Protestant clergy undoubtedly exercised considerable influence over the social attitudes of their congregations. As the pulpit offered the only regular instruction available to the large numbers of illiterate English men and women, it was potentially one of the most powerful teaching mediums within Elizabethan and seventeenth-century England. The need for the laity to conform to the orthodox moral code and accepted social norms of the day was a constant theme of homilies and sermons, and many believed them to be very effective in helping to maintain the social order. The MP Sir John Eliot, for example, commented in the early seventeenth century that 'Religion is that which keeps the subject in obedience'; and, explaining his reluctance to surrender control of the established church to his parliamentarian enemies, Charles I later declared that 'the people are governed by the pulpit more than the sword in time of peace'. Care must be taken, however, not to exaggerate the influence of these sermons and homilies, for lay men and women frequently ignored or defied clerical advice; thus, while homily after homily read by the Elizabethan clergy denounced wife-beating, the court records reveal a number of brutal incidents of wife abuse.

During the post-Reformation period, the church exerted further influence over the literate section of the population through the publication by individual churchmen of their sermons, catechisms, and a number of highly influential books which contained both the basics of orthodox theology and a great deal of practical advice on questions of moral and domestic conduct. In the course of Elizabeth's reign, around 100 catechisms and over 130 sermons were printed, prescribing correct Christian behaviour on matters ranging from everyday dress to sexual propriety. During the half-century which preceded the civil war, books such as Arthur Dent's *The Plain Man's Path-Way to Heaven*, Stephen Egerton's *A Brief Method of Catechizing*, John Dod and Robert Cleaver's *A Plain and Familiar Exposition of the Ten Commandments*, and William Gouge's *Of Domesticall Duties* proved extremely popular and played a major role in the shaping of individual attitudes and conduct. Even during the revolutionary years of the civil war and Interregnum, the traditional social and moral code continued to be championed by conservative clerics such as Henry Hammond, Robert Sanderson, and Jeremy Taylor. In 1645, Hammond published a *Practical Catechism* aimed specifically at a popular audience, and in 1652 he followed this with *A Letter of Resolution to Six Queries of Present Use in the Church of England*, a spirited defence of traditional Anglican doctrinal and liturgical practice. Fourteen of Sanderson's popular sermons were published in 1657, and the following year saw the appearance of another hugely influential work, *The Whole Duty of Man*, probably written by Richard Allestree, who was later one of Charles II's chaplains and professor of divinity at Oxford. Perhaps most widely read of all, however, were *Eikon Basilike*, which contained the last prayers and meditations of the martyred Charles I, and Jeremy Taylor's two major works, *Holy Living* and *Holy Dying*. By emphasizing the need for a return to traditional political, social, and religious values, these books did much to undermine the regimes of the Interregnum and bring about the return of the monarchy in 1660. Many of them, in particular *Holy Living* and *The Whole Duty of Man*, retained their popularity throughout the remainder of the seventeenth century.

The second and more institutionalized vehicle for moral regulation was the church courts. During the late medieval period, these tribunals had concerned themselves with three types of business: instance cases, which were suits between parties rather like civil litigation in the secular courts; *ex officio* or office cases, which were disciplinary prosecutions of wrong-doers initiated by the ecclesiastical authorities; and record business, which dealt mainly with probate (the proving and administering of wills). Appeals against decisions in the local archdeacons' and bishops' courts could be made to higher courts in England and ultimately to the papal court or Rota at Rome, although only the most wealthy could afford to take matters this far.

During 1529 and the early 1530s, this system of ecclesiastical justice came under heavy fire from the members of Henry VIII's Reformation Parliament. Numerous MPs complained in 1529 of the high costs and inefficiencies of probate, and three years later a general attack on ecclesiastical jurisdiction was included in their 'Supplication against the Ordinaries'. Whether or not the specific criticisms listed by the MPs were justified has recently been a matter of debate among historians. From her study of the diocese of Lincoln, Margaret Bowker[1] has argued that most of the complaints contained in the 'Supplication' were in fact unfair. In her view, the hostility of the Commons to the courts was aroused not by the stated reasons of their high costs or lengthy procedures, but rather as a direct result of their efficiency in confiscating the property of convicted heretics. The researches of some other historians, however, have revealed that in a few dioceses, such as Canterbury, the courts were charging what could be considered excessive fees, and that in some major urban centres, especially London, they may have been disappointing the more wealthy and respectable sections of society by their failure to deal adequately with pimps, prostitutes, and other hardened criminals. On balance, however, it seems likely that the parliamentary assault on the courts did not reflect a general dislike of their existence or procedures, but was inspired in the main by particular interest groups with a specific axe to grind. Foremost among these were the common lawyers, who resented the ecclesiastical courts as rivals for business; it was indeed one of their number, Christopher St German, who led the literary attack upon the ecclesiastical courts, arguing in a number of tracts that their jurisdiction should be limited to 'mere spiritual things'.

Because of the hostility of the lawyers, MPs, and others, there was some doubt during the 1530s as to whether the church courts would survive. Thomas Cromwell had given serious consideration to proposals to abolish a separate spiritual jurisdiction, or at the very least to prohibit all *ex officio* cases except those involving accusations of heresy. The study of canon law at the universities had also been forbidden in 1535, leaving ecclesiastical lawyers unsure of the status of their proceedings. Consequently, the number of *ex officio* and instance cases going through the courts declined dramatically during the middle decades of the sixteenth century, as plaintiffs became reluctant to take their disputes to courts that might soon be abolished, and demoralized diocesan officials curtailed the amount of business they were prepared to handle. In the diocese of Chichester, for example, Bishop Sherburne's ecclesiastical officers cut back on the number of *ex officio* prosecutions and held fewer court sessions; the consistory court met forty-five times in 1524, but only twenty-three times in 1536. As late as the 1550s the amount of office business in the courts remained below their pre-Reformation levels.

At the same time, a number of diocesan courts appear to have been operating less efficiently. In Norwich, for example, the administration of probate was a cause for concern, as wills were sometimes being approved too hastily without sufficient inquiry into possible fraud. This may well have been the main cause of the noticeable increase in testamentary suits, from an average of twelve every year in the mid-1530s to twenty-nine every year in the early 1550s. Similarly, in the Prerogative Court of Canterbury, there were so many contemporary criticisms of the slack administration of probate that a new set of regulations had to be introduced in 1587. Nor were instance and office cases always handled satisfactorily during these middle decades of the century. In the 1520s, most office cases in the diocese of Chichester had been completed within one session, but by the 1560s many were spreading into two or more. Bishop Parkhurst's diocese of Norwich saw a similar prolongation of cases. Contemporary accusations that such delays were deliberate – 'a point of cunning', for material gain – were not without some foundation; Elizabethan prelates, who had received little if any training in canon law themselves, frequently allowed a free rein to entrenched court personnel who had a vested interest in prolonging cases and encouraging litigation, especially in the lucrative areas of probate and instance business.

As time went on, however, the courts in most dioceses gradually began to recover from the doldrums of the mid-sixteenth century, and were once again able to employ officials who were at least moderately capable and honest. By the end of the century efficiency had certainly improved markedly from the low point of the mid-century, and recent detailed studies of the work of the courts in the dioceses of York and Canterbury and the archdeaconries of Essex, Wiltshire, and Salisbury during the later Elizabethan and early Stuart periods, have revealed a level of efficiency and probity which was certainly no worse than that of most other contemporary institutions. Furthermore, from the 1570s onwards the number of ecclesiastical suits grew rapidly, a trend largely attributable to the dramatic rise in the number of cases of alleged defamation, as those involved in incidents of slander and name-calling became increasingly anxious to protect their reputations by publicly clearing themselves in the courts. In 1561, only one defamation case had been heard in the consistory court of York, but by the 1580s such suits were very common, and during the period from 1580 to 1640 they regularly constituted nearly half of the court's business. A large number of these cases involved sexual defamation – accusations of loose living, or the labelling of a woman as a whore or harlot. Women appear to have been sexually defamed far more often than men, and even in those cases where husbands were being defamed as cuckolds, the reputation of their wives was of course under attack too.

The courts were also more active during the late sixteenth and early seventeenth centuries in the hearing of *ex officio* cases, the great majority of which also involved alleged sexual misconduct. Accusations of fornication, adultery, and extra-marital pregnancy were all heard before the church courts, although the particularly grave sexual offence of buggery, which was by now considered a felony, was dealt with by the secular courts. As well as damaging the spiritual and moral health of the individual, these sexual sins could lead to strife within the local community, and on occasions provoke bitter quarrels and violence between neighbours. They also frequently resulted in the birth of bastard children who became a financial charge upon the parish. The second half of the sixteenth century saw an extremely high number of sexual cases coming before the courts, a trend which no doubt reflected the increase in illegitimacy during the later part of Elizabeth's reign. As illicit sexual activity was much more difficult to hide once it had resulted in conception, it was often the discovery that an unmarried woman was pregnant that led to her appearance before the courts. For the same reason it was women who most frequently received the punishment for any sexual indiscretions, especially as a large proportion of their male partners tended to flee the avenging parish. It has been estimated that in Essex alone nearly 10,000 people were summoned to appear on sexual charges during Elizabeth's reign, and as the records of the archdeacon's court are incomplete, the actual figure could be considerably higher. It is not surprising, therefore, that the tribunals were known colloquially as 'the bawdy courts'. None the less, those incidents that were brought to the attention of the ecclesiastical courts were probably merely the visible tip of a large iceberg of undetected extra-marital copulation, for there is no evidence that the church was ever able to inflict an effective reign of moral terror on the English people, or to restrict to any significant degree the general freedom of most individuals to enjoy the company of the opposite sex.

Attitudes towards the sin of fornication were complicated by the widespread prevalence of the phenomenon of pre-nuptial pregnancy. During the sixteenth and seventeenth centuries, it was very common for couples who intended to marry to indulge in sexual intercourse prior to the solemnization of their union, and as a result large numbers of brides arrived at the altar pregnant. Many other women were impregnated by men who had promised to marry them, but who subsequently abandoned them. Although the church courts extended little sympathy to this latter group of unfortunate women, they did often display a lenient attitude towards a pregnant woman who was about to be married. A significant change in attitudes appears to have occurred, however, in the early 1620s, when churchwardens in many areas began to present increasing numbers of women for pre-nuptial pregnancy, and the courts began to hand out stiffer penalties for the offence. Some historians have suggested that this new repressive attitude was the product of the moral crusading of Puritan clergy and laity, but the fact that it is also evident in parishes untouched by Puritan influence suggests that a more fundamental reason for the adopting of this tougher line may have been the worsening economic climate. The widespread economic recession of the 1620s led to a rapid increase in the scale of poverty in the English countryside, and made the authorities particularly anxious to discourage any pre-marital sexual activity which might result in bastardy and add to the strain on the already overburdened poor rate.

Another significant aspect of the courts' work involved matrimonial disputes. Most of these cases involved the formation rather than the termination of marriage, as, perhaps surprisingly, the laws concerning the dissolution of marriage were not reformed after Henry VIII's break with Rome over his own divorce. Continental reformers, such as Martin Bucer, had advocated that divorce and remarriage be allowed to the innocent party in cases of adultery or wilful desertion, and during Edward VI's reign changes along these lines had been incorporated in a proposal to reform the canon law entitled the *Reformatio legum ecclesiasticarum*. Elizabeth, however, subsequently refused to authorize the *Reformatio*, and her bishops shared her suspicion about such a radical revision of the law of divorce. Consequently, England was one of the few Protestant countries not to see a relaxation in the divorce laws during the sixteenth century. During the 1640s, the poet John Milton launched another vigorous campaign in favour of liberalization, but this too ended in failure.

The majority of the matrimonial cases heard in the church courts resulted from the widespread confusion over the correct canonical procedures for the contracting and solemnizing of marriage. Although by 1600 most marriages were solemnized by a church wedding conducted by a clergyman, it was still technically possible to contract a valid marriage without setting foot in a church through a procedure known as spousals – the public exchange of vows by a man and a woman – which had constituted a canonically valid means of contracting a marriage since the middle ages. As a result, the courts were regularly called upon to make judgments about the validity of marriages and to hear accusations of breach of promise. They also frequently dealt with cases of clandestine marriage, where the partners and their clergyman had failed to observe the detailed canonical injunctions for church weddings, often by neglecting to obtain the necessary parental consent for the marriage of minors.

As well as continuing to exercise their traditional function as regulators of sexual morality and social behaviour, the Elizabethan and early Stuart church courts were given the additional role of enforcing conformity to royal policy in matters of religion. Following the issuing of the 1559 injunctions, church court officials were expected to ensure that copies of the Bible, the Paraphrases, and the new Prayer Book were purchased and installed in every parish church. They were responsible for ensuring that the laity attended church services on Sunday and that the clergy preached regularly to them. It also fell to them to discipline Puritan ministers who refused to conform in matters of dress or ceremonials. Such duties were onerous and time-consuming, and depended on the co-operation of parish churchwardens. As a result, they were frequently not performed with any great diligence. This was especially true where churchwardens and court officials did not approve of the changes that they were being required to impose, or sympathized with those facing prosecution for non-compliance.

Elizabeth and her bishops were quick to recognize the limited potential of the existing church courts in enforcing conformity and eradicating Catholic survivalism, and early in her reign special ecclesiastical commissions of laymen and clerics were created to assist in these tasks. They were thought to be more effective than the established church courts, not least because they had stronger powers of coercion and could fine, imprison, and take bonds to enforce attendance at their hearings. The most notorious of these new commissions were the two courts of High Commission which were permanently established at Canterbury and York. These bodies had jurisdiction over the whole of England and Wales, but were supplemented by a number of local commissions meeting in provincial centres. Although intended to strengthen the disciplinary machinery of the bishops in *ex officio* cases, they soon began to attract instance work, but not probate business as they were not authorized to deal with disputes involving property. Although they employed the same administrative procedures as the lesser church courts, they were apt to be taken more seriously as they were more rigorous in their application of oaths, able to impose more meaningful penalties, and could depend upon the backing of the Court of Star Chamber and the privy council. Indeed, it was the very effectiveness of High Commission that led to its extreme unpopularity among radical Protestants, especially after 1583 when Archbishop

Whitgift made extensive use of it in his campaign against both Puritans and Presbyterians, and again in the 1630s when Archbishop Laud used it in his attempt to enforce conformity to his conservative orthodoxy. Criticism was directed mainly at High Commission's procedures, and in particular its use of the *ex officio* oath, for to have questioned the right of existence of a body expressly founded by the queen would have constituted a direct attack on royal authority.

The popularity and effectiveness of the church courts during the period 1560 to 1625 has been hotly debated by both contemporaries and historians. Throughout this period they were frequently criticized for delays and inefficiencies, and for charging excessive fees. Foremost among the contemporary critics were the common lawyers who from the 1590s onwards mounted a concerted campaign against the church's jurisdiction by regularly taking out writs of prohibitions, which had the effect of suspending ecclesiastical cases and transferring them to the common law courts. In addition, many Puritans resented the entire panoply of the church courts, condemning them even before they were specifically used against them as a popish institution inappropriate to a reformed church. They disliked the impersonal nature of the disciplinary procedures and the use of professional lawyers who had little interest in their spiritual function. Some criticized the courts for their use of 'toyish censures' for serious sins, such as public penance for adultery, while most railed against the imposition of the penalty of excommunication for trivial offences. Some Puritan critics wished to replace the existing system with a personal discipline exercised by elders and ministers over individual congregations, supplemented where necessary by the intervention of the godly magistrate or bishop to deal with the obdurate offender. In the absence of this kind of discipline within the church as a whole, individual Puritan ministers acted unilaterally and imposed it upon their own parishes. For example, after Edward Snape of Northampton had tried unsuccessfully to bring a man accused of sexual misconduct to private penance, he preached a 'very bitter sermon' against him, and eventually forced him to do public penance and marry the girl with whom he had transgressed. Similarly, at Dedham in Essex the task of promoting godliness was shared by the Puritan ministers and lay representatives of the townspeople, who sat together in a form of consistory court.

In some areas, Puritan reform initiatives also depended heavily on the efforts of the godly magistrate, who, particularly when supported by local ministers, could be a devastating instrument of social control.

In 1578, the justices of the peace of Bury St Edmunds drew up and displayed in the town's parish churches a penal code covering a wide range of offences from blasphemy to gaming. Compared to the penalties imposed by the church courts, the punishments for offenders were draconian; fornicators, for example, were to have their hair shorn, to be tied to a post for twenty-four hours, and to receive thirty strokes of the whip 'till the blood come'. In a number of other counties too, including Kent, Lancashire, Nottinghamshire, and Somerset, sexual offenders were regularly whipped during the late Elizabethan period. Puritan magistrates also maintained a close watch on the poor, who were considered especially prone to immoral behaviour. In 1570, the justices of Norwich declared that the new orders for the idle poor of their town were aimed at preventing them sliding 'from idleness to drunkenness to whoredom to shameful incest and abominable life, greatly to the dishonour of God and ruin of the commonwealth'. In many other centres too, it was the godly element upon the bench of justices that took the lead in punishment of the 'idle' or 'impotent' poor, incarcerating them in houses of correction where the daily prayers included an acknowledgement that 'the punishments wherewith we be now scourged is much less than our deserts'. Many urban magistrates relished this extension to their civic control, and took full advantage of the opportunity to regulate important aspects of the social life of their communities.

The view shared by many contemporary Puritans that the Elizabethan and Jacobean church courts were largely ineffective has been reiterated more recently by a number of historians, who have produced evidence to suggest that a large and growing proportion of defendants and witnesses in disciplinary cases treated the courts' proceedings and punishments with an only thinly veiled contempt. Ronald Marchant[2] calculated that in the diocese of Chester in 1595 barely 30 per cent of defendants in disciplinary cases both appeared to answer charges and subsequently obeyed court orders, while in the diocese of York in 1623 the corresponding figure was only 33 per cent. F. D. Price[3] likewise found that by the middle of Elizabeth's reign, two-thirds of those summoned to appear before the consistory court of Gloucester were failing to turn up. Admittedly, Gloucester was at this stage a particularly badly run diocese, while both York and Chester posed exceptionally severe administrative problems. Nevertheless, Ralph Houlbrooke[4] has suggested that by the beginning of the seventeenth century the average percentage of non-attenders throughout the whole country was as high as 60 per cent.

According to these historians, the problem of contumacy was the natural outcome of a widespread lay disrespect for ecclesiastical penalties, and particularly for the ultimate sanction of excommunication, which was used more and more frequently as Elizabeth's reign progressed. As the lesser penances imposed by the courts apparently held few fears for the laity, officials were increasingly obliged to resort to excommunication even for a first offence, with the inevitable result that this ultimate sanction itself soon ceased to hold any great terrors. The secular authorities became reluctant to confirm or enforce the penalty, and large numbers of excommunicates escaped any disciplinary proceedings and did not even bother to seek absolution. In the archdeaconry of Colchester in June 1594, for example, no fewer than eighty-six persons were designated as excommunicates, while Marchant[5] has calculated that at the beginning of the seventeenth century at least 5 per cent (or 10 per cent if their families are included) of the population of the dioceses of York, Chester, and Norwich were excommunicates. Christopher Hill[6] has similarly argued that the pre-civil war church courts were anachronistic institutions, which were not only ineffective and inefficient but also extremely unpopular. On the one hand, he claims, they failed to pursue either sexual offenders or the poor with sufficient rigour, and on the other, they represented an intolerable intrusion into people's private lives and were a particular nuisance to the 'industrious sort', whose business activities were hamstrung by the outdated restrictions against practices such as usury and Sunday working.

Recent research, however, into the court records of several dioceses in southern England suggests that this picture may be unduly pessimistic. Martin Ingram[7] has estimated that in normal years non-attendance at the courts in these areas was only around 40 per cent, not very different from the non-attendance record at the secular courts. He has further demonstrated that the majority of excommunicates had been indicted for major sexual offences; from his study of the records of the diocese of Ely and the archdeaconries of Salisbury, North Wiltshire, Leicester, and Chichester, he found that 'very commonly' well over 50 per cent of those charged with adultery, fornication, or bastard-bearing were subsequently excommunicated for contumacy. Many of these unregenerates were young, single people with little stake in society and a tendency to move on when they found themselves in trouble, while a number were members of the criminal underworlds which operated in most large urban centres. Thus, according to Ingram's evidence, there was no widespread alienation from ecclesiastical justice, since the majority of settled householders both appeared before the courts and accepted its discipline. Nor was there a sub-group of disaffected 'ethical dissenters' who preferred to live as excommunicates rather than conform to the church's moral standards, for, Ingram believes, many excommunicates returned to the church and put their pasts behind them, once they grew older and took on greater responsibilities.

Nor can Christopher Hill's blanket condemnation of the courts be accepted any longer, for, as we have seen, many English men and women remained eager to resort to the church courts in cases of defamation of their character by a neighbour, and through their arbitration in these extremely common local disputes, the courts continued to fulfil a highly useful social function. Furthermore, as even *ex officio* prosecutions were initiated through the presentments of local churchwardens, here too the scope and intensity of the courts' activities were to a great extent determined by the level of social concern within the local community itself. Indeed, it would appear that, far from being unpopular institutions, throughout the second half of the sixteenth century and the first quarter of the seventeenth the ecclesiastical courts remained one of the most convenient vehicles for the public resolution of community disputes and the disciplining of offenders against communal ethics.

After 1625, however, this generally favourable image and opinion of the courts was to be adversely affected by their association with the ecclesiastical innovations introduced by William Laud. During the 1630s, the provincial church courts began to impinge on the lives of the laity in new and provocative ways, as more and more court time was spent on prosecutions for failure to implement the Laudian reforms. Moreover, during Charles I's reign the politically influential gentry and aristocracy found themselves with their own particular causes of grievance against ecclesiastical justice. Before 1625, the church courts had directed their attentions almost exclusively towards the lower orders, and as long as they were relatively discreet, more socially elevated transgressors had normally been able to avoid the discovery and punishment of their moral faults. Only very occasionally, such as in 1611 when Sir William Chancey was imprisoned by High Commission for adultery, and in 1613 when Sir Pexall Brocas was obliged to do public penance in a white sheet at St Paul's Cross in London after being convicted of repeated adultery, did the ecclesiastical courts bring prosecutions against members of the landed classes. After Charles I's accession, however, such disciplinary action against the socially elevated intensified. In 1625, High Commission publicly excommunicated Sir Robert Howard for refusing to appear to answer a charge of adultery, and in 1631 the same court fined Sir Giles Allington £12,200 for incestuously marrying his niece. Throughout the remainder of the 1630s, the court continued to exact heavy fines from peers and gentlemen convicted of adultery and fornication. It also concerned itself in a number of cases of marital breakdown, showing some sympathy for the plight of estranged wives and allocating them levels of alimony which most male observers considered excessively generous. These activities did little to endear High Commission to the landed classes. As the Earl of Clarendon later pointed out:

> persons of honour and great quality of the court and of the country were every day cited into high commission court upon fame of their incontinence or other scandal in their lives, and were there prosecuted, to their shame and punishment; and as the shame (which they called an insolent triumph upon their degree and quality, and levelling them with the common people) was never forgotten but watched for revenge, so the fines imposed there were the more questioned and repined against, because they were assigned to the rebuilding and repairing of St Paul's church.

Following the meeting of the Long Parliament in November 1640, the representatives of the landed classes quickly set about taking their revenge on the church courts. The Court of High Commission was abolished by the MPs in 1641, and during the next few years, as the Puritan critics of the pre-war courts gained increasing power at Westminster, the local courts too abandoned their activities, not to function again until after the Restoration. In the short term, the result may have been some increase in illicit sexual activity; in 1647, Thomas Fuller declared in his *Good Thoughts in Worse Times* that 'Vice these late years hath kept open house in England'; and Sir Philip Warwick later claimed in his memoirs that in the period following the abolition of High Commission, adultery and fornication had been committed 'barefacedly'. Whether the civil war years did indeed see an increase in illicit behaviour is debatable, but if any wartime permissiveness did occur it was to prove short-lived. Although the anti-clerical rulers of Interregnum England continued to exclude the church from any involvement in measures of social control, they none the less regarded the reform of the nation's morality as one of their chief priorities. During the 1650s, secular justices of the peace throughout the country assumed the function of the church courts, and during 1655 and 1656 they were assisted in this work by Cromwell's major-generals, some of whom engaged in concerted campaigns to achieve a reformation of manners in their regions.

Although the restoration of the monarchy in 1660 failed to bring about the return of the hated Court of High Commission, it did lead to the rapid resumption of the activities of the local ecclesiastical courts. Probate and instance work resumed within months of the king's return, and *ex officio* proceedings recommenced in late 1661 and 1662 as bishops and archdeacons once more began to conduct parochial visitations. Although the theoretical powers of the Restoration church courts remained unchanged from those of the pre-civil war courts, in practice their influence had been substantially eroded. The eighteen-year hiatus in the middle of the century had allowed the secular magistracy to replace the courts as the prime constraint upon a whole range of social impropriety. After 1660, churchwardens increasingly deflected enquiries from the ecclesiastical courts about the state of their communities with the bland phrase *'omnia bene'* – 'all is well'; by 1680 this trend was so marked that the Bishop of Peterborough declared in a letter to the Archbishop of Canterbury: 'defects can never be known by the presentments of the churchwardens. . . . They will forswear themselves over and over rather than bring expense on themselves or their neighbours.'

To compensate for this loss of corrective influence over the social and moral behaviour of the laity, the church courts assumed a new role – the identification and prosecution of the many groups of Presbyterians, Baptists, and Quakers, which had proliferated in the religious freedom of the 1650s, only to be ejected from the established church in the aftermath of the Restoration. The harassing of dissenters came to occupy more and more of the courts' time during the period 1660 to 1689, so much so that, when the penalties against nonconformists were at first suspended by James II in 1687 and then abolished altogether by the 1689 Toleration Act, the ecclesiastical courts were left high and dry with no other compelling *raison d'être*. During the 1690s, the position of the church courts was further undermined by the public disrespect shown them by a series of unsympathetic Whig governments. When a Plymouth shipwright was presented to a church court in 1693 for working on a Sunday, the government intervened to prevent the prosecution, making no secret of its irritation at the court's obstruction of the national war effort. Furthermore, in 1689, 1694, and again in 1708, parliament passed acts of general pardon, which had the effect of terminating all existing proceedings in the courts and annulling the temporal penalties against all those under excommunication. The role of the ecclesiastical courts as an organ of social control died, therefore, with the seventeenth century. After 1700, all the important functions of social control were exercised by justices of the peace, and the church courts were left only with the more peripheral functions of adjudicating in tithe disputes, investigating matters relating to the fabric of churches, and disciplining their own clergy.

NOTES

1 Margaret Bowker, 'Some archdeacons' Court Books and the Commons' Supplication against the Ordinaries', in D. A. Bullough and R. L. Storey (eds), *The Study of Medieval Records* (Oxford, 1971).
2 Ronald Marchant, *The Church under the Law: Justice, administration and discipline in the diocese of York 1560–1640* (Cambridge, 1969).
3 F. D. Price, 'The abuse of excommunication and the decline of ecclesiastical discipline under Queen Elizabeth', *English Historical Review* 57 (1942).
4 Ralph Houlbrooke, 'The decline of ecclesiastical jurisdiction under the Tudors', in Rosemary O'Day and Felicity Heal (eds), *Continuity and Change: Personnel and administration of the church in England 1500–1642* (Leicester, 1976).
5 Marchant, *The Church under the Law*.
6 Christopher Hill, *Society and Puritanism in Pre-revolutionary England* (London, 1964).
7 Martin Ingram, *Church Courts, Sex and Marriage in England 1570–1640* (Cambridge, 1988).

SUGGESTIONS FOR FURTHER READING

For views expressed in sermons, catechisms, and books written by the clergy, Richard L. Greaves, *Society and Religion in Elizabethan England* (Minneapolis, 1981), is useful, but his central thesis that there is a distinction between Puritan and Anglican outlooks must be discarded. The church courts are discussed as part of the machinery of government in Penry Williams, *The Tudor Regime* (Oxford, 1979), but the most valuable studies of their organization and influence in Tudor and early Stuart England are Ralph Houlbrooke, *Church Courts and the People during the English Reformation, 1520–1570* (Oxford, 1979); and Martin Ingram, *Church Courts, Sex and Marriage in England 1570–1640* (Cambridge, 1988). The differences of emphasis and opinion between these two historians are discussed above and also in Ingram's introduction.

Both historians have also written articles in collections of essays, which highlight some of their main conclusions: Ralph Houlbrooke, 'The decline of ecclesiastical jurisdiction under the Tudors', in Rosemary O'Day and Felicity Heal (eds), *Continuity and Change: Personnel and administration of the church in England 1500–1642* (Leicester, 1976); and Martin Ingram, 'The reform of popular culture? Sex and marriage in early modern England', in Barry Reay (ed.), *Popular Culture in Seventeenth-century England* (London, 1985).

The Restoration church courts can best be approached through I. M. Green, *The Re-establishment of the Church of England 1660–1663* (Oxford, 1978); A. Whiteman, 'The re-establishment of the Church of England', *Transactions of the Royal Historical Society*, fifth series, vol. 5 (1955); and G. V. Bennett, *The Tory Crisis in Church and State* (Oxford, 1975).

There are now a number of detailed studies of the church courts in particular dioceses. These include Ronald Marchant, *The Church under the Law: Justice, administration and discipline in the diocese of York, 1560–1640* (Cambridge, 1969); J. A. Sharpe, *Defamation and Sexual Slander in Early Modern England: The church courts at York*, Borthwick Papers 58 (York, 1980); F. D. Price, 'The abuses of excommunication and the decline of ecclesiastical discipline under Queen Elizabeth', *English Historical Review* 57 (1942); Stephen Lander, 'Church courts and the Reformation in the diocese of Chichester 1500–1558', in Rosemary O'Day and Felicity Heal (eds), *Continuity and Change*; R. M. Wunderli, *London Church Courts and Society on the Eve of the Reformation* (Cambridge, Mass., 1981); and M. Bowker, 'Some archdeacons' Court Books and the Commons' Supplication against the Ordinaries', in D. A. Bullough and R. L. Storey (eds), *The Study of Medieval Records* (Oxford, 1971).

For an older, more negative view of the courts, see Christopher Hill, *Society and Puritanism in Pre-revolutionary England* (London, 1964).

11　Conclusions

While the primary purpose of this study has been to reflect and synthesize the large amount of recent research into the religious history of early modern England, before concluding it seems appropriate for the authors to summarize their personal views on some of the more important controversies discussed in the previous chapters. The issue that has recently caused the most disagreement between early Tudor historians is the crucial question of why the English Reformation happened. As we have seen, the immediate cause of the schism with Rome was Henry VIII's determination to divorce his wife and marry Anne Boleyn. Had the pope allowed Henry his annulment and remarriage, there would have been no need for the king to have asserted his imperial power over the church in so revolutionary a way. Once, however, the arguments of imperial power had been formulated and publicized, and the financial advantages of the supremacy had been experienced, a Pandora's box had been opened, and Henry was not seriously able to contemplate a return to the papal fold, even after the death of Catherine of Aragon and the execution of Anne Boleyn. In this sense, the English Reformation was certainly an official process, an 'act of state'.

This official Reformation did not stop with the jurisdictional revolution of the early 1530s, but moved on to encompass first evangelical reform and later doctrinal change. During the later 1530s, Henry was pushed into moderate evangelical reforms both by the influence of humanists at court and by a range of political and financial pressures. Similarly, the doctrinal and liturgical changes of Edward's reign were the product of the factional battles at court, and came about mainly as a result of the unexpected seizure of power by prominent Protestant courtiers, first on Henry's death in 1547 and again after Somerset's fall in 1549. The fact that by 1553 England was officially Protestant

was, therefore, the direct result of the successful political manoeu-
vring of individual reformers and their allies, who were able to
acquire the power to impose their reforms upon the English people.
That the Protestant regimes they led were able to enforce outward
conformity and overcome any active opposition through propaganda
and coercion is a testimony to the efficiency and power of Tudor
government.

It is difficult to see how without this official Reformation there
could have been any popular Reformation. On balance, the evidence
from wills indicates that in the early sixteenth century the vast majority of the laity remained well satisfied with Catholic forms of worship,
while the records of ecclesiastical courts suggest that heresy possessed
only a very limited appeal, and was a minor nuisance, rather than a
major threat to the Catholic church. Even after Henry's break with
Rome, there is little evidence of any early or rapid haemorrhage to
Protestantism. On the contrary, it seems clear that the laity continued
to demonstrate a deep attachment to Catholic beliefs and practices
right up to the moment when they came under attack from the
government.

There were, none the less, a few men and women within early
sixteenth-century England who were strongly attracted to Luther's
ideas, and who would probably have become Protestants whatever
attitude had been taken by Henry's government. Many of these
individuals were characterized by a marked independence of outlook,
which made it difficult for them to participate happily in the collective rituals of Catholic spirituality, and led them to prefer instead
the introspective approach of private biblical study and *ex tempore*
prayer. Most early converts to Protestantism were literate, and many
of them were also either common lawyers who had imbibed the
anti-clerical environment of the Inns of Court, or young unbeneficed
priests who were employed as academics or family tutors. Although
they became fervent and life-long Protestants, without the schism
they would have faced the united Catholic forces of the church,
government, and universities, and would have remained a small
minority with relatively little influence.

Although the government injunctions of the 1530s and 1540s calling
for the dismantling of the apparatus of Catholic worship were obeyed
speedily enough, Protestant beliefs do not appear to have been fully
accepted by a majority of the population until the middle years of
Elizabeth's reign. Before 1547, Protestants were few and far between,
more evident at court than in the country at large. During Edward
VI's reign, their numbers grew steadily and they became so densely

concentrated in some regions that Mary's bishops were subsequently unable to eradicate them totally. None the less, when Edward died in 1553 they were still a minority; historians remain divided about exactly how substantial this minority was – perhaps because this is a question which in the last analysis they do not possess the means to answer.

Although Mary failed to revitalize all aspects of Catholic life, many waverers and less committed Protestants did re-embrace the old faith during her reign. When Elizabeth came to the throne at the end of the 1550s, therefore, a strong residual attachment to Catholic belief and ceremony remained, and this was to continue to exist throughout the 1560s. The new queen soon discovered that a great many of her lay subjects were indifferent to the 1559 Protestant settlement, while others were positively hostile to it. Converting large numbers of the laity to the Protestant beliefs and practices of the church created in 1559 was to be no easy task, for the early Elizabethan clergy were inadequately trained and motivated for a large-scale evangelizing effort, and the material they were working on was initially far from promising. In the light of this inauspicious beginning, one of Elizabeth's primary achievements as monarch was the creation of not only a Protestant church but also a Protestant nation.

Elizabeth's success in this area could be attributed to a number of initiatives on the part of her secular and ecclesiastical advisers, some of which have been discussed in previous chapters. However, a more fundamental, albeit more prosaic reason for the ultimate victory of Protestantism might be the simple passage of time. There is a strong tendency for people to retain a preference for the cultural norms familiar to them from childhood. For this reason, many of the Elizabethans of the 1560s who had been brought up with the Catholic ritual of the Henrician church found the new English services, the austere church interiors, and the emphasis on preaching with which they were confronted on the sabbath, alien and uncongenial. However, once the Protestant establishment had outlasted the transitional generation of the mid-century, the task of cementing Protestantism became increasingly easier. By the mid-1570s, those reared in the Protestant environment of Edward VI's reign had come of age, and those born into the Elizabethan church who had known no alternative to Protestantism were already in their teens. From this point onwards the formative religious experiences of a growing majority of Elizabeth's subjects had occurred within a Protestant setting and their rudimentary knowledge of their faith had come from Protestant catechisms. As a direct consequence, they were generally much more strongly committed to the Elizabethan church than their fathers and mothers. For this reason, it was in the mid-1570s that the tide began to turn in favour of Protestantism. By the end of Elizabeth's reign, a second generation of Protestants had reached adulthood, and the church which had been greeted with little enthusiasm on its establishment in 1559 had gained so strong a hold on the popular imagination that neither the Laudians of the 1630s nor the reforming Puritans of the Interregnum would be able to detach the English people from it.

Some historians, however, still deny that the post-Reformation church was ever popular. Christopher Haigh, in particular, has continued to argue that the Elizabethan ecclesiastical establishment was out of touch with the needs and desires of the laity, and as a result was responsible for creating both an endemic lay hostility towards ministers and a widespread indifference towards organized religion. In the absence of any early modern opinion polls to register the views held by ordinary people about the clergy, all historians are left to piece together an incomplete and speculative picture from fragmentary and indirect evidence, and in such circumstances they often come up with conclusions that suit their personal biases. However, if one applies to the Elizabethan and Jacobean churches the same sort of definitions and sources which Haigh employed in his study of the pre-Reformation church, it then becomes clear that the case for the existence of a widespread anti-clericalism in the late sixteenth and early seventeenth centuries is as unconvincing as it is for the late fifteenth century.

There is, for example, little evidence of clerical corruption, and Haigh's comment, 'There were scandals, it is true – but they were very rare', applies as much to the post-Reformation clergy as it does to their pre-Reformation predecessors. In addition, just as fifty years earlier, much of the evidence for lay discontent with the Elizabethan church comes from writers representing interest groups with a particular axe to grind, such as Puritans or common lawyers. As for the evidence of tithe disputes, it would be unwise to argue that the expansion in tithe litigation from the 1540s onwards was either a symptom or a cause of increased anti-clericalism. Most of these cases did not arise from objections to the payment of tithes as a matter of principle, but were rather related to specific tithing customs or arrears in payment. More importantly, because tithes were paid to the laity as impropriators as well as to the clergy, refusal to pay often led to a dispute between two laymen; such cases prove that it was taxation rather than the church that was unpopular. Finally, the most recent research into the records of the church courts has revealed that there was a general return to both lay respect for ecclesiastical discipline and high attendance rates at church in the 1570s.

Comparing the respective quality and attractiveness of pre- and post-Reformation worship is another problematic area. Haigh may well be right to suggest that Elizabethan Protestant services were more boring and demanding than the old Catholic liturgy, but it must not be forgotten that some of the laity welcomed these new demands and found the new participatory services more relevant and accessible. Again, while many of the sermons and homilies delivered by Elizabeth's ministers were no doubt tedious, some may have been interesting or even inspirational, and their quality is not easily assessed by reading a printed version. As modern students know all too well, the attractiveness of listening to a lecture varies enormously, and depends heavily on the abilities and personality of the speaker.

There was undeniably some parochial anti-clericalism in the late sixteenth and early seventeenth centuries. At the same time, how-ever, many ordinary lay people held a positive regard for the clergy, and a strong attachment to their local churches and national reli-gion. As for corporate anti-clericalism, outside the Inns of Court this was much less strong than it had been on the eve of the Reformation, for in the course of the religious changes the laity had acquired substantial ecclesiastical assets and greatly extended their influence over the church. From Henry VIII's reign onwards, lay property-owners had purchased ecclesiastical land, income, and rights of presentation; in Elizabeth's reign alone they acquired the tithes and advowsons of over 2,200 parishes. In addition, despite Elizabeth's insistence that ecclesiastical reform was the responsibility of her bishops in convocation, at a national level there was a consider-able parliamentary involvement in ecclesiastical affairs. Similarly, at a local level individual laymen sat on ecclesiastical commissions and endowed lectureships, while town corporations initiated measures to improve the economic viability of livings and worked closely with the clergy to impose moral discipline upon the urban population.

The Elizabethan church, which was constructed during the period from 1559 to 1625, strongly reflected both the queen's personal religious preferences and her assessment of the appropriate political role of a church. As a consequence, its contemporary Protestant critics were able to complain with some justification that it was only 'halfly-reformed', and that its hierarchical structure, Erastian nature, and 'Catholic' ceremonial rendered it inferior to the best continental Reformed churches. But if its liturgy and governmental structure set it apart from Europe, at least its theology was closely in line with that of the Calvinist churches abroad. There can be little doubt that the outlook of the overwhelming majority of the higher clergy and university theologians was unequivocally predestinarian. However, to argue that these influential men determined that the official theology of Elizabeth's church would be predestinarian is not to argue that they were responsible for successfully disseminating this doctrine to the large mass of ordinary, uneducated parishioners with only a passing interest in theology. Indeed, believing that the theory of predestination was too complex and subtle for the uneducated and had the potential to create great confusion and anxiety, some of the clergy deliberately kept the laity in the dark about this central doctrine of their church. As a result, predestinarianism made only modest headway at grass-roots level. Even as late as the 1620s, large sections of the population either did not know of it at all, or at best experienced it in the diluted form of a belief in providence. Only among the Puritans was there a strong attachment to predestinarianism. For these small but influential groups of individuals it was both the central tenet of their faith and the litmus test by which they judged the established church. As long as that church remained officially predestinarian, they were prepared to accept its ungodly liturgical and ceremonial features, and discount the alternative of separating from it and forming their own sectarian congregations outside the parochial structure.

This highly successful *modus vivendi* came to an abrupt end with the rise of English Arminianism. As we have seen, the Arminians made significant changes to the doctrine of salvation in order to emphasize the importance of works. While this development caused dismay among the Puritans and the university academics, the vast majority of ordinary men and women were little affected or bothered by the doctrinal adjustment. This does not mean, however, that the Arminian takeover was welcomed by the laity, for if the majority were not particularly alarmed by the new Arminian theology, they were greatly disquieted by the accompanying alterations to ceremonials, the liturgy, and above all the visual appearance of their parish churches. The installation of altars and rails, and the imposition of practices such as genuflection and the wearing of veils during the churching ceremony, were bitterly opposed, both because the English people had grown unaccustomed to 'the beauty of holiness' and also because they were viewed as popish innovations which represented the first stage in a return to Rome. To borrow the analogy of one of his contemporaries, Laud was widely seen as the little boy put through an open window to unlock the house for a thief. This mistaken identification of the Arminian reforms with popery alienated large numbers of mainstream Protestants from the episcopal authorities, and drove the moderate Puritans into an alliance with the radical, sectarian extremists. During the 1630s, therefore, Laud and his colleagues shattered the consensus which had existed within the Elizabethan church over the form of visual and communal expressions of religious belief. It is for this reason that the rise of the Arminians must be regarded as a major, if not *the* major cause of the English civil war.

The subsequent parliamentarian victory in that war left the country in the hands of Laud's most committed Puritan and sectarian opponents. While these rigid predestinarians allowed most of their fellow Protestants a considerable degree of freedom in organizing their own external worship, they also attempted to impose upon the English people their own particular brand of experimental Calvinist spirituality. This involved the promotion of predestinarian beliefs, strict sabbatarianism, iconophobia, and a rejection of 'ungodly' folk festivals, rural pastimes, and traditional rites of passage. The mass of the laity, however, decisively turned their backs on this attempt at Calvinist cultural revolution. While a few demonstrated their rejection of it by joining the rapidly growing ranks of anti-predestinarian sects such as the General Baptists and Quakers, large numbers of others did so by retaining a marked preference for the liturgy and more muted dogma of the pre-1625 Elizabethan church. As a result, for all its powerful backers, the Directory of Public Worship was quite unable to dislodge the Elizabethan Book of Common Prayer from the unique position it had gained in the affections of the English people.

Given this continued attachment to the liturgy and ceremonials of the Elizabethan church, it is not surprising that the return of monarchy and church in 1660 was closely followed by an Anglican backlash. The Restoration bishops and their parliamentary allies rejected predestinarianism, brought back many of the liturgical practices that had been outlawed by the Interregnum Calvinists, and decisively expelled from the state church all those who were not prepared to adhere to their narrow orthodoxy. While these actions were generally applauded at the time, in the long term the decision to repudiate the comprehensive traditions of the Elizabethan church was to prove a major mistake. Although the numbers of nonconformists remained relatively small, their staunch commitment to their faith and persistent refusal to bow to the pressure of persecution meant that it was impossible to destroy them. Furthermore, educated lay opinion grew increasingly hostile to the coercion of dissenters, who were often now respectable and law-abiding members of the community. In these circumstances, the ending of the Anglican religious monopoly was only a matter of time. With the passing of the Toleration Act of 1689, separatism finally achieved its objective and nonconformists were given the right to go their own way outside the established church. Anglicanism would remain the dominant influence over English religious life for the next two centuries, but by 1700 it had squandered its last chance of regaining the allegiance of the entire nation.

Like all childhoods, the early years of the church of England were marked by a long struggle towards independence and identity. This process was rarely free from conflict and on occasions, as in the 1580s and the mid-seventeenth century, it involved great upheaval. By 1689, however, the church created in 1559 had come of age. Its boundaries and fundamental characteristics had been established, its continued existence was assured, and it was ready to embark on a career which would eventually see it emerge as a leading Christian denomination with an influence extending throughout the modern world.

Glossary

adiaphora: literally 'matters indifferent'; thus beliefs not central to faith.

adultery: sexual intercourse involving a person married to a third party; in practice most condemnation was reserved for adultery involving a married woman.

advowson: right of appointment to a clerical living.

affinity: kinship by marriage; the laws of affinity regulated the marriages of relatives by marriage.

alb: a full-length tunic of white cloth worn by the priest at mass.

anabaptists: radical Protestants who practised the baptism of adult believers; widely regarded as social revolutionaries, they were persecuted throughout Europe by Catholics and more moderate Protestants.

annates: a payment which new holders of important benefices, such as archbishops or bishops, were obliged to hand over to the pope, comprising the revenue they received during their first year of office.

annulment: a judicial decision by the church that a marriage had not been valid when it was contracted, and that any children born from that union were illegitimate.

antinomian: literally 'against the law'; thus the belief that there was no obligation upon those predestined for heaven to obey the moral law.

appropriations: rights held by monasteries to appoint the holder of a clerical living and collect its tithes.

archdeaconry: an administrative subdivision of a diocese under the jurisdiction of an archdeacon.

auricular confession: the private confession of sins to a priest.

benefice: an ecclesiastical living, most commonly a parish; unbeneficed clergy did not hold a parish of their own, but were employed as curates, chantry priests, chaplains, or schoolmasters.

benefit of clergy: the privilege enjoyed by the clergy of exemption from the jurisdiction of the secular courts in criminal cases.

buggery: sexual intercourse between two men; often also used to describe sexual relations between a human and an animal.

canon: an ecclesiastical regulation; thus canon law, the law of the church.

catechism: a method of instruction in the main tenets of doctrine (or a book containing such instruction) which employs a question and answer format.

celibacy: the unmarried state; usually taken to mean living without sexual relations.

censer: a vessel in which incense is burnt during mass. The burning of incense was a symbol of sacrifice.

chantry: an endowment which maintains a priest or priests to say masses for the soul of the founder and other designated individuals after their deaths, sometimes in a purpose-built chantry chapel.

chasuble: a sleeveless mantle covering the body and shoulders worn over the alb by the priest at mass.

chrism: consecrated oil, used particularly for anointing the child during baptism.

churching: the ceremony by which a woman was received back into the church following childbirth; seen by many as a thanksgiving rite, it also involved suggestions of purification.

church-papist: a Catholic who attended the services of the post-1559 Protestant state church.

churchwarden: a lay officer of the parish church, usually elected annually by a rotation basis; they performed a variety of tasks, including making presentments on oath to the church courts about the physical state of the church buildings, and the religious and moral behaviour of the local clergyman and his parishioners.

clerestory: the upper wall of a large church containing a series of windows.

consistory: an ecclesiastical court composed of lay elders and pastors which disciplined offenders; an important feature of the church founded by Calvin in Geneva.

contumacy: persistent disobedience to, or defiance of, the orders of a court, often involving the failure to appear to answer charges.

convocation: the general assembly of the clergy, consisting of an upper and lower house, which met at the same time as parliament.

cope: a long, semi-circular cloak, usually richly embroidered, worn by the clergy for processions.

crucifix: a wooden or metallic cross with a representation of the suffering Christ.

curate: an assistant to a beneficed clergyman, who sometimes deputized for him in his absence.

cure: the charge of the care for the spiritual health of a parish or congregation; thus the spiritual responsibilities of the parish clergyman.

decretal commission: a commission which allowed provincial ecclesiastical courts to pass judgments against which there was no appeal to Rome.

dispensation: a licence granting an exemption from ecclesiastical law.

episcopacy: government of the church by bishops.

episcopate: the bishops as a group.

Erastian church: a church subordinated to the state.

eucharist: the celebration of the Lord's Supper.

evangelical reformers: Catholic reformers who emphasized the doctrine of salvation through faith rather than the penitential system of the medieval church, the authority of scripture rather than that of the church hierarchy, and the importance of sermons; during Henry VIII's reign they supported governmental measures aimed at reducing superstitious practices and making the Bible more accessible to the laity.

excommunication: the exclusion of an offender from participation in the life of the church, and in particular from receiving communion; in theory those who had been excommunicated were to be treated as outcasts.

ex officio **oath**: an oath administered to all defendants accused of serious disciplinary offences in the church courts; those to whom it was tendered were obliged to swear to answer truthfully questions of which they had no prior knowledge.

ex tempore: spontaneous; without a set formula; composed for the occasion.

feoffee: a trustee; one to whom property is granted in trust.

first fruits: a payment paid to the crown after the Reformation by new holders of all ecclesiastical benefices of the revenues received during their first year of office.

font: the receptacle that holds the water used for baptism; it was normally situated at the rear of the church.

fornication: sexual intercourse between an unmarried man and an unmarried woman.

genuflection: a gesture involving the bending of one knee made when entering or leaving church as a sign of reverence.

glebe: a piece of land farmed by the parish clergyman.

grace: an unmerited favour granted by God; divine influence or spiritual fuel which operates within individuals to sanctify and purify them.

homily: a prescribed discourse read by the parish minister to his congregation; collections, or books of these homilies were published in 1547 and 1563.

humanism: an educational theory stressing the importance of studying the works of the writers of classical Greece and Rome; in the Christian context humanists emphasized the importance of the critical study of the scriptures in their original languages of Hebrew and Greek as the basis of theological truth.

iconoclasm: the removal from churches or smashing of religious images by those who consider them idolatrous.

iconophobia: the fear or hatred of religious images.

images: visual representations of Christ and the saints, in the form of statues, paintings, and stained glass.

incumbent: the holder of an ecclesiastical benefice.

indulgence: remission of the punishment for sin which remained after absolution by a Catholic priest in confession.

Jesuit: a member of the Society of Jesus, a Catholic religious order founded in 1540 under the leadership of St Ignatius Loyola; dedicated to missionary work and the struggle against Protestantism, the order was a major instrument of the counter-Reformation.

lay fraternity: an association of Catholic lay people which conducted regular acts of collective piety, often under the patronage of a specific saint; they undertook to provide members with a funeral and organized the saying of regular masses for the souls of departed members; sometimes they also ran schools and charities for the benefit of members.

lay impropriations: the rights enjoyed by those who acquired ex-monastic land after the dissolutions to appoint ministers to clerical livings and to collect the impropriated tithes which had formerly come to the monks.

liturgy: the form of public worship; thus church services.

millenarianism: the belief that the end of the world and the second coming of Christ were imminent.

missal: a book containing the text and readings of the mass.

nepotism: the practice of giving preferential treatment to one's own relatives.

obit: an annual mass said for the soul of a deceased person often on his or her saint's day or the anniversary of the death.

ordinand: a candidate for ordination (entry into the church's ministry).

ordinary: a cleric who exercised jurisdiction in ecclesiastical cases, most commonly used of bishops and their deputies.

papal bull: a sealed papal letter, often containing a papal decree or directive.

papal legate: a churchman acting as the deputy of the pope, who was either appointed on a temporary basis for a specific mission, or as in the case of Thomas Wolsey, given a permanent status. A legate *a latere* was commissioned directly by the pope and given authority over all other churchmen in his provincial area.

papal nuncio: an official papal envoy or messenger.

pluralism: the practice of holding more than one church position at the same time; it led inevitably to absenteeism and non-residence by clerics.

praemunire: the criminal offence of introducing into England a foreign or papal jurisdiction which might limit royal authority.

prophesyings: meetings of the clergy of a local area to expound and discuss scripture; part of the discussion took place before a lay audience.

pyx: the vessel in Catholic churches which contained the host or consecrated wafer.

rector: a person or corporate body which received the tithes due from a benefice; often therefore parish priests or ministers who received for their own use the tithes due from their parishes.

recusant: one who refused to attend the Protestant services prescribed by the state church; most commonly used of Roman Catholics after 1559.

Reformed theology: the theology associated with the southern German and Swiss Protestantism of Zwingli, Bucer, and Calvin, rather than with that of Luther.

regular clergy: those clergy who have taken vows to follow the rule of a religious order; thus all monks, friars, and nuns.

relics: the supposed remains of the bodies of, or other physical objects associated with, Christ or the saints; housed in boxes or shrines known as reliquaries, these were the object of great veneration among Catholics.

reredos: a screen, often elaborately carved or decorated, which stood at the back of an altar.

rites of passage: religious rituals marking the important stages in the life of the individual, for example baptism and marriage.

rood screen: the screen separating the chancel from the nave in a pre-Reformation church. Above the screen there was often a crucifix flanked by carved images of the Virgin Mary and St John, and a gallery known as the rood loft which was used for preaching and reading prayers.

rosary beads: a string of 165 beads used by Catholics as a memory aid in the recitation of the rosary cycle of prayers to the Virgin Mary.

sabbatarianism: the practice of keeping Sunday (the Christian sabbath) holy by refraining from all work and leisure activities, and devoting the day to a round of church attendance, private prayer, and Bible study.

sanctification: the action or process by which something or someone is made holy.

sanctuary: the right of those accused of crimes to take refuge on church property, usually for a limited period.

schism: a formal breach in the unity of the Christian church.

sect: a group of men and women who have separated from the established church and voluntarily come together to worship as a gathered church.

secular clergy: clergy who were not bound by a religious rule; normally they served in a parish.

simoniacal: from simony, the act of buying or selling ecclesiastical office or assets for profit.

surplice: a loose, long, white vestment with long sleeves worn by the clergy.

tenths: an annual tax of one-tenth of the value of ecclesiastical benefices received by the crown after the Reformation.

tithes: the payment made by the laity to the parish church of one-tenth of their agricultural profits or personal income. Originally the great tithe was paid as arable crops, the lesser tithes as chickens or eggs, but by the sixteenth century many parishioners paid money or commuted tithes. Designed for the maintenance of the parish clergy, many tithes were impropriated and were received by the laity after the Reformation.

tympanum: the triangular or semi-circular panel over the door of a church; in post-Reformation churches a tympanum was sometimes placed above the framework of the rood screen.

vestments: the robes worn by the clergy when conducting church services; following the Reformation, Protestant reformers bitterly criticized the continued use of the alb, cope, and chasuble, which they closely associated with the celebration of the mass.

vicar: a priest or minister serving in a parish where the revenues had been appropriated, either to a monastery before the dissolutions or to a lay person thereafter. As a result, such clergymen did not receive the tithes due from their parishioners, but were paid an often meagre stipend by whoever did receive them; they thus generally received a smaller income than rectors.

visitation: the inspection of a parish or diocese by a bishop or his representative. Following the break with Rome, a visitation could also be carried out by someone appointed by the monarch; thus in the 1530s Thomas Cromwell organized visitations as Henry VIII's vicar-general.

Important dates 1529–1689

1529 Meeting of legatine court at Blackfriars; Thomas Wolsey charged with praemunire; opening of Reformation Parliament; Acts against pluralism and non-residence and limiting probate and mortuary fees.

1530 Arrest and death of Wolsey; charge of praemunire against clergy.

1531 Pardon of clergy for praemunire on payment of fine; convocation acknowledges Henry VIII as 'Protector and Supreme Head of the English Church and Clergy so far as the law of Christ allows'.

1532 House of Commons' 'Supplication against the Ordinaries' drawn up; surrender by convocation of its independent legislative power; Act for Conditional Restraint of Annates; death of William Warham; Anne Boleyn pregnant.

1533 Secret marriage of Henry VIII to Anne Boleyn; Thomas Cranmer appointed Archbishop of Canterbury; Act in Restraint of Appeals; Cranmer pronounces Henry VIII's marriage to Catherine of Aragon invalid.

1534 Act of Succession; Act in Absolute Restraint of Annates; Act of Dispensations; Act for the Submission of the Clergy; Act of Supremacy; Treason Act; Act awarding first fruits and tenths to crown.

1535 Thomas Cromwell appointed vicegerent in spirituals; *Valor Ecclesiasticus* drawn up; execution of John Fisher and Thomas More.

1536 Execution of Anne Boleyn; dissolution of smaller monasteries; Act against papal authority; issuing of Ten Articles and Cromwellian Injunctions; Pilgrimage of Grace.

1537 Surrender of first of larger monasteries to king; publication of authorized English translation of Bible.

1538   Issuing of second set of Cromwellian Injunctions.

1539   Act of Six Articles; Act authorizing dissolution of larger monasteries; publication of Miles Coverdale's Great Bible.

1540   Execution of Thomas Cromwell; suppression of last monastery.

1546   Arrest of Duke of Norfolk and Earl of Surrey.

1547   Death of Henry VIII and accession of Edward VI; Edward Seymour, Duke of Somerset, appointed Lord Protector; issuing of injunctions against images; repeal of heresy laws; Act introducing communion in both kinds; Act dissolving chantries; publication of first Book of Homilies.

1548   Order for removal of all images from churches.

1549   Issuing of first Edwardian Prayer Book; Act of Uniformity; Act allowing marriage of priests; rebellions in West Country and East Anglia; fall of Somerset.

1550   John Dudley, Earl of Warwick and later Duke of Northumberland, dominant in government.

1552   Execution of Somerset; issuing of second Edwardian Prayer Book.

1553   Issuing of Forty-Two Articles; death of Edward VI and succession of Mary following short 'reign' of Northumberland's relative Jane Grey; repeal of religious legislation of Edward's reign.

1554   Wyatt's rebellion; royal order for removal of married priests; marriage of Mary to Philip of Spain; repeal of royal supremacy and revival of heresy laws; England formally reunited with Rome.

1555   First fruits and tenths handed over to church; burning of first Protestant martyrs, including John Hooper, Hugh Latimer, and Nicholas Ridley; deprivation of Cranmer.

1556   Burning of Cranmer; Reginald Pole appointed Archbishop of Canterbury.

1558   Death of Mary and accession of Elizabeth I; Elizabethan Prayer Book; death of Pole.

1559   Acts of Supremacy and Uniformity; deprivation of Marian bishops; Matthew Parker appointed Archbishop of Canterbury.

1560   Publication of English translation of Genevan Bible.

1563   Approval by convocation of Thirty-Nine Articles; publication of John Foxe's *Acts and Monuments* or *Book of Martyrs*.

1564   Dispute over clerical dress within church precipitated by Elizabeth's insistence on conformity.

1565 Issuing of order by Elizabeth demanding uniformity in the rites and ceremonies of the church.

1568 Foundation of Catholic seminary at Douai in Spanish Netherlands.

1569 The Rebellion of the North.

1570 Excommunication of Elizabeth I by papal bull *Regnans in Excelsis*; Presbyterianism advocated by Thomas Cartwright in lectures at Cambridge University.

1571 Confirmation by statute of Thirty-Nine Articles.

1572 Publication of *Admonition to the Parliament*.

1574 Arrival in England of first Catholic missionary priests.

1575 Edmund Grindal appointed Archbishop of Canterbury.

1576 Royal order suppressing prophesyings defied by Grindal.

1577 Grindal suspended from office for defiance over prophesyings.

1581 Arrival in England of first Jesuit missionaries.

1583 John Whitgift appointed Archbishop of Canterbury.

1588 Publication of Martin Marprelate tracts.

1591 Trial and imprisonment of leaders of Presbyterian movement.

1593 Execution of leaders of separatist movement.

1595 Publication of first part of Richard Hooker's *Laws of Ecclesiastical Polity*; drawing up of Lambeth Articles.

1603 Death of Elizabeth I and accession of James I.

1604 Meeting of Hampton Court Conference; Richard Bancroft appointed Archbishop of Canterbury; issuing of new ecclesiastical canons.

1605 Gunpowder Plot by English Catholics to murder James I and his MPs.

1611 George Abbot appointed Archbishop of Canterbury; publication of Authorized Version of Bible.

1618 Beginning of Thirty Years' War signalled by revolt in Bohemia; opening of Synod of Dort in United Provinces; issuing of *Book of Sports* by James I.

1621 William Laud appointed Bishop of St David's.

1625 Death of James I and accession of Charles I; beginning of war with Spain; setting up of Feoffees for Impropriations.

1626 Laud appointed Bishop of Bath and Wells.

1628 Laud appointed Bishop of London.

1629 Passing of resolutions against Arminianism by House of Commons; parliament dissolved by Charles I; beginning of Personal Rule.

1631 Appeal launched by Charles and Laud for funds for the repair of old St Paul's Cathedral.

1633   Laud appointed Archbishop of Canterbury; suppression of Feoffees for Impropriations; reissue of 1618 *Book of Sports*.

1637   Mutilation of Puritans John Bastwick, Henry Burton, and William Prynne for attacks on bishops; John Williams imprisoned for opposition to Laudian innovations; new Laudian Prayer Book imposed on Scots.

1638   Resistance in Scotland to Prayer Book; national covenant drawn up by Scots.

1639   Beginning of Bishops' War.

1640   Meeting of Short Parliament; issuing of new Arminian canons by convocation; victory of Scots over Charles I; meeting of Long Parliament; arrest and impeachment of Laud; Root and Branch Petition calling for the abolition of episcopacy presented to parliament.

1641   Court of High Commission abolished; beginning of insurrection by Catholic inhabitants of Ulster.

1642   Beginning of civil war; local church courts no longer active; London theatres closed on orders of parliament.

1643   Meeting of Westminster Assembly of Divines; parliament and Scots agree upon Solemn League and Covenant.

1645   Publication of Directory of Public Worship and banning of use of Book of Common Prayer; execution of Laud.

1646   Ending of civil war in parliamentary victory; abolition of episcopacy.

1648   Long Parliament's Blasphemy Act.

1649   Execution of Charles I and declaration of English republic; appearance of a number of Ranter tracts.

1650   Adultery and Blasphemy Acts passed by Rump.

1651   Early stages of Fifth Monarchist and Quaker movements.

1653   Civil Marriage Act passed by Barebone's Parliament; Cromwell appointed Lord Protector.

1654   Setting up of committees of triers and ejectors.

1655   Appointment of major-generals to carry out a number of tasks in localities, including improving morality.

1656   Blasphemy of Quaker leader, James Nayler, at Bristol.

1658   Death of Cromwell.

1659   Widespread fear among conservatives about the activities of the Quakers.

1660   Return of Charles II and restoration of monarchy and episcopal state church; William Juxon appointed Archbishop of Canterbury.

1661   Failure of Fifth Monarchist rising in London; return of church courts; Corporation Act; failure of Savoy Conference to agree upon return of comprehensive church.

1662 Act of Uniformity.

1663 Gilbert Sheldon appointed Archbishop of Canterbury.

1664 First Conventicles Act.

1665 Five Mile Act.

1666 Destruction of old St Paul's Cathedral and many parish churches in capital by fire; rebuilding programme entrusted to Christopher Wren.

1670 Second Conventicles Act; secret treaty of Dover between Charles II and Louis XIV.

1672 Issuing of Declaration of Indulgence by Charles II.

1673 Test Act.

1677 William Sancroft appointed Archbishop of Canterbury.

1678 Anti-Catholicism fuelled by revelation of Popish Plot.

1679 Meeting of first Exclusion Parliament.

1681 Defeat of call for exclusion.

1685 Death of Charles II and accession of Catholic James II.

1687 Issuing of first Declaration of Indulgence by James II.

1688 Issuing of second Declaration of Indulgence by James II; Seven Bishops' case; invasion of William of Orange and flight by James II.

1689 Throne offered jointly to William and Mary; Toleration Act.

Index

Numbers in italic type denote an entry in Glossary.

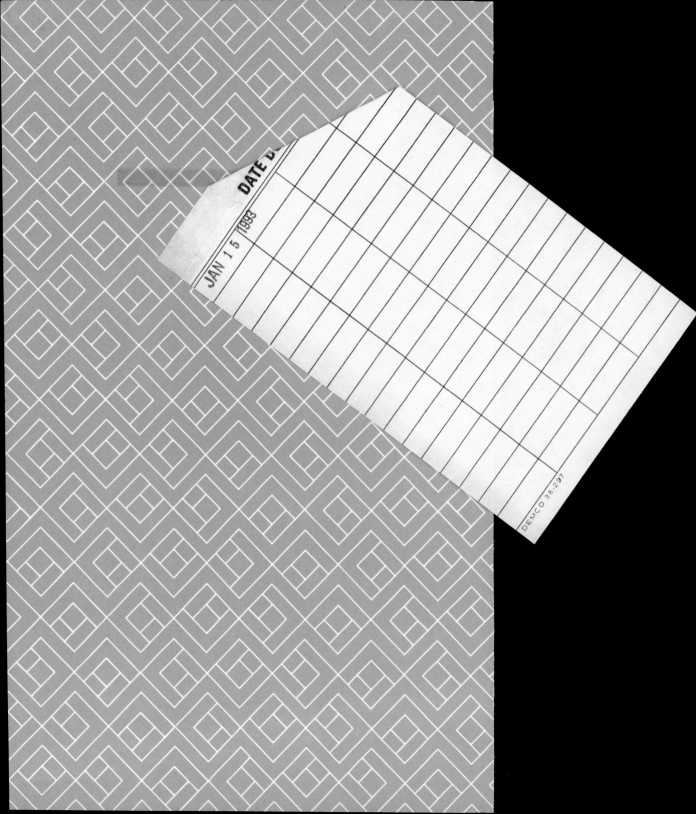